CREATING
THE PEACEABLE KINGDOM

CREATING
THE PEACEABLE KINGDOM

And Other Essays on Canada

Edited by
Victor Howard

Michigan State University Press
East Lansing

Michigan State University Press
East Lansing, Michigan 48823-5202

04 03 02 01 00 99 98 1 2 3 4 5 6 7 8 9 10

Library of Congress Cataloging-in-Publication Data

Creating The peaceable kingdom and other essays on Canada /
    edited by Victor Howard.

            p.   cm. —(MSU Press Canadian series ; # 8)
        Includes bibliographic references.
        ISBN 0-87013-430-2 (alk. paper)
Canada—History—Congresses. 2. Canada—Politics and government—
Congresses. 3. Québec (Province—History—Autonomy and independence
movements—Congresses. 4. Canada—Foreign relations—Congresses. I. Howard,
Victor, 1933- . II. Series.
F1026.6.C74 1998   97-39431
971—dc21   CIP

The cover design includes the painting by Edward Hick, *Peaceable Kingdom*, gift of Edgar William and Bernice Chrysler Garbisch, © 1997 Board of Trustees, National Gallery of Art, Washington.

Canadian Series Editor: Victor Howard

CONTENTS

Quebec! Quebec!

Matters of Defense

Of Newspapers and Narratives

PREFACE

Once upon a time, in 1969, I overheard an exchange between two Canadian undergraduate women, "Ellen, why don't other folks know anything about Canada?" "Hush, Diane, we don't want them to know anything about Canada." Implicit in Ellen's response is the belief that Canada was a wonderful place in which to live, perhaps, who knows? A Peaceable Kingdom. Keep it a secret, Diane. Don't tell "the others" about us or they'll want some too! They might just move in and take over!

About the same time, in response to the news that an American university counted a Canadian Studies Program in its larger international studies ambition, the inimitable artist/critic/wag from London, Ontario, Greg Curnoe, was heard to mutter that "Before the Yanks take over a country, THEY STUDY IT."

What Diane, Ellen, and Curnoe could not possibly anticipate was the wave of interest in Canada as a subject of academic inquiry that would reach prominent colleges and universities around the world. Pretty soon, everyone would know about Canada!

For one thing, Trudeau's government decided that external affairs might as well include "educational outreach." By the mid-1970s, a substantial program of support abroad for the educational systems of "the other folks" had settled into place: grants for curriculum design, research, conferences, library development, etc.

In the United States, a sizable league of "Canadianists" emerged which included an old guard made up of the Russell Nyes, the Alice Stewarts, the Mason Wades, and the Annette Baker Foxes, folks who had been in the business forever, or so it seemed.

They trained or inspired a new generation including a few Canadians who had moved south, Dick Beach, Peter Kresl, Lee Thompson, Robert Babcock, Jane Moss, and Gordon Stewart. Programs flourished at Western Washington, Duke, Michigan State, Maine, Vermont, Bowling Green, and more. The Association for Canadian Studies in the United States started up.

Happily, current events came to the aid of these folks and their enterprise. Canada was where one had gone if he wanted to avoid the Draft! Pierre Trudeau bore a certain charisma. Montreal and Toronto agreed to play baseball. A Canadian foreign service officer rescued some Americans in flight from Iranian despots. Neil Young comes from Canada, doesn't he? Pay attention students!

Still, a whole lot of Americans were sure that Canada had a president for a chief executive officer and that Canada was basically just like the States. Canadian watching the 1967 Detroit Riots from the safe haven of Windsor, Ontario, might disagree with that judgment, as might my student Ellen who understood that Americans, in her time, were indeed "the other."

There was a lot of hostility, not to say sadness, felt by Canadians toward Americans in the late 1960s and early 1970s. The United States was on the eve of destruction, so it seemed. The Vietnam War. Political assassinations. Race conflict. Economic imperialism. Cold War stuff. Now, as the century ends, Canada has so many local anxieties that no one has time to worry about the States who have enough problems with China, Bosnia, you name it, but not Canada.

The essays collected here are all about Canada. From them, the reader might just gain a sense of that country which he or she has not had before. And I mean the professional as well as the student. The reason I used Philip Kokotailo's essay as the title of this collection is that creating Canada is the work of the scholar just as it has been the work of the Canadian citizen, the poet, and the politician. Every time a scholar writes up the new interpretation of Canada — that new history, that new judgment — he or she has created another Canada, ideally one not discovered previously. Now the interpretation, the history, and the judgment may be dismissed, overturned, sent packing, by another legion of scholars. And thus, another Canada emerges. All the while, Canada is trying to be "peaceable" while these scholars are trying to rearrange it. to make something new.

My thanks to the contributors who waited patiently in the wings. The Michigan State University Foundation, the Government of Canada, and the Canadian Studies Centre at Michigan State University for their assistance. To Lyall Powers for his commentary on the enterprise. To my poor relation, Jesse Howard, who, along with the MSU Press editor in chief, Julie L. Loehr, managed the production of this book.

Victor Howard

THE HISTORICAL MOMENT

CREATING *THE PEACEABLE KINGDOM*: EDWARD HICKS, NORTHROP FRYE, AND JOE CLARK

Philip Kokotailo
University School, Hunting Valley, Ohio

When Edward Hicks died in 1849, he was one of the most popular and esteemed Quaker ministers of his day. Between three and four thousand people attended his funeral, the largest then held in Bucks County, Pennsylvania. Yet shortly before his death, Hicks wrote in his journal: "I have nothing to depend on but the mercy and forgiveness of God, for I have no works of righteousness of my own. I am nothing but a poor old worthless insignificant painter" (qtd. in Arkus 1972).

A hundred and fifty years later, Hicks has become an even more popular and esteemed painter than he was a minister. Today, his pictures command prices far beyond those of other American folk artists. In Canada, the value of his work may be still greater, though no Canadian, so far as I know, has ever purchased one of his paintings. But without knowing it, many Canadians have purchased one of his ideals. Northrop Frye calls it a pastoral ideal, and Frye is largely responsible for its popularity in Canada. In 1965, he transformed the title of Hicks's best known works, *The Peaceable Kingdom*, into an emblem of Canadian cultural aspiration. That title quickly became an accepted part of Canadian cultural currency. Like a coin minted by Frye, it has been widely circulated in Canada, circulated in social contexts that have little to do with pictorial art, and much to do with national self-definition. Hicks's title—Frye's coin we might say—has also been used to promote

3

specifically political ends, most notably by Joe Clark. So how did this transnational transformation happen?

In 1780, Hicks was born into a wealthy family of Anglican, Tory magistrates in what is now Langhorne, Pennsylvania.[1] His mother died when he was 18 months old, on the day that Cornwallis surrendered at Yorktown, 19 October 1781. Hicks effectively lost his father the same day, for the end of the Revolutionary War meant that the family's status and wealth were irretrievably lost, too. The father went into hiding, leaving the son to be raised by his mother's close friend, the wife of a well-to-do Quaker farmer. At age 13, he was apprenticed to a carriage maker. At age 23, he himself joined the Society of Friends, and he married.

Religion quickly became the driving force in Hicks's life. When his carriage-building partnership failed, he turned to painting carriages and coaches. He soon began to paint household objects and signboards, too. But Quaker affairs preoccupied him. He meditated; he attended meetings; he gained a reputation by speaking. Because his fellow Quakers recognized a special light within him, he became, at age 33, a minister, travelling and preaching on behalf of the Friends. But because it seemed inappropriate to the plainness required of a Quaker minister, he also stopped his elaborate ornamental painting.

Hicks did not return to painting — this time to the easel — until he was 40 years old. Again, religion appears to have been the driving force. He began by copying an engraved illustration of a drawing by Richard Westall, *The Peaceable Kingdom of the Branch*, which appeared in many Bibles used in the United States at that time.[2] Westall's work was itself inspired by well known verses from the Book of Isaiah: "The wolf also shall dwell with the lamb, and the leopard shall lie down with the kid; and the calf and the young lion and the fatling together: and a little child shall lead them" (11.6).

For Christians, Isaiah is the most revered of the Hebrew prophets, because he appears to foretell the coming of Christ, the messiah who will redeem his people and lead them to the peaceable kingdom. Hicks conflated this prophecy with history, specifically with a mythologized view of Quaker history, as his own verse paraphrase of Isaiah makes clear.

> The wolf did with the lambkin dwell in peace
> His grim carnivorous nature there did cease
>
> The leopard with the harmless kid laid down

And not one savage beast was seen to frown

The lion with the fatling on did move
A little child was leading them in love;

When the great PENN his famous treaty made
With Indian chiefs beneath the Elm-tree's shade.
(Mather, 34)

For Hicks, we can see, Isaiah's Old Testament prophecy was fulfilled at least once here on earth. When William Penn signed a treaty with the Delawares and established the Quaker settlement of Pennsylvania, the peaceable kingdom, in his view, was made real.

Into his painting, therefore, Hicks introduced a small representation of the treaty being signed. The result is a mythologized view of Quaker history, because no such ceremony ever took place. But Hicks did not invent it. He copied it instead from an engraved illustration of Benjamin West's famous painting, *William Penn's Treaty with the Indians*. This second model had a more lasting influence than the first one, Westall's drawing. Hicks did at least 60 versions of *The Peaceable Kingdom* from the early 1820s until the late 1840s. Westall's child disappeared from the center of the composition in the early 1830s, when it was replaced by a seated lion. West's treaty appeared first in the second oldest *Peaceable Kingdom* (c. 1822–25). It disappeared for a while in the late 1820s, when it was replaced by a group of historically important Quakers carrying banners. It reappeared for good in the early 1830s. The versions painted in the mid-1830s, often called *The Peaceable Kingdom with Seated Lion*, eventually become the best known.

Critics have said that in the nineteenth century, Hicks's paintings must have been regarded "either as pious Biblical statements or the vagaries of a disordered mind" (Mather, 15). They did not gain popularity until well into the twentieth century. In our troubled, modern world, the serenity of his great lions and leopards, with their almost human eyes, has become much more appealing. That serenity certainly appealed to Northrop Frye, a critic of art as well as literature, and, like Hicks, a minister. Frye effectively introduced Hicks to Canada, upholding his *Peaceable Kingdom* in the resonant, conclusive cadences of what is still often called the most important single essay about Canadian literature, his conclusion to the 1965 *Literary History of Canada*.

Hicks is called a primitive painter because he was self-taught, not professionally trained. Critics who value the work of such

painters typically praise their simplicity, their freshness of expression, or their innocence of vision, despite their lack of sophistica-
tion. Though Frye found these qualities in *The Peaceable Kingdom*, he
did not attribute them to Hicks's lack of formal training. He saw
them instead as the effects of a powerful tradition in art and literature, the pastoral tradition. He also believed that the pastoral
vision has been crucial throughout history to the formation of society, particularly Canadian society. Frye says:

> At the heart of all social mythology lies what may be called, because it usu-
> ally is called, a pastoral myth, the vision of a social ideal. The pastoral myth
> in its most common form is associated with childhood, or with some earlier
> social condition—pioneer life, the small town, the *habitant* rooted to his
> land—that can be identified with childhood. The nostalgia for a world of
> peace and protection, with a spontaneous response to the nature around it,
> with a leisure and composure not to be found today, is particularly strong
> in Canada. It is overpowering in our popular literature. . . . (840)

Many of these qualities are clearly evident in *The Peaceable
Kingdom*, though at this point in his essay Frye has not yet mentioned Hicks's painting. With three children in the foreground, it
too emphasizes childhood. In the background, the treaty scene
evokes the "earlier social condition." And both background and
foreground are worlds of peace, leisure, and composure. Most importantly, the center of *The Peaceable Kingdom* conveys what Frye
finds "Close to the centre of the pastoral myth" — "the sense of
kinship with the animal and vegetable world" prophesied by Isaiah
and represented by Hicks (841).

As Frye illustrates these qualities with specific examples from
Canadian literature, he distinguishes between the "sentimental or
socially stereotyped form" of pastoral, on the one hand, and the
"genuinely imaginative form" on the other (841). *The Peaceable
Kingdom* is clearly one of the latter. Frye saves it for his last example, and he uses it as an emblematic summary of his argument.
About the painting, he says:

> Here, in the background, is a treaty between the Indians and the Quaker
> settlers under Penn. In the foreground is a group of animals, lions, tigers,
> bears, oxen, illustrating the prophecy of Isaiah about the recovery of inno-
> cence in nature. Like the animals of the Douanier Rousseau, they stare past
> us with a serenity that transcends consciousness. It is a pictorial emblem of
> what Grove's narrator was trying to find under the surface of America: the
> reconciliation of man with man and of man with nature: the mood of

Thoreau's Walden retreat, of Emily Dickinson's garden, of Huckleberry Finn's raft, of the elegies of Whitman. (848)

The passing reference to Frederick Philip Grove is crucial. Earlier, Frye called Grove's *A Search for America* a "genuinely imaginative form" of pastoral. He also called attention to "a hint" dropped by Grove "in a footnote near the end that what his narrator is looking for has been abandoned in the United States but perhaps not yet in Canada" (842). Frye quickly adds, "This is not our present moral." But notice the list of writers in his concluding comments about *The Peaceable Kingdom*: Thoreau, Dickinson, Twain, Whitman — all, like Hicks himself, nineteenth-century Americans. They stand in contrast to Grove, the twentieth-century Canadian. In this context, Frye's final words about Hicks's painting come as no surprise. Its mood, he says:

is closer to the haunting vision of a serenity that is both human and natural which we have been struggling to identify in the Canadian tradition. If we had to characterize a distinctive emphasis in that tradition, we might call it a quest for the peaceable kingdom. (848)

It did not take long, in Canada, for Frye's transnational transformation to gain widespread recognition and acceptance. The first sign it had done so was the title of an anthology edited by the historian William Kilbourn, *Canada: A Guide to the Peaceable Kingdom*, published in 1970. In his introduction, Kilbourn called it "a book about the Canadian identity" (xii). The title, he explained, was chosen to suggest both "a travel companion for explorers of the Canadian spiritual landscape," and "a guide to other peoples who seek a path to the peaceable kingdom" (xi). He acknowledged that this phrase is the title of a painting, though he did not say by whom, stressing instead that Northrop Frye used it "To identify that which is most essentially Canadian in our literature" (xvii). But Kilbourn's own use of the title shows that another transformation has taken place. Frye's "quest" is over. Canada has *become* the peaceable kingdom, in spite of Frye's insistence that "pastoral myths, even in their genuine forms, do not exist as places" (842). As we have already seen, even Frye foresaw, and partly gave in to, this temptation. In his comments about Grove, he acknowledged that "the conception 'Canada' can also become a pastoral myth in certain circumstances."

Two more titles suggest that in the 1990s these circumstances are still prevalent. The first is Graeme Mount's book, *Canada's Ene-*

mies: Spies and Spying in the Peaceable Kingdom, published in 1993. The second is Jonathan Lemco's *Turmoil in the Peaceable Kingdom: The Quebec Sovereignty Movement and Its Implications for Canada and the United States,* published in 1994. Since neither book mentions Hicks or Frye, the pattern is now complete. In 30 years time, *The Peaceable Kingdom* has been transformed from the title of a primitive American painting into an unattributed metaphor, in English Canada, for the Canadian nation itself. More importantly, it has become a *useful* metaphor *within* Canada, particularly in the political realm.

In March 1990, for instance, three months before the deadline for ratification of the Meech Lake Accord, then Secretary of State for External Affairs Joe Clark delivered a speech in Edmonton which received widespread media attention, because it alluded to the possibility of violence following any breakup of Canada due to the Accord's failure. No attention, so far as I know, was paid to the language in which Clark made his allusion. He said: "No one here can guarantee that our children will inherit a kingdom so peaceable as that in which we grew up" (17).

Clark was clearly using the metaphor of Canada, *The Peaceable Kingdom,* to summon last-minute support for the Meech Lake Accord; but some of my friends scoff at this allusion. The only thing it proves, I have been told, is that Clark had a Canlit student as his speech writer. So I wrote to Clark, asking if he had ever read Frye, if he knew the source of the metaphor he used. But Clark did not write back. In the wake of the Meech Lake Accord's failure, he had been appointed Minister Responsible for Constitutional Affairs, and he was actively investigating the possibility of achieving a new accord.

Three years later, I got a second chance to ask my questions. At the 1993 biennial meeting of the Association of Canadian Studies in the United States in New Orleans, standing on the deck of the *Natchez,* a Mississippi River excursion "event," looking out on the petro-chemical wasteland south of New Orleans, feeling through the floorboards the thumping zydeco beat of Bruce Daigrepont's Cajun Band, I suddenly found myself being introduced to Joe Clark.

"I wrote you a letter once," I began.

"Oh, ohhhh," he replied.

But then we had a very interesting and rewarding conversation. I asked if he had ever read Frye. "Yes," he said, and he volunteered the title of Frye's book, *The Bush Garden*. I quoted the relevant sentence of his Edmonton speech, and asked if he was deliberately quoting Frye. "No," Clark replied. He did not know that the phrase came from Frye. He could not remember where he first heard it, showing once again that *The Peaceable Kingdom* has become an anonymous unit of Canadian cultural currency. I should add that when I told him my story, Clark took offense at the suggestion that a Canlit student must have written his speech. Months later, when we exchanged letters about our meeting, that suggestion still bothered him. "You reported," he wrote:

> the surmise of one of your colleagues that a speech writer was more likely to have read Frye than an active politician. In my experience, that particular scepticism is misplaced although, clearly, there is not enough collaboration between the Canadian artists and politicians who share an interest in what you call a "tradition of community in the search for national values."[3]

I should have used the word *reconciliation*, rather than *community*, because reconciliation is Frye's key word. We might even call it the theme of his analysis. *The Peaceable Kingdom*, he says, is a pictorial emblem of "the reconciliation of man with man and of man with nature."

For most of us, Frye's use of the word *man* here is outdated and no longer acceptable. But what about the word *reconciliation*? What about Frye himself? And what about Clark? Clark succeeded in negotiating the Charlottetown Accord, and he was given much credit for what initially appeared to be its imminent success. When the House of Commons was recalled to debate it, the CBC's Joe Schlesinger reported that Clark was applauded "as warmly by members of the opposition as he was by members of his own party." The accord he brought about, we should remember, was also more inclusive than its predecessor. It brought the native peoples as well as Quebec into the constitutional fold, and it granted Frye's "thinly" or "sparsely" populated provinces equal voice in a reformed Senate.

Though Charlottetown was later rejected by popular vote, its potential realization of constitutional reconciliation, I am suggesting, owes something, perhaps much, to the values upheld by a literary critic, Northrop Frye. In his own response to the Meech Lake crisis, Frye asserted that it called for the "Reconfederation" of Canada ("Cultural," 128). Though he did not live to vote on such a reconfederation, his criticism had already made a significant cultural contribution toward that end. In it, he articulated an ideal of peaceful reconciliation, an ideal to which many Canadians subscribe, and which clearly influenced the significant political actions of Joe Clark. That ideal conveys from the past the value of a quest for the peaceable kingdom, a quest to which Clark remained loyal in the present, for the sake of the future: "our children," as he put it in 1990, and their inheritance.

Five years later, that inheritance is still doubtful. In 1991, Frye passed away. In 1993, Clark stepped down from elected office. Who will now inherit their ideal, or has the word *ideal* also become outdated and no longer acceptable? I wonder, especially when an accepted definition of myth, for people who study literature, is "any religion in which people no longer believe" (Abrams, 102). Furthermore, with the passing of time, any painting, any essay, any speech tends naturally to disappear. Some survive, only because certain people care enough to preserve them, to reproduce them, to quote them, even to teach them. This paper is my own modest attempt to keep *The Peaceable Kingdom* alive.

Notes

1.   For biographical information about Hicks, I have relied on Arkus and Mather.

2.   Reproductions of all the artworks cited in this paper can be found in Mather.

3.   Correspondence with Joe Clark, 15 January 1994.

Works Cited

Arkus, Leon Anthony. Introduction. *Four American Primitives: Edward Hicks, John Kane, Anna Mary Robertson Moses, Horace Pippin, February 22–March 11, 1972*. New York: ACA Galleries, n.d.

Clark, Joe. "Why Canada Is Worth Saving." *Canadian Speeches/ Issues: Informed Thought* 4, no. 2 (1990): 16–21.

Frye, Northrop. "The Cultural Development of Canada." Pp. 124–35 in *The Modern Century: The Whidden Lectures, 1967.* New ed. Toronto: Oxford University Press, 1991.

———. Conclusion. Pp. 821–49 in *Literary History of Canada: Canadian Literature in English.* Edited by Carl F. Klinck et al. Toronto: University of Toronto Press, 1965.

Edward Hicks. *The Peaceable Kingdom.* c. 1833. Worcester Art Museum, Worcester, Mass. Mather, 126.

———.*The Peaceable Kingdom of the Branch.* c. 1822–25. New Haven: Yale University Art Gallery. Mather, 95.

Kilbourn, William. Introduction. Pp. xi–xviii in *Canada: A Guide to the Peaceable Kingdom.* Edited by William Kilbourn. Toronto: Macmillan, 1970.

Lemco, Jonathan. *Turmoil in the Peaceable Kingdom: The Quebec Sovereignty Movement and Its Implications for Canada and the United States.* Toronto: University of Toronto Press, 1994.

Mather, Eleanor Price, and Dorothy Canning Miller. *Edward Hicks: His Peaceable Kingdoms and Other Paintings.* American Art/Kennedy Galleries. Newark: University of Delaware Press; New York: Cornwall, 1983.

Mount, Graeme S. *Canada's Enemies: Spies and Spying in the Peaceable Kingdom.* Toronto: Dundurn, 1993.

Schlesinger, Joe. *The National.* CBC Television. Toronto. 8 September 1992.

West, Benjamin. *William Penn's Treaty with the Indians.* 1771. Pennsylvania Academy of the Fine Arts, Philadelphia. Mather, 48.

Westall, Richard. *The Peaceable Kingdom of the Branch.* Mather, 18.

EARLY NINETEENTH-CENTURY MILITARY FRONTIERS ON THE LAKE HURON BORDERLANDS

Paul A. Demers
Michigan State University

While Canada and the United States may indeed share the longest undefended border in the world, this is a relatively modern convenience. Two hundred years ago, the Canadian-American boundary was ill-defined, representative more of an idealized concept than of the political and geographic circumstances of the time. Yet border enforcement became a critical issue in relations among the British, the Americans, and the Indians. The ambitions of various military and civilian groups along this border made for conflicting perceptions of group identities and varying uses of social space played out at the local and regional levels.

The constructed environment and the documentary record of border area sites such as the British post at Drummond Island, Michigan, provide data for fresh insights into the agenda and the nature of interaction among Indians, British military and colonial governments, post officials, the U.S. and Michigan territorial governments, and civilian fur traders. From these sources, we can begin to comprehend the perceptions of social space and attempts to define and manipulate the space on this emerging frontier. The British station on Drummond Island and the adjacent Lake Huron borderlands during the late eighteenth and early nineteenth centuries, are the areas under consideration.

This border area encompasses the St. Mary's River and the Straits of Mackinac which together form the junction of Lakes

Huron, Michigan, and Superior and has functioned as an important transportation corridor and gateway into the heart of the North American continent for several thousand years. European intervention begins in the early seventeenth century with the Jesuits Joques and Raymbault who visited Sault Ste. Marie in 1641 and reported that approximately 2,000 Indians had gathered at the Rapids.[1] In 1668 Pere Jacques Marquette established the Jesuit mission near that site; the threat of Iroquois attacks forced its closure in 1689.[2] The French shifted their focus to the Straits of Mackinac with the construction of a mission at St. Ignace in 1671 and at Fort du Baud in 1685. In 1715 a garrison was established on the south side of the Straits of Mackinac.

By the middle of the eighteenth century, the British were actively competing in the lucrative fur trade of the Northwest Territory. British political control began after 1760, when they defeated the French in the Seven Years' War. The British occupation of Michilimackinac began in 1761 and continued until 1780, when the fort was deemed indefensible in the event of U.S. attack. The garrison was then moved to Mackinac Island. The construction of Fort Mackinac further attested to the strategic importance of the Straits in the eighteenth and nineteenth centuries.

After the Revolutionary War, the British retained this post, in direct violation of the 1783 Treaty of Paris, in order to maintain their alliances with the Indians and their fur trade interests. Fort Mackinac finally surrendered to American troops in 1796 under the terms of Jay's Treaty which specified the restoration of all territory according to the Treaty of Paris. The British were forced to move their post to nearby St. Joseph Island. Despite the loss of Fort Mackinac, the British hoped that the new installation would become the center of the fur trade and protect British North America from possible attacks from American posts.

Throughout the late eighteenth and early nineteenth centuries, international conflicts fused with local issues and culminated in the War of 1812 in North America. The Treaty of Ghent, which ended this conflict in 1815, provided for the return of several key posts to the United States, including Fort Mackinac which had fallen into British hands. The loss of this post was a crucial blow to British hopes for control of the area. When the treaty terms were announced, Lieut. Col. Robert McDouall, British commandant of Mackinac, commented, "Our negotiators as usual have been egregiously duped . . . they have shown themselves profoundly ignorant of the concerns of this part of the Empire.[3] McDouall expressed further concern over the loss of influence with Native American groups: "It will retire us out of the reach of the Indians altogether, and give the finishing blow to whatever influence we yet possess amongst them. The surrender of this most important island, the key to the whole western country. . . ."[4]

The Treaty of Ghent reflected an attempt on the part of the British government to scale back military operations in the western Great Lakes and to concentrate on the St. Lawrence River area and the Maritime Provinces. This policy was not popular with the local British military nor with civilians in the British sphere of influence in the western Great Lakes who had fought in the War of 1812 to consolidate the fur trade territory. In fact, the export of furs and their profitability reached a peak in this area between the end of the War of 1812 and the 1820s.[5] The strategic and economic agenda of local military officials and civilians began to contradict the British policy of phasing out installations in the western Great Lakes.

Despite these local protests, Mackinac Island was handed over to the United States on 18 July 1815. The British had been searching already for a site for a post to counteract the American influence at Fort Mackinac in the northern Lake Huron basin. Drummond Island, thought of as part of the Manitoulin Chain of Lake Huron, seemed ideal. This island, some forty-five miles northeast of Mackinac Island, commands approaches to the Straits from the north as well as the entrance to the St. Mary's River from both the east and west (figure 1). In June 1815 Colonel McDouall described the site in a letter to Sir George Murray:

> The new post on Lake Huron has been at length fixed upon by Capt. Payne, R. Engineers (who arrived here the 13th) Capt. Collier, R. N. and myself. The situation combines several important advantages viz- an admirable harbor, proximity to the Indians, and will enable us to command the passage of the Detour, giving our vessels the double advantage of a good anchorage in that strait in addition to the fine harbor adjoining. The ground fixed upon for the new post, and which was best calculated for the protection of the harbor.[6]

Although there are no detailed returns of the actual number of people who came to the island in July of 1815, a reliable estimate is that between 350 and 400 people were evacuated to Drummond Island.[7] This number included a company of the Eighty-first Regiment of Foot, two companies of the Royal Newfoundland Regiment,

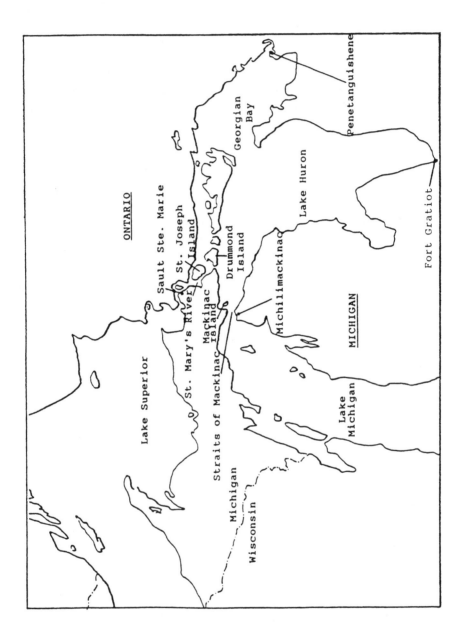

Figure 1. Project Area

Indian Department officials and fur traders. Since these regimental companies were isolated and not at full strength at the end of the war, they might have accounted for 150–200 of this total. If the estimate is accurate, then approximately the same number, 150–200, were civilians. Later, in the fall of 1815, both of these regiments were relieved by two companies of the Thirty-seventh Regiment of Foot sent from Fort Malden at Amherstburg, on the Detroit River.

A conceptual plan of the new installation was drafted by post staff in 1816 (figure 2) and portrayed a large settlement with massive fortifications and shipyards. This depiction represented the post officials' vision of a powerful fort, a fur trade center, and a base of operations should hostilities break out once again. But the British government was reducing its presence in the Old Northwest and so Sir John C. Sherbrooke halted construction of the fortifications on Drummond Island.[8] It was argued that since the Boundary Commission had not yet determined the fate of Drummond Island, only temporary quarters and stores should be constructed.[9]

Despite these government directives, Lieut. Col. Durnford, commander of the Royal Engineer Department of the Canadas, reluctantly agreed to commission a blockhouse in 1816, at the insistence of post officials.[10] Despite Sherbrooke's order which forbade this construction, post engineer Lieutenant Portlock began construction after returning to the post.[11] Post officials vigorously petitioned for the blockhouse on several occasions thereafter. When permission finally was granted to build the blockhouse, Major Howard, commandant of Drummond Island, assured the assistant adjutant general, Lieut. Col. Foster, that the site would be examined by senior engineer officers before any expense was incurred, and before any work would begin.[12] (Howard did not mention that the project had been initiated two years earlier. In a spring 1820 inspection report, Portlock reported that a forty square-foot fortified blockhouse had been damaged previously by fire.[13]) Such discrepancies illustrate the conflict between government policies of cutbacks, a shifting military emphasis away from this area, and the vested interest of local military and civilian post inhabitants.

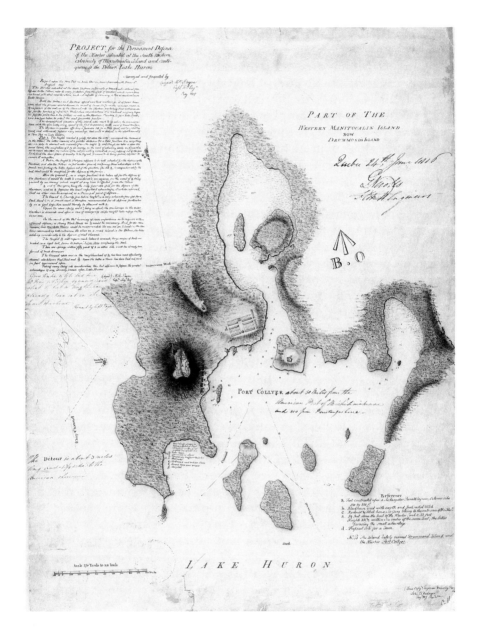

Figure 2. Proposed Settlement Plan for Drummond Island, 1816. (K.R. Payne, *Part of the Western Manitoulin Island Now Drummond's Island.* Courtesy of National Archives of Canada.)

A number of post officers and civilians had private interests in the fur trade. Some had married into Indian families, creating both economic advantages and further obligations in the fur trade network. Still, the attempt to make Drummond Island a vital British post for the fur trade ran counter to official policy. It would appear that this local priority necessitated concealment from higher ranking officials.

An important aspect of civilian-military relations at the post was the new settlement which had come to be known as the village of Collier. A variety of fur traders, post staff, Indian Department officials, and tradesmen secured lots in this settlement. The 1816 plan map for the post showed surveyed lots for the village (figure 2). Licenses to occupy village lots were granted with stipulations regarding standardization in the size of lots and the form of the dwellings. United States Boundary Commissioner Major Joseph Delafield passed through the area in 1820, and placed the size of the village at fifteen structures laid out along a single street.[14] This account of the settlement layout differs from the original 1816 grid pattern survey plan of the town.

Another source of information regarding the village was the "return" or exit report prepared by the deputy assistant commissary General, James Wickens, upon the evacuation of Drummond Island in 1828.[15] The size of the village was estimated by Wickens to be about forty dwellings, a threefold increase between 1820 and 1828. Archaeological reports have confirmed the Wickens estimate.[16] The fact that the actual settlement pattern did not conform to the grid pattern proposed by the military authorities, and the variety in the size of structures, construction techniques, and spacing between structures (figure 3) all suggest that the strict control proposed for the village was not carried out by the military.

A similar discrepancy between the survey and settlement patterns was observed by Kenneth Lewis at the eighteenth century British military town of Camden, South Carolina.[17] Lewis suggested that the two-row settlement with a single main street and two cross streets, similar to the pattern for the village of Collier, had evolved in order to maximize access to the primary routes of transportation and communication. These adjustments in spatial organization represent degrees of control exercised by village inhabitants over the military post authorities.

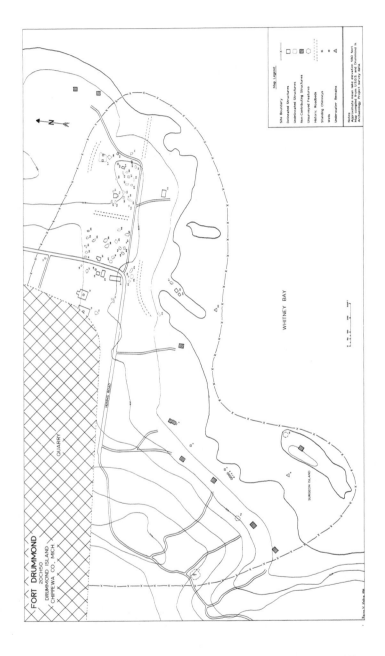

Figure 3. Fort Drummond Archeological Site Settlement Plan.

Commercial interests located at the post were responsible for a series of eight private buildings situated between the Officers' Quarters and messroom and the townsite. The buildings labeled "private" do not appear on the 1816 plan map, but they do appear on site maps dated 1819 and 1823 (figure 4). The meaning of the term "private" in this context is unclear. The term would seem to exclude government buildings which were almost always identified on maps by their function. Yet, the civilian-owned buildings, located within the townsite, were not labeled individually on any of the site maps.

Archaeological excavation of the four northernmost private buildings[18] suggests that these structures (16, 17, 19, 20) were storehouses connected with the fur trade (figure 3). The ownership of the buildings is difficult to determine at this juncture. However, if the structures were the property of a government agency such as the Indian Department, they should have been identified as such on the maps. Hence, the buildings were more likely the property of independent fur traders or fur trade companies. If these structures were indeed privately-owned, it would seem that the post officials had relaxed the traditional, segregation policies toward civilians, or at least, toward some civilians. The nature and location of the "private" structures suggests certain civilians such as fur traders interacted more closely with the military. Given the similarity of their agenda and the convergence of their interests, it is not surprising that this settlement pattern favored some fur traders over other civilians. Conversely, this frontier situation represented the breakdown of the military-civilian dichotomy in terms of functions and partitioning of space.

The post was also a treaty negotiation center and depot for the British Indian Department. This unit of the British Army, established in 1755, spent vast sums of money for gifts and annuities issued during Councils to court Indian allegiance and to protect fur trade interests.[19] Prior to the War of 1812, this relationship resulted in the Indians holding a balance of power in the Old Northwest Territory.

Certainly, the British needed Indian assistance in their struggles with the United States. Yet, the British also viewed Indians as a buffer between the Americans and the trading establishments such as the Hudson's Bay Company and the North West Company. Conversely, the Indians realized that the British had proven to be unreliable allies, and previous Euro-American boundary lines negotiated after previous conflicts had not protected their interests.

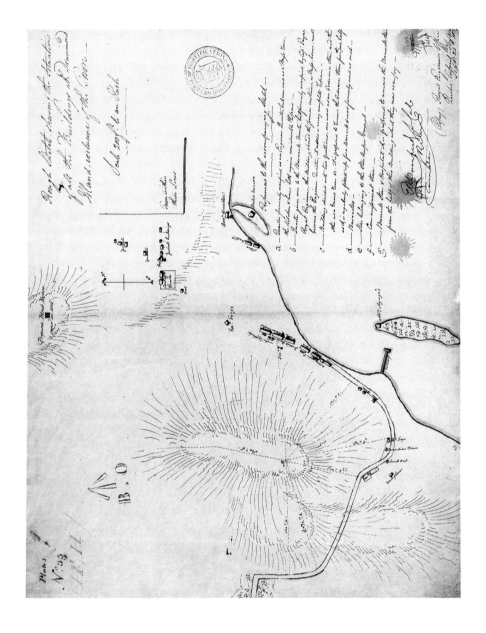

Figure 4. Drummond Island Post Sketch Map, 1823. (Anon. *Rough Sketch Showing the Situation of All the Buildings at Drummond's Island Exclusive of the Town.* Courtesy National Archives of Canada.)

Nevertheless, many Indians entered into alliances with the British in order to stem the tide of incursions into their lands. These continued since the fledgling Republic had not yet committed to monitoring this border area.

Neither the Americans nor the British were anxious to go back to war. During an Indian Council held on Drummond Island on 29 June 1816, the British offered no direct assistance to an Indian league organized to combat U.S. fort-building in Indian territory. Further, the British suggested the Indians should not take violent measures against the U.S. although they were encouraged to continue visiting the British posts.[20] Contrarily, the Indians continued to frequent Drummond Island and Amherstburg in an effort to place pressure on the British to take a more active role against the U.S. During one such Council, Sauk Chief Blackhawk admonished the British:

> You was not afraid to bring us our Great Father's bounty when our hatchet was still red with blood. Why can you not do it when our women and children are poor and we are threatened with the loss of our lands.[21]

Yet the British-Indian connection, demonstrated by such councils, was but one of the strategies used by Indian groups to play off both powers against each other. They easily fueled the paranoia of American officials such as Michigan Territorial Governor Lewis Cass and Secretary of War John C. Calhoun, both War of 1812 veterans who interpreted British-Indian rendezvous as opportunities to conspire against the United States.

The strategy of pitting the British and the American governments against each other proved successful in temporarily altering American Indian policy in the Northwest Territory. While the United States was forced to offer the Indians increased rations and other incentives at Mackinac Island, the government also threatened to withhold any benefits from those Indians who visited British posts.[22] However, British Indian Department records show that in 1823, one year after Drummond Island was awarded to the United States, a total of 3,333 Indians visited Drummond Island to trade and to receive gifts and rations from the British.[23]

Certainly, there was no single set of responses or strategies employed by Indian groups to address the complex events which threatened their culture. In fact within most Algonquian tribes, there was disagreement over allegiances and strategies to deal with the U.S. and the British.

Rather than turning to direct military confrontation, the United States reoccupied old forts and constructed a chain of new forts in the Western Great Lakes. In Michigan the Americans occupied Fort Mackinac (Mackinac Island), Fort Brady (Sault Ste. Marie), Fort Gratiot (Port Huron), and Fort Saginaw, in order to surround and isolate British posts in its territory. American interests also employed a variety of other strategies to sever this British-Indian connection and reduce the British presence in the borderlands.

Certainly, the American Fur Company headed by John Jacob Astor represented one of the most powerful economic and political interests. Many American government officials and private entrepreneurs believed the success of this enterprise would end the British presence in American territory, and hence, conclude their dominance of the fur trade. Astor lobbied for the exclusion of foreign ownership of companies and so in 1816, a law was passed to license only U.S. citizens for trade with the Indians. This newly enacted legislation enabled Astor to buy out his Canadian partners in the South West Company.

Yet both the American Government and Astor knew that British and Canadian field personnel had to be hired in order for U.S. companies to succeed. In the 1817 and 1818, Ramsay Crooks, Chief Factor of the American Fur Company, employed more than 125 traders from Montreal. Crooks himself was a British subject and needed a special passport to travel in the United States.[24]

Some American officials saw the British and Canadian employees as a security risk which undermined their authority. William Puthuff, Indian Agent at Mackinac, vehemently opposed such practices and called into question the loyalty of Astor and the American Fur Company. He was soon removed from office by John Calhoun. Colonel Talbot Chambers, Commander of Prairie du Chien and Missouri Governor William Clark also received reprimands for their actions against the American Fur Company.[25]

The conflicts between American private enterprise and the American government were further complicated by the Factory System. Government trading houses or factories were established to eliminate unscrupulous trade practices with Indians, to lure Indian allegiance away from the British at posts such as Drummond Island and to provide a more powerful American presence on the frontier. Further, many hoped the factories would persuade Indians to adopt sedentary agriculture, thereby freeing surplus land for settlers. The factories maintained a liberal trade policy offering material incentives to the Indians for adopting Euro-American agriculture and husbandry. Continuing in the Jeffersonian tradition, Thomas McKenney, superintendent of the Indian Trade, sought to educate and Christianize Indians via the factory system. He felt that many of the practices of private traders were immoral and served to incite Native Americans.[26] Yet Astor bitterly complained that a government subsidized competitor represented an unfair advantage and hindered private enterprise. Astor took every opportunity to lobby against the factory system. In 1822, the system was abolished due to efforts of the American Fur Company lobby, mismanagement, post-war losses and the lack of Congressional support.

In that same year the Boundary Commission decided that Drummond Island lay within U.S. territorial waters. Discussion of a replacement for this post began immediately after the news was made public. The Smyth Commission of 1825 concluded all of the buildings were "more or less decayed, and totally unworthy of repair."[27] After a discussion of all possible alternative locations, the Commission recommended that the inhabitants remove to the military and naval establishment at Penetanguishine on the eastern shore of Lake Huron. The report also suggested diverting the Indians to Amherstburg for their annual visits.

The final decision to evacuate the post on Drummond Island came in 1828, six years after the edict of the Boundary Commission was handed down. On 14 November 1828, the United States took possession of the island and a brig carried the garrison to Penetanguishene, arriving a week later on 21 November 1828.

The return of the Deputy Assistant Commissary General James Wickens showed that seven officers, forty men, fifteen women, twenty-six children, and three servants departed for their new post.[28] This return also showed that during the winter of 1828–29, only three families remained on the island. The evacuation of Drummond Island drew to a close the final episode of the Old Northwest Territory. The long term importance of this area has been highlighted by the two and a half century struggle among Indians, France, Britain, and the United States. For all of its strategic importance it was never again occupied as a military post.

This study underscores the complexity of social relations involved in the border area during this period. It is clear that simple rubrics such as nationalism or ethnicity cannot be used to categorize the range of behaviors within social groups. Further, the application of a single stereotypical identity to an individual or social group cannot reflect the complexities of interaction over a broad range of social situations. Individuals or groups may promote or ignore certain aspects of their identity or the identities of others.

Certainly, these differing perceptions of social space and resultant conflicting agenda are linked to the larger phenomenon of expansion, and the nature and organization of the economic system. These behaviors reflect the complex social processes of cultural interaction, and the formation of new socio-political identities and their subsequent boundaries. In this sense, they can be studied as adaptations to changing social circumstances.

The challenge is to decipher this social complexity in order to understand the roles these groups played in border formation, and in turn, to assess the impact of the international border upon these groups. Yet, all to often, these complexities are treated as merely a series of directional, historical events.

The study of border areas is by necessity a multidisciplinary pursuit. While an individual site functions as the interface between political, economic, and social issues, a regional framework must be adopted to incorporate all parties concerned to discover how these groups interacted over time and space. Data can be derived from a variety of sources including historic documents and archaeological remains, each form having its own advantages and limitations. The reconciliation of contradictions between these lines of evidence produces a more dynamic understanding of past events.

Notes

1. Ruben G. Thwaites, ed., *The Jesuit Relations and Allied Documents: Travel and Explorations of the Jesuits and Missionaries in New France, 1610-1791* (New York: Pageant, 1959), 52:201.

2. W. J. Eccles, *France in America*, rev. ed. (East Lansing: Michigan State University Press, 1990), 91.

3. Lt. Col. Robert McDouall to Capt. Andrew Bulger, 5 May 1815. National Archives of Canada, RG 8, C3171, 230–31.

4. Lt. Col. Robert McDouall to Lt. Col. C. Foster, 15 May 1815. National Archives of Canada, RG 8, C688, 49.

5.   Charles E. Cleland, *Rites of Conquest: The History and Culture of Michigan's Native Americans* (Ann Arbor: University of Michigan Press, 1992), 179.

6.   Lt. Col. Robert McDouall to Sir George Murray, 24 June 1815. National Archives of Canada, RG 8, vol. 688, 138–40.

7.   Samuel F. Cook, *Drummond Island: The Story of the British Occupation, 1815–1828* (Grand Rapids: Black Letter Press, 1974), 42.

8.   Lt. J. E. Portlock, *Report of the State of the Posts of Amherstburg, Drummond's Island and St. Joseph's* (1820). National Archives of Canada, RG 8, vol. 406, 38–45a.

9.   Lord E. W. Durnford, *Report of the State of Several Barracks and other Public Buildings to be Transferred from the Barrack Commissary of the Medical Departments Throughout the Canadas to that of the Ordnance and those to be Retained by the Commissary* (1823). National Archives of Canada, RG 8, II, vol. 81.

10. Lord E. W. Durnford to Lt. Col. J. Harvey, 22 August 1818. National Archives of Canada, RG 8, C400, 29.

11. Lt. J. E. Portlock to Lord E. W. Durnford, 19 January 1817. National Archives of Canada, RG 8, C398, 104.

12. Major Thomas Howard to Lt. Col. C. Foster, 20 March 1819. National Archives of Canada, RG 8, C263, 40.

13. Portlock, *Report, 1820.*

14. Major Joseph Delafield, *The Unfortified Boundary,* edited by Robert McElroy and Thomas Riggs (Privately Printed: New York, 1943).

15. Deputy Assistant Commissary General James Wickens to Lt. Col. C. Foster, 13 February, 1829. National Archives of Canada, RG 8, vl. 675, 151–52.

16. Paul A. Demers, *Report on the Fort Drummond Archaeological District Survey, 20CH50 and 20CH55,* photocopy (Lansing: Bureau of History, Michigan Department of State, 1992).

17. Kenneth Lewis, "Sampling the Archeological Frontier," in *Research Strategies in Historical Archaeology*, edited by Stanley South (New York: Academic Press, 1977), 151–202.

18. Paul A. Demers, *Report on the 1992 and 1994 Excavations at the Fort Drummond Site (20CH50) Drummond Island, Michigan*, photocopy (East Lansing: Department of Anthropology, Michigan State University, 1995).

19. Robert S. Allen, *His Majesty's Indian Allies: British Indian Policy in the Defence of Canada, 1774–1815* (Toronto and Oxford: Dundurn Press, 1993).

20. Lt. Col. William McKay, speech to Drummond Island Council, 29 June 1819. National Archives of Canada, RG 8, C260, 329.

21. Blackhawk, speech to Drummond Island Council, August 1817. National Archives of Canada, RG 10, Vol. 32, 19172–77.

22. John C. Calhoun to Lewis Cass, 30 August 1819, in *The Territorial Papers of the United States*, edited by C. E. Carter (Washington, D.C.: Government Printing Office, 1942), 10:854.

23. Col. William Claus, *A Return of Indian of Upper Canada for Whom Presents Specified in the Annexed Estimates* (1823). National Archives of Canada, RG 10, vol.15: 12184–88.

24. John Haeger, *John Jacob Astor: Business and Finance in the Early Republic* (Detroit: Wayne State University Press, 1991), 195.

25. Ibid, 197–98.

26. Francis Paul Prucha, *The Great Father* (Lincoln: University of Nebraska Press, 1984), 1:115–58.

27. Sir James Carmichael Smyth, *Report to the Duke of Wellington Relative to His Majesty's North American Provinces*. National Archives of Canada, RG 8, II, vol. 6.

28. Wickens letter, 13 February 1829.

THE QUEBEC MODEL, TOPOGRAPHICAL POETRY, AND THE CONSTRUCTION OF CENTRAL CANADA

D.M.R. Bentley
University of Western Ontario

> *[E]ach society offers up its own peculiar space . . . as an "object" for analysis and overall theoretical explication.*
>
> —Henri Lefebvre, *The Production of Space* (1974; trans. 1991, p. 31)

In his account of his visit to Lower Canada in 1808, the English author and artist John Lambert laments the absence of "literature, the arts, and the sciences" in the province, and characterizes Canada as a country seemingly more capable of supporting than creating genius" (1:318, 330). As an exception to these judgments, he cites the maps and drawings of Jean-Baptiste Duberger (1762-1821), a "native" of Canada, "a self-taught genius," "an officer in the corps of engineers and [a] military draughtsman" (1:331). As well as being responsible for the "only correct chart of Lower Canada," Duberger was the author of "several . . . large draughts of the country, and many other drawings, some of which were beautifully done, and are deposited in the Engineer's office" (1:331). "But the most important of his labours," concludes Lambert, is a beautiful model of Quebec, upon which he is at present employed, in conjunction with a school-fellow of mine, Captain By of the engineers. . . . The whole of the model is sketched out, and a great part is finished, particularly the fortifications and public buildings. It is upwards of 35 feet in length, and comprises a considerable portion of the plains of Abraham, as far as the spot where Wolfe died. That which is done is finished with exquisite neatness; cut entirely out of wood, and modelled to a certain scale, so that every part will be completed with a singular correctness, even to the very space and projection of the rock, the elevations and descents in the city, and on the plains, particularly those eminences which command the garrison. It is to be sent to England when finished, and will, no doubt, be received by the British government with the approbation it merits. (1:332)

A note to this passage in the third edition of Lambert's *Travels* (1816) states that Duberger's model of Quebec was indeed sent to England and, by 1813, placed in the Royal Military Repository at Woolwich.

Now the genesis and provenance of the Quebec Model (fig. 1) has attracted the attention of several amateur and professional historians. In the nineteenth century, the most important of these was a Quebec lawyer, H.H. Miles, who provided a comprehensive and influential account of its history in "Some Observations on Canadian Chorography and Topography, and on the Meritorious Services of the Late Jean-Baptiste Duberger, Senr.," a paper read before the Literary and Historical Society of Quebec in 1873. In particular, Miles substantiated Duberger's authorship of the Model against the rival claim of Captain—later Colonel—John By, who participated in its assembly in 1806-8, superintended its removal to England in 1811, and received sole credit for its "construction" in the first catalogue of the Woolwich Museum (see Pothier, *Quebec Model*, 24). Without endorsing the so-called "Duberger legend"— the myth that By drove Duberger to an early grave by taking credit for his work—Miles does suggest that certain aspects of By's character and circumstances in 1811—most notably his "concern" that "the British authorities" should appreciate his work on the "Martello Towers on the west side of Quebec"—are "not wholly incompatible with the idea of his having dealt wrongfully by Duberger" (106-7). He also makes an eloquent plea for the return of the Quebec Model to its "native place": "Year by year the visible memorials of old Quebec . . . are passing away; but the restoration of this model would serve, for generations to come, to exemplify native Canadian genius, to preserve a useful link in the connection between the past, the present, and the future of the famous city, and also as a lasting attraction to the visitors who flock to it annually in quest of objects of historical interest" (109-10). Despite Miles's plea for its repatriation, the Quebec Model was not "return[ed] to Canada as a gift to the Dominion until 1908" (Pothier, *Quebec Model*, 2). Thereafter it was exhibited in Ottawa, first at the Dominion Archives (1910-67) and then at the Canadian War Museum (1967-81), before being moved to its present location at Artillery Park in Quebec City (Pothier, "Duberger" 224).

Figure 1. The Quebec Model. (Courtesy of Parks Canada, Artillery Park National Historic Site, Québec.)

The most important twentieth-century historian of the Quebec Model is Bernard Pothier, whose study of its "origins and construction, . . . the circumstances of its removal to England and its return to Canada, and . . . [its] integrity and credibility as a document of the early nineteenth-century topography of Quebec" (*Quebec Model*, 65) was published in 1978 as Canadian War Museum

Drawing on Lambert, Miles, and others, as well as on archival materials unavailable to earlier writers, Pothier adds a wealth of detail
and interpretation to the history of the Quebec Model. Authorized
by Isaac Brock, then the commander of the Quebec garrison in
October 1806, the model was begun in November of the same year
and completed almost exactly two years later in November 1808
(Quebec Model, 10-16). Although Duberger was supervised by By,
the two worked on it "jointly" (Duberger's word), building sections
of it in Duberger's residence and assembling them in By's, where
"four rooms . . . [were made] into one" to accommodate it.
Duberger and By did not work in isolation, however, but
"benefitted from the active support and advice of the senior officers of the Artillery and Engineer Corps: Brock and [Colonel Ralph
Henry] Bruyeres," the commander of the Engineers at Quebec,
"Colonel George Glasgow, Commanding the Royal Artillery, Major
John Robe, R.A., and others" (12). That one of these advisors —
Robe — also wrote a topographical poem entitled "Quebec" at about
this time[1] gives a preliminary hint of the intriguing literary parallels and cultural implications of the Quebec Model.

Pothier's monograph contains two further pieces of information
that add to the significance of the Quebec Model as a cultural arti-
fact. The first is that during its construction the Model did not
"enjoy . . . support from every quarter" of Quebec society but, on
the contrary, generated "opposition from certain civilians" who
may have perceived it as a means of identifying and curtailing their
"incroachments" on Crown lands (13). As Duberger himself observed in a letter of 16 February 1807, "[n]o Body has had the sight
of [the Model] as yet although it is much spoken of, except Colonels
Brock, Glasgow, Vezey and Bruyeres, the business being too delicate for any others" (qtd. in Pothier, *Quebec Model,* 67). It should be
remembered, however, that the Model was constructed during the
early years of the Napoleonic Wars when Britain had reason to fear,
not only an invasion of Lower Canada by the United States, but
also an insurgence of the French inhabitants of the province. Perhaps more than at any time before or since, the garrisons at Quebec
City and elsewhere in British North America were burdened during
the Napoleonic period with the dual responsibility of defending
and dominating Britain's Canadian subjects and possessions. One
thing is clear from the mixed purposes and emotions surrounding
its construction and reception: the Quebec Model served as a con-
denser for the tension between the authorities and the residents of

Lower Canada which, *mutatis mutandis*, continues to the present day. The second piece of significant information provided by Pothier concerns the response of Governor General Sir James Craig to the Model after his arrival at Quebec in November 1807. "Though he pronounced himself 'highly pleased with [its] correctness,' [Craig] . . . suggested to By that its usefulness as a planning model would be significantly enhanced were it to include the high ground commanding the town from the Plains of Abraham" — a proposal that "doubl[ed] the size of the undertaking" and apparently necessitated the Model's removal to the ball-room of the Governor's residence, the Chateau St. Louis. "It was perhaps here," suggests Pothier, "that . . . John Lambert admired the model in May or June of 1808. . . . As it finally appeared, the model of Quebec was nearly double the length originally planned, extending into the Plains of Abraham, and beyond Saint John's suburb (as it existed at that time) approximately to the present Avenue des Erables" (*Quebec Model*, 14-16).[2] As these facts about its reception and augmentation indicate, the Quebec Model reflected in miniature the panoptic and expansive aspects of the imperial authorities in Lower Canada after the conquest.

It is tempting to proceed directly to these engaging issues, but before doing so a few moments may usefully be taken to discern the conception of art — the aesthetic — embodied in the Quebec Model and to ponder its relation to the ideological underpinnings of such poems as Robe's "Quebec." Clearly, Lambert's ascription of artistic merit to the work of Duberger and his colleagues in the Artillery and Engineer Corps relies on the general and pre-Modern meaning of "art" as "skill" (Williams, 32-33). But was there a particular skill, or set of skills, operating in the design and execution of the Model? In his *History of the Corps of Royal Engineers* (1889), Whitworth Porter provides a broad definition of the tasks faced by a military engineer after a conquest: "[h]e was to make a general survey of the position, to estimate for the restoration of the fort, and to prepare designs for other necessary works, such as barracks, storehouses, and a residence for the Governor" (1:138; and see Legget, *John By*, 9). To prepare engineers for these tasks, the training at the Royal Military Academy at Woolwich in the eighteenth century included "Mathematics . . . Fortifications . . . Arithmetic . . . Drawing for Landscape . . . [and] Figures," and modelling (Cattermode qtd. in Legget, *John By*, 6-7). Thus the training of Royal Engineers included, not only methods of calculation, but also techniques of representation in two and three dimensions — in short, accurate mimesis. When Lambert and Craig praised the Quebec Model for its "neatness" and "correctness" they were attesting to its creators' precise workmanship: to the extent that it accurately replicated a military position, the Quebec Model was both "useful" and "beautiful" — a praiseworthy manifestation of the mimetic skills and aesthetic of the Corps of Royal Engineers.

In the terms developed by Henri Lefebvre for the critical "analysis and theoretical explication" of space in *La production de l'espace*, the Quebec Model belongs in the category of "representations of space" — that is, "the space of scientists, planners, urbanists, technocratic subdividers and social engineers, as of a certain type of artist with a scientific bent. . . . This is the dominant space in any society (or mode of production) . . . [and it is] shot through with . . . a mixture of understanding *(connaissance)* and ideology which is always relative and in the process of change" (38-39, 41). The aim of Lefebvre's project is "to elucidate the . . . rise, . . . role, and . . . demise" of the "logic of visualization" — the "coded language" of "classical perspective and Euclidean space" — that permeated the "relationship between town, country, and political territory" in Western Europe "roughly from the sixteenth . . . to the nineteenth century" (17, 41). The relevance of such a line of inquiry to the Quebec Model is obvious and promising. An attempt to uncover the logic and ideology of this and other productions by the Royal Engineers could well yield valuable insights into what Lefebvre calls "the social (special) practices" of the "users and inhabitants, . . . the authorities and . . . technicians" (18, 17) of colonial Canada.

As a skillful imitation of Quebec City and its environs, the Quebec Model has obvious parallels in the various topographical poems that were written in and about portions of Upper and Lower Canada around the turn of the nineteenth century. In the Preface to *Abram's Plains* (1789), Thomas Cary endorses similar mimetic objectives and criteria when he "pronounce[s] descriptive poetry, that exhibits a picture of the real scenes of nature, to be the most difficult to excel in" and proceeds to assess Pope and Thomson on the basis of their "comparative merits . . . in description" (7-8, 27-28). So, too, does J. Mackay when he allows in the Preface to *Quebec Hill* (1797) that "the Poem might have been rendered . . . more poetical, if less attention had been paid to veracity" and adds that "to lovers of truth, no apology is necessary on this head, and to those of a contrary disposition, none is due" (15-18). Since Mackay's aim is to dispel the illusion that the Canadas are fit for European habitation, he gives scant attention either to Wolfe's victory or to the fortified city that it delivered into British hands. To him the Plains of Abraham evoke thoughts of the cruelty of war, the vanity of "Martial Fame," and the brevity of peace (1:187-206). Indeed, only marginally more lines are allotted in Quebec Hill to the spot where Wolfe "fought . . . bled . . . conquer'd, and . . . died" (1:184) than to a Thomsonian vignette of an "artful swain" shooting a covey of "trembling" birds on the otherwise desolate "Plain" (1:199-206).

Writing on the thirtieth anniversary of the Battle of the Plains of Abraham and as a patriotic inhabitant of British North America, Cary's aims and emphasis are very different. Not only does Wolfe's self-sacrificing victory provide the title and centerpiece of Abram's Plains, but the poem's avowedly peace-loving muse devotes several passages to earlier and later British victories in North America: Sir William Johnson's defeat of the French under Dieskau in 1755 and Sir Guy Carleton's route of the Americans under Montgomery in 1775-76. That Montgomery's campaign was aimed at Quebec is but one indication of the City's continued importance as a strategic site in the years following the conquest. Until well into the nineteenth century, "the city founded on the rock that proudly holds the height of the hill" was seen as the "Queen of the West" (Moodie, 38, 35), as "a translated Britannia asserting British tradition and might" (Sinclair, xiii). Abram's Plains is the product of an aspiring clerk and journalist rather than an engineer, an artilleryman, or a strategist, but it nevertheless parallels and, indeed, anticipates the Quebec Model in its detailed representation of the City and its sur-roundings, not least its extensive fortifications and adjacent battle-field.

In the extension of the Quebec Model to include Abraham's Plains and, more capriciously, the subsequent "loss" of this addi-tion can be read the tension between the centrifugal and centripetal forces that were active in Britain's imperial endeavors. Both expan-sive and contractile, the British Empire dotted the world with nodes of a central authority — "translated Britannia[s]" — to which personnel and materials were regularly dispatched and, as the case might be, recalled (Colonel By) or extracted (the Quebec Model). Such nodes of authority were, in turn, staging-posts for further ex-pansions and acquisitions, the preliminary agents of which were explorers, traders, soldiers, missionaries, and engineers. With the British Empire, as with the Quebec Model, the ultimate questions raised by the centrifugal urge to expansion were logistical: how far from the center or the node to extend, and where to stop. In the global — which is to say, spherical — space of British imperial dreams and practices, there was theoretically no limit to expansion: the Empire would extend eastward and westward until it encircled the world. A manifestation of this conceptual monad can be found in Cornwall Bayley's *Canada. A Descriptive Poem, Written at Quebec, 1805* and published there some six months before Brock authorized the construction of the Quebec Model. "[H]alf the convex world intrudes between" Europe and North America, observes Bayley, but "British sons" are nevertheless successfully transporting British "peace . . . science," freedom, and civilization across "uncounted leagues" to "hemispheres" unknown "to Caesar's eyes" (*418-24*). Almost as worthy of praise as Wolfe from Bayley's Romantic-imperialist perspective is Alexander Mackenzie, the Montreal-based explorer whose "exalted mind . . . scan[ned] / Millions of regions undescribed by man[!]; / Circling the globe from wide Atlantic's bound, / To where Pacific meets the joining round!" (*427-30*). As if replicating in small the centrifugal and centripetal vectors of British imperialism, Bailey concludes this portion of *Canada* by celebrating British expansion into Upper Canada and focusing on the Union Jack above Quebec City:

> . . . Kingston tow'rs o'er vast Ontario's sheet,
> Here too Toronto, now an Empire's seat;
> And here impending Albion's signal plays,
> O'er the rude rock from whence my fancy strays! (*451-54*)

The "here" to which this last couplet refers is Cape Diamond, the "most elevated part" of the Quebec promontory and the location of the British garrison. "The Cape is strongly fortified," explains Isaac Weld in his *Travels* (1799 f.), "and may be considered as the citadel of Quebec. . . . The evening and morning guns, and all salutes and signals, are fired from hence" (1:349). As what Benedict Anderson would call the "high centre" (25) of the British Empire in North America, Quebec City is both signalized and subordinated by the agents and emblems of imperial authority.

A variation of this hierarchy of exaltation can be seen at work in the Quebec Model. By its very nature as a miniature simulacrum mounted on a work-bench, the Model places its creators and viewers high above Quebec City and Abraham's Plains in a position similar — indeed, superior — to the British garrison and flag, a position otherwise physically impossible prior to the invention of the passenger balloon and the aeroplane. In effect, the Model allowed the British authorities to "read" the City and its surroundings with "a solar Eye, [or] . . . like a God" (Certeau, 92). The fact that the entire civic and military landscape of Quebec could now be scanned and assessed panoptically helps to explain both the suspicion and the secrecy that surrounded the Model during its construction. Thanks to the Quebec Model, it had become much easier to *oversee* and "rule . . . *over*" (Lefebvre, 21; emphasis added) the layout and development of the colonial capital. The physical reality of the place had been captured both accurately and, as important, transportably. It would now be possible to study Quebec City, not just in Colonel By's house or in the governor general's mansion, but also in Woolwich Barracks in the imperial capital; the Duke of Wellington or King George himself could assess the fortifications of Quebec and the Crown's holdings in and around the city. A sense of the Model's place in the surveillance network (Certeau, 96) — the remote control system — of imperialism can be gained from the fact that when it was removed from the barracks to the Rotunda Museum at Woolwich in c. 1820 it "was joined by a model of Gibralter" and "a further thirty-two such models — of fortifications and dockyards mostly — from the personal collection of George III" (Pothier, *Quebec Model*, 23-24).

An obvious cognate of the panoptic and transportable overview provided by the Quebec Model is the celestial or angelic perspective adopted by several of Canada's topographical poets. Near the beginning of Abram's *Plains,* Cary surveys the entire Great-Lakes-St. Lawrence System as if following its outlines on a map (21-41) and near the end of *Talbot Road* (1818) Adam Hood Burwell, whose brother Mahlon had surveyed the region north of Lake Erie for Colonel Thomas Talbot in 1809-11, invites the reader to "see, as on a single sheet, / The Talbot Road unbroken and complete" (*485-89*).[3] More fancifully, Thomas Moore — a guest of Isaac Brock and other government officials during his visit to Canada in 1804 (see Bentley, "Thomas Moore") — invites a Puckish Indian Spirit to describe a flight over the Appalachian Mountains and the Great Lakes in the central portion of "To the Lady Charlotte Rawdon from the Banks of the St. Lawrence." As obvious as the perspectival parallel between these topographical poems and the Quebec Model is the reliance of both genres on the maps of various Canadian regions and localities that were produced by explorers, surveyors, and engineers in the post-conquest period. Both Cary and Moore knew the

"New Map of North America" in Jonathan Carver's *Travels* (1778); Burwell may also have known the map in Michael Smith's *Geographical View of the Province of Upper Canada* (1813); and, of course, the Quebec Model was based on Duberger's own maps and drawings of the area.

When not aspiring to quite such elevated and comprehensive overviews as Cary, Moore, and Burwell, most topographical poets ascended promontories like Cape Diamond in order to survey and describe Canada's natural and human landscapes. A little less effectively than the Quebec Model, Cape Diamond afforded a view from the top which minified the objects and people below and, in doing so, permitted a recognition of the structure of the City and its surroundings. As Mackay repeatedly observes in *Quebec Hill*, distant prospects are composed of "waving orchards" and "varied foliage" rather than "crab . . . apples" and "pointed thistles" (*1:269-98*), large forms rather than minute particulars. A vivid sense of what is lost and what is gained by the adoption of an elevated perspective is provided by Bayley's description of the view from Cape Diamond in the opening lines of *Canada*:

> The tide-resisting wharf — the busy shore —
> The bulky vessel — and the crowded store —
> Half-undistinguish'd by the naked eye,
> Low at my feet, in pigmy semblance, lie!
> Onwards — whilst not a shade intrudes between,
> Expands the area of the checquer'd scene;
> All that Creation's rural sceptre yields
> The bloom of vales — the garniture of fields,
> All that of Beauport's crops — of Orlean's charms
> Majestic Lawrence circles in his arms. (15-24)

The details of the Lower Town and the surrounding towns — lower-class and predominantly *Canadien* zones below and beside the "high centre" — become just indistinct enough to permit a recognition of Quebec's mercantile and agricultural wealth — its busy port and warehouses, its fertile fields and abundant crops. No less than the creators of the Quebec Model, the authors of such poems as *Canada* cast themselves as giants in a drama of imperial superiority.

Nor was Cape Diamond the only promontory in Lower Canada that afforded Bayley and others a panoramic view of the province's riches. After enthusing about William Grant's "industrious" development of his seigneury on the Île St. Hélène near Montreal, Bayley ascends Mount Royal to survey the "plenteous farm — the field — the busy mill, / . . . the azure distant hill," and other "un-numbered beauties" of the "exhaustless view" (*180-94*). The precise spot chosen for this second poetic survey of Lower Canada's richness and potential is a "romantic cave" on the lower slopes of Mount Royal: the "tomb on the mountain" which fulfilled the wish of the wealthy fur-trader Simon McTavish to be buried near the mansion that remained unfinished on his death in July 1804. As well as being used for poetic surveys and military installations, the "high centres" of Lower Canada were (and are) the sites of the status-charged homes and retreats of the commercial and administrative elites that dominated the province's "social superstructures" (Lefebvre, 85).[4] In the early nineteenth century, McTavish's mansion and the Chateau St. Louis repeatedly commanded the attention of travelers and poets. Of the former, Lambert observed that it was "[a] large handsome stone building . . . at the foot of the mountain, in a very conspicuous situation" (2:68). Of the latter (which was rebuilt in 1810-11), John MacTaggart observed in 1826 that it was "placed in a very fine and lofty situation" (*Three Years in Canada*, 1:33). Very obviously both houses were carefully sited and landscaped so as to permit their inhabitants to look down on their surroundings and, by the same logic, to encourage the remainder of the population to look up at (and to) them. Less obvious is the care taken in *Canada* and elsewhere to associate the McTavish and governor's mansions with domestic affection and physical health. By Bayley's account, it was "window'd love [that] . . . rais'd a husband's grave" on "Montreal's mountain heighth" (*283-86*), and in *Abram's Plains* Cary associates the "villa of fair Dorchester" (governor, 1786-94) with domestic felicity — "the tender sweets of life / That in the mother centre and the wife" — and with the "breeze-inviting plains" — the airily healthy uplands (*485-91*). In Cary's application of the rural retirement theme to Dorchester, the Chateau St. Louis is simultaneously an official residence and a modest retreat, a substantial neoclassical edifice ("villa") far from "parade . . . crowds" and "the glare of equipage" (social trappings). The implication is that the mansions of the wealthy and powerful in Lower Canada are not the seats of ostentation but the abodes of an overclass that is affectionate, stable, healthy, and, despite certain appearances, modest. Who could fail to look up to such people? Or as Cary puts it earlier in the poem, in an address to Canada's "swains" that is unlikely to have reached many French-Canadian ears: "Grateful, ye peasants, own your mended state, / And bless, beneath a GEORGE, your better fate" (450-51).

Of course, the most imposing or "dominant" (Lefebvre, 164) manifestation of Georgian authority in Lower Canada was the star-shaped citadel that sits astride the upper plateau of Cape Diamond above the old city and the Plains of Abraham, and which now contains both the headquarters of the Royal 22nd. Regiment and the Quebec residence of the governor general. "The great fortification is on the highest situation," enthused MacTaggart, adding that "of course, [it] commands the whole town" (Three Years in Canada, 1:33). Although envisaged as early 1762, a year before "British military officials reserved . . . 535 acres . . . for [its] construction" (Noppen, 42-43; Ruddel, 206), the citadel was not in fact built until 1820-30, on the recommendation of the Duke of Richmond and the authority of the Duke of Wellington. Almost certainly the selection of the final design and precise location of the citadel was assisted by the Quebec Model (Legget, John By, 12), whose principal purpose, of course, was "to assist the authorities in England in improving the defenses of the City" (Pothier, Quebec Model, 17).[5] Between the proposal and construction of the citadel, Quebec's defenses were continually being restored and augmented, most notably in 1797 with the addition of Prescott's Gate near the entrance to the Upper Town (Noppen, 55). It may simply be a coincidence that in 1798-99 Governor Robert Prescott's secretary was none other than Thomas Cary. But the possibility of it being something more is scarcely ruled out by the numerous references to the "works," "bastions," and other fortifications of Quebec in Abram's Plains, or by the poet's coy insistence that his muse "comes [as] no spy to draw the secret plan" of the City's defenses (454-69). At the very least Cary's detailed knowledge of the existing and planned fortifications of Quebec points once again to the overlapping interests and attitudes of Lower Canada's topographical poets and military engineers.

In considering these shared characteristics, it is important to remember that most of the defensive structures mentioned by Cary in Abram's Plains belong to a broad category of built forms — walls — that the Royal Engineers regarded as a special area of expertise. Nowhere is this proprietary attitude to walls in general more apparent than in "The Engineer," an unfinished and as yet unpublished long poem[6] by the same John MacTaggart who commented favorably on the locations of the citadel and the governor's mansion in his Three Years in Canada: an Account of the Actual State *of the Country in 1826-7-8* (1829). Before coming to Canada in 1826 as By's clerk of works on the Rideau Canal project, MacTaggart had published *The Gallovidian Encyclopedia* (1824), a compendium of antiquarian and folkloric materials pertaining to southern Scotland, and, more to the point, worked on the enormous breakwater that sheltered Plymouth Sound, a project designed by the innovative Scottish civil engineer John Rennie (Emmerson, 481).[7] "Our temples and our towns / Require strong walls flung round for their defence," proclaims MacTaggart in "The Engineer," for "Discord growls amongst Mankind / When scarce two nations think or act alike" (71).[8] Whether as breakwaters, for defense, or around orchards,

> Walls of themselves are wonderful Engines:
> •   •   •
> By them we keep our cattle to their fields,
> Sheep on their hills and oxen in their vales,
> Without the which confusion would ensue . . .
> •   •   •
> And Desolation grasp the country wide.
> Landlords about their Marches would to war,
> The greedy eat the simpletons away
> By field and Field till their estates were gone.
> Back from the shallow flats when tides o'erflow
> With walls of mud we press the wat'ry world. . . . (73)

In MacTaggart's analysis, walls maintain peace and maximize productivity by keeping animals, people, and the elements in their proper place; walls embody and protect the rational and moral order.[9] Little wonder that MacTaggart envisages the creation of order out of chaos in Genesis 1 as God's originary engineering project, and conceives of engineers as a caste uniquely entrusted with the ability to "mitigate" the effects of the Fall (87, 23). The heirs to the (masonic) knowledge that produced the pyramids, MacTagart's "Engineer" is nothing less than the agent of providential design.

A less prominent and, in central Canada, less utilized element in the technical repertoire of the Royal Engineers was road construction. "Good roads are glorious for they hasten haste" and thus provide numerous social benefits, particularly to aspects of "trade and commerce needing quick dispatch" (MacTaggart, "The Engineer," 79). "At least in Britain," MacTaggart continues, "paved and cambered roads have made "Ruts" and "mud" things of the past. That this was not the case in early nineteenth-century Canada is confirmed by numerous writers[10] including William Robe at several points in "Quebec." "Canadian roads! how much to be admired," Robe exclaims ironically,

> Canadian laws much more! which mend those roads,
> Or leave them to be mended as they can!
> While wheels and carriages; and necks, and limbs Of horses and of
> men endanger'd are Almost at ev'ry step: surely 'tis shame
> While ample means are found in every rock
> For forming good and solid roads, that here
> Th' approach to Britain's first Provincial Town
> Should ev'ry way be miserably bad!
> Yet, let us hope, 'twill not be always so;
> The spirit of improvement once begun,
> will soon extend itself around the town,
> And mend the rugged ways. (1: 43-56)

The status of Quebec as the foremost British "Town" outside Britain makes the condition of Lower Canada's roads especially reprehensible. A system of "good and solid roads" in the province would reduce danger and confirm the presence of British law and order. As consistent with the ethos of imperial engineering as Robe's comments on Canadian roads is his perception that "improvement" is already beginning to "extend . . . around the town" — outwards and downwards from the "high centre" of Quebec City.

Similarly consistent with the ethos of imperial engineering is Robe's subsequent emphasis on the hierarchical structure and civic architecture of Quebec City. With the arrival of spring, the Lower Town begins to bustle with activity as vessels arrive from the West Indies, from "Greenock's rising port, or [from] Liverpool" and "the shops display their earliest store / Of Britain's fashions, and of Britain's goods" (1:80-86). Meanwhile, in the Upper Town "The troops their gay attire again display" and

> The builders now
> Their summer occupations recommence,
> Wither the public edifice to rear,
> Houses, for numbers still increas'd, to build
> Or old ones to repair. . . . (1:87-97)

Quebec's builders are not hailed as the agents of improvement, however, but as the practitioners of backward-looking and "dim-sighted" architectural prejudice who, despite "successive years" of devastating fires, continue to use traditional and dangerous designs in the construction of chimneys (1:97-106). Like his earlier suggestion that stricter laws might hasten the improvement of Canada's roads and his later appeal to the British authorities to counteract the dissipation and poverty that he finds rampant in Lower Canada (2:116-201), Robe's call for better building codes in the province rests on the imperialistic assumption that legal and practical remedies emanating from the "high centre" are crucial to the colony's material and moral progress.

It is entirely consistent with Robe's moralistic application of the engineering ethos that, before participating in the construction of the Quebec Model, he was the architect in charge of building the Church of the Holy Trinity in Quebec City, a "public edifice" modeled on St. Martin's-in-the-Fields in London (with elements . . . drawn from the Coliseum and the Pantheon in Rome) and destined to be the first Anglican cathedral outside the British Isles (Wurtele, 75-79). Robe must have been well-pleased with Alexander Spark's pronouncement in the 17 August 1805 issue of Cary's *Quebec Mercury* that the civic buildings recently completed in Lower Canada indicated the province's speedy ascent of the ladder of social development from "rude[ness] and barbarism" to "refinement" and "wealth" (262). "The gradual steps by which societ[ies] advance . . . may be traced, with tolerable accuracy, in the improvement of their buildings," proclaims Spark, "[a]nd . . . several Edifices . . . lately erected in this province, and various works of public utility which have been undertaken and executed, indicate a degree of public spirit highly auspicious to the state of the country, and . . . seem to promise a rapid progress of colonial Improvement." A sadly ironical coda to Robe's career is contained in the fate of the other major architectural project of his design, a grandly Palladian circular market in the Upper Town. Begun at about the time of the writing of "Quebec" (which contains a brief description of Lower Canada's produce markets [1:259-62], Robe's highly "refined" market was neither built to his original designs nor popular with the towns people, and in 1815 the Assembly passed a bill ordering its demolition on the pretext that its wooden dome constituted a fire risk (Noppen, 55).

Of greater consequence for the construction of central Canada than any other component of the Royal Engineers' technical repertoire was their mastery of the means of controlling and utilizing water. After describing the construction of a "quay" below Quebec City in the seventeen eighties, Cary anticipates MacTaggart in likening the power of "British spirits" over "the wave" to that of Moses or God:

> At their command floods back their billows heave,
> And a bold shore their cozy bottom leave:
> High flinty rocks descend to level plains,
> Whence, on both sides, commerce a footing gains. (*104-7*)

The probable reference here is to the use of landfill below Quebec City to increase the number of wharves and warehouses — Bayley's "tide-resisting wharf . . . and . . . crowded store" — along the shoreline of the St. Lawrence between the St. Charles River and Ansedes-Meres. As David T. Ruddel notes, the number of wharves in this area "increased from eleven in 1785, to twenty-one in 1804, and thirty-seven in 1829" (202). MacTaggart could be commenting on these developments when he asks his reader to behold the "Engineering Architect":

> See how he plans the villages and towns
> To suit their various trafficking and trade:
> For foreign commerce seaports are laid out;
> Harbours and docks inclose the placid flood,
> Where ride secure the couriers of the deep. . . . (69)

The ability of the Royal Engineers to build wharves, harbors, and docks, to create additional land for agricultural and commercial use, and, above all, to construct better and bigger canals such as the Rideau — in short, to manipulate fresh and salt water enabled the British to adapt and "improve" Canada's natural environment for their military and mercantile purposes. In the manipulation of Canada's coastal and inland waters lay a crucial key to the future of both the country and the empire.

Apart from Cary's brief reference to the building of a "quay" below Quebec City, there are no direct treatments of the manipulation of water in early topographical poems about Canada. Rivers, rapids, and waterfalls make frequent appearances in these poems, however, and often with metaphorical accretions that resonate with the attitudes and activities of the Royal Engineers. Abram's *Plains* derives its very structure from what Donald Creighton once called the "Commercial Empire of the St. Lawrence" (see Bentley, Introduction to Cary, xiii-xiv), and early in the poem the "rude rocks" and loud "rushing" rapids (76) that would eventually be eliminated by a series of large canals are associated metaphorically with the rude cultures and social discords that had already given way to British refinement and the *pax Britannica*. No doubt Cary's approval of the taming of the "savage soil" and the "savage mind" (54, 57) would have extended to the control of savage water. Looking down on the "rich meadows" beside the St. Charles, he draws a standard Augustan comparison between the waters of the river and the conduct of human life:

> The slow meand'ring stream that tardy moves,
> Dispenses fatness through the meads and groves:
> Whilst rushing floods that downward eager drive,
> The meadows of their needful dews deprive.
> So, in life's course, who with wise caution treads,
> Tho' slow, yet sure his influence widely spreads:
> Whilst him who headstrong, thoughtless whirls away,
> Of cheated views, useless, becomes a prey. (*400-7*)

Like slow-moving rivers, people should control their passions, for by so doing they increase their productivity and prospects ("views"). In *Quebec Hill*, Mackay similarly councils the rational control of human nature when, after describing the fate of "savage beasts" and "ev'n birds" that venture too close to Niagara Falls, he applies the lesson to "careless, roving men, devoid of thought" who become caught "in the rapids of their passions" (*1:109-22*). No more than "rapids" or "passions" are human nature and physical nature identical, but in an age obsessed with rational control they are so intimately interconnected as to be homologous.

Bayley introduces another level to the subjugation of Canadian water when, between celebrating Mackenzie's "discoveries" and saluting "Albion's signal," he identifies the waters of the St. Lawrence with the benefits that flow from the British monarch:

> Hail . . . Majestic King of rivers, hail!
> Whether amid the placid-winding vale,

Thy waters ripen nature's every bloom; Or, thro' the bosom of the
forest's gloom, Their swelling currents with resistless tide,
Break o'er the rocks, and lash their craggy side;
Where ere thy waves reflect the face of day,
Wid — rich — romanticis thy regal sway! (437-44)

Using the coronation of a new monarch as an analogy for the
inauguration of a "golden reign" (435) in Canada, Bayley invests
his "regal" river with the topographical equivalents of the orb, the
scepter, and the crown: a "placid-winding vale" suggesting peace,
"ripen[ing]" waters productive of fertility, and the "swelling currents" of a power that is as "resistless" as it is enlightened. To reinforce his identification of the St. Lawrence with the British
monarch, Bayley calls attention to the renaming of Toronto and
Sorelle as York and William Henry in honor of the brother and son
of George III, whose troubled reign (1760-1820) began shortly after
the fall of Quebec and should have coincided with the inception of
the new golden age in Canada's history.

After such an elaborate conceit, it is almost disappointing to
turn to Burwell's *Talbot Road* where the perception of Upper
Canada's rivers and lakes is more practical than poetic. Less interested in elaborate metaphorical comparisons than in water-
powered mills (499-502), Burwell looks to the day when the
notorious "storms" that "often vex the bosom" of Lake Erie (444-
45) will have been conquered by the presence of large vessels "deep
laden . . . with wealth from India's distant shores" (569-71). As they
"plough the liquid plain" and "Stem the rude winds" of the Lake
(179-81), the immigrants of the Talbot Settlement have already begun to master the water as well as the land of Upper Canada. By
the time Burwell's poem was published in 1818, their efforts had
been well augmented by Talbot's mill-wrights and road-builders. In
1829, the fulfillment of their mercantile ambitions came a huge step
closer with the completion of the Welland Canal. The Falls that had
prompted Mackay to expiate on the dangers of thoughtless passion
lay beyond human control, but they had been bypassed to allow the
quick and easy passage of vessels into the center of the Great Lakes
System.

The engineer most closely associated with the manipulation of
Canadian water in the early nineteenth century was, of course, By.
The son of at least two generations of Thames watermen who broke
with family tradition when he entered the Royal Military Academy
at Woolwich, By did his first tour of duty in Lower Canada when

British canal-building in the province was beginning to gain momentum. When he arrived in August 1802, work had just begun on "the reconstruction of the . . . small and crude canals in the Soulanges section of the St. Lawrence. . . [between] Lake St. Francis [and] Lake St. Louis," and by 1804-5 he was himself in charge of the construction of "an entirely new canal at the Cascades" that would be "capable of holding six batteaux" (Legget, *John By*, 10).[11] But it was not until his return to Canada in May 1826, after a posting to the Peninsula War and several years in England, that By received his most important commission: the construction of the Rideau Canal between Kingston and what is now Ottawa. On 13 July 1826, By wrote a report to his superior, General Gother Mann, in London, which reveals his military and mercantile vision of the canal: "it appears self-evident that, by forming a steam boat navigation from the River St. Lawrence to the various Lakes [we] would at once deprive the Americans of the means of attacking Canada; and would make Great Britain mistress of the trade of that vast population on the borders of the Lakes, of which the Americans have so much boasted" (qtd. in Legget, *John By*, 29). Some six years later in May 1832, By had the pleasure of traveling the full length of the completed canal on a steam boat, and in June of the same year he reported to Lord Dalhousie that he had already witnessed as many as "35 cribs of Timber" pass through it in a single day (qtd. in Legget, *John By*, 41-42).

But for a full — indeed, giddy — assessment of the implications of the St. Lawrence, Rideau, and more westerly Canadian canals, it is impossible to do better than By's most literary and visionary clerk of works. Once the Welland Canal around Niagara Falls and the Grand Canadian Canal at Sault St. Marie are completed, MacTaggart suggests, "steam-boats may go up from Quebec to Lake Superior . . .; from thence with little trouble, they will pass through the *notch* of the rocky mountains and be locked down . . . to the Pacific Ocean. . . . The town of Nootka [Vancouver] is likely yet to be as large as London, and ought to be laid out on an extensive plan, as the trade between it and the Orient world may become wonderfully great. Then when the steam-packet line is established between Quebec and London . . . we may come and go between China and Britain in about two months" (*Three Years in Canada*, 1:169). MacTaggart's "prophecy" is more "foolish" and less "practicable" than he suspected, but with the partial replacement of canals by railways it translates into the imperial dream that gov-

erned the development of Canada in the decades following Con-
federations.[12]

Less risible are MacTaggart's remarks on the engineering
achievement and developmental importance of the Rideau and
other western canals. Unlike "any other in the known world," he
writes in *Three Years in Canada*, the Rideau Canal is "not ditched or
cut out by the hand of man, [but] natural rivers and lakes are made
use of . . ., and all that science or art hard] to do . . . is in the lock-
age of the rapids or waterfalls" (1:162). As well as being a means of
"transporting stores safely, either in times of war or peace," the
Rideau Canal "might also be the means of opening an important
tract in the interior of Canada" (1:104). Although MacTaggart laments certain aspects of the development of what is now Ontario —
the destruction of indigenous plants, the colonization of people "as
good as ourselves," and the division of the province into townships
on the basis of concession lines "laid out artificially, without attending in any respect to the laws of nature" (1:92-94; 2:100-2) — he
does not question the civilizing value of either canals or engineers
around "the huge Canadian reservoirs":

> Down from those Lakes in humid regions high
> Canals they cut, extending traffic's scope,
> Transforming wastes and wilderness drear
> To cheerful lands of animated life.
> The plowman whistles where the Indian hunted,
> And love notes chaunt where warsongs savage yell'd.
> Our industry can even the climates tame. . . .
> •   •   •
> Morasses drained or forests fell'd invite
> The weather warm, while floods and trees rebuff
> The solar fires and cool the hectic breeze. . . .
> ("The Engineer," 117)

In *Abram's Plains*, the Great Lakes are scarcely more than distant cartographical forms. In *Quebec Hill*, the "foetid fens" of Upper
Canada are the source of "fever and ague" (1:87 and n.). In *Canada*
the preliminary signs of settlement can be seen on the shores of
"wild Erie" (351-54). And in *Talbot Road*, the prophetic poet looks
to the day when the Talbot Settlement will be fully integrated into
the mercantile system of the British Empire. Looking back on these
developments in "The Engineer," MacTaggart sees gloomy

"wastes" transformed by the white magic of engineering into productive, peaceful, and even congenially temperate "lands" inhabited by happy British settlers.[13]

If one public works project were to be chosen to sum up the contribution of the Royal Engineers to the construction of central Canada, it could well be the Union Bridge across the Ottawa River at Chaudeire Falls. "[A] Bridge from land to land . . . Connect[s] shores by easy intercourse / Which distant lay and were to other strange" (76-77) writes MacTaggart in "The Engineer," and in *Three Years in Canada* he confirms that the Union Bridge was intended "to connect Upper and Lower Canada" (1:326), a union not in fact enacted until 1839. Begun in 1826 and completed in 1829, the Union Bridge consisted of a wooden truss mounted on dry-stone pillars, a design that seems to have been adapted from an illustration in the 1738 translation of Palladio's *Four Books of Architecture* (Legget, "First Bridge," 53, 59). According to a letter in the Montreal *Herald* on 21 February 1827, its "beautiful arch was suggested by Lieutenant-Colonel By; planned by Mr. [John] MacTaggart; and executed under the appropriate superintendence of Mr. [Thomas] MacKay, of Montreal, [the] architect" and—MacTaggart adds—the master mason who "built the locks on the Lachine Canal, from the plans of . . . the engineer" (*Three Years in Canada*, 1: 344-47). At Lord Dalhousie's request, By had a model of the bridge made and sent to the earl's home in Scotland (Legget, *John By*, 38). Given its wooden frame and dry-stone construction, it was perhaps inevitable that the Union Bridge would succumb to the rigors of the Canadian climate. This it did in the winter of 1836, leaving the Rideau Canal as what By himself had hoped would be "a lasting monument of [his] perseverance" (qtd. in Legget, *John By*, 42). The Union Bridge served its practical and symbolic purposes for less than ten years, and By's model of it has not survived. But in John Burrows' watercolor, now in the National Archives of Canada in the city that once bore By's name, it still stands as a testament to the constructive arts of the Royal Corps of Engineers (fig. 2).

The story of the Royal Engineers' construction of Canada does not begin or end in Upper and Lower Canada in the period between the conquest and confederation. During the same period and earlier, they left their mark on several parts of Newfoundland and the Maritime provinces, and from 1858 to 1863 their Columbia detachment "compiled and printed at least 20 maps of parts of the new colony of British Columbia." On the west coast, adds William G. Dean, "[t]heir major tasks, besides military peacekeeping, were exploring, surveying, and road building. . . . They also made cadastral [landownership] surveys of 11 townsites, principally New Westminster and Sapperton" (166). Not least of their tasks in British Columbia was to locate and mark the boundary laid down by the Oregon Treaty of 1846. As George F.G. Stanley explains, this meant "ascertaining points" and erecting cairns at "convenient intervals on or near the boundary" and then "cutting a track" of at least "twenty feet in width" along the parallel on both sides of the markers (10). Thus the Royal Engineers demarcated the southwestern limits of the country that they had earlier helped to consolidate and extend.

Figure 2. The Union Bridge. (Courtesy of National Archives of Canada, Ottawa.)

Notes

I am grateful to the taxpayers of Ontario and Canada through the University of Western Ontario and the Social Sciences and Humanities Research Council of Canada for their support of my teaching and research, to Victor Howard for his interest in this essay, and to Lise Fournier, I.S. MacLaren, the Very Reverend James D. Merrett and several others for assisting me with my enquiries and theorizing about the Quebec Model and related matters. I am also grateful to Kerry Breeze and Tara Stephens for their word processing skills.

In parenthetical references, italicized numbers refer to parts and lines of poems.

1.   The fact that the poem is written on paper watermarked 1806 and contains an address to Henry Caldwell (*1:119-26*), who died in May 1810, suggests that it was composed between these dates.

2.   Pothier notes that the "spot where Wolfe died" was "marked on the model itself by a piece of the original marking stone" (*Quebec Model*, 16n.).

3.   A little later in the poem, Burwell regrets his earthly location and limitations: "my weak efforts scarcely rise to praise. / Had I an angel's wing, a seraph's fire, / How would my muse to daring flights aspire!" (530-32).

4.   The spatial/social division of Montreal and Quebec City into above and below, Upper and Lower town, anticipates the stratification and segregation of Canadian urban centers into hierarchical districts and zones that, as Graeme Wynn observes in "Forging a Canadian Nation" (1987), occurred between 1850 and 1930 with the arrival and spread of modernity. Wynn notes that by 1930 "both large and small places [in Canada] bore the specialized, differentiated stamp of the modern urban centre" and that the phrase "the other side of the tracks" had achieved "meaningful currency" (397-98). Modernity arrived belatedly in the Maritimes, but from almost its beginnings, Wynn suggests, Shaughnessy Heights in Vancouver B.C. was a "haven of conspicuous consumption" "[d]ownslope" from which were the "wooden tenements close to the work-places on the banks of False Creek" (398). Much the same point could be made about Uplands in Victoria, B.C. Tuxedo Drive in Winnipeg, Manitoba and any number of districts in Canadian towns and cities that have earned such designations as "Pill Hill" on account of their high concentrations of doctors and other professionals.

5.   In a letter to William Lyon Mackenzie-King on 5 July 1925, the Dominion Archivist, Sir Arthur Doughty, informed the Prime Minister that he was "setting up" the Quebec Model in the Archives' "new building" on Sessex Drive· in

Ottawa, adding: "I . . . have spent a great deal of time in restoring it. It requires a canvas at the back and it should be painted. I wish you would speak to the Minister of Public Works about having this done for us. It is well worth making the most of this model because it is intensely interesting to the Architects of Canada. It was a serious piece of work made for the British Government in order that they might decide what form of defense was best for the city of Quebec and it was on this model that the works at Quebec were begun in 1815 at the cost of thirty million dollars."

6.   The manuscript of "The Engineer" is held in the Stewartry Museum, Kircudbright, Scotland. A photocopy of the manuscript, which runs to 154 pages, was very kindly supplied by the Museum's Curator, Dr. F. D. Devereux. In some ways a verse precursor of Samuel Smiles' *Lives of the Engineers* (1861-62), MacTaggart's poem touches only sporadically on engineering in Canada, but it does, among other things, liken bridges constructed of "Iron" to "those in frigid climes the work of Frost" and refer to Niagara Falls in an account of the dynamics of rivers and oceans (76, 91).

7.   See *Three Years in Canada*, 1:170-76 for the letter that MacTaggart wrote to the Montreal *Herald* in 1826 urging the establishment in Quebec of a Society for the Promotion of Natural History and the compilation of a Canadian encyclopedia. As a result of this letter and similar articles, the Natural History Society of Montreal was founded in 1827 and MacTaggart was "elected . . . to membership" (Emmerson, 481). In *Inventing Canada: Early Victorian Science and the Idea of a Transcontinental Nation* Suzanne Zeller could be describing MacTaggart when she writes that the "Royal Engineers' surveys for canals and roads offered unique opportunities to observe the geology of the country" (16) and its natural history.

8.   Capitalization has been regularized, punctuation added, and ampersands changed to "and" in quotations from both "The Engineer" and Robe's "Quebec."

9.   See *Quebec Hill*, 1: 245-46, for Mackay's notion that "The pointed fence each peasant's right contains, / And forms a barrier to the neighb'ring swains" and 2:127-32 for his horror at the ability of northern winds to "pierce . . . [the] walls" of houses.

10.   Catharine Parr Traill's comments on the badness of Upper Canadian roads are well known (see *The Backwoods of Canada*, 113-14, for example). See also Standish O'Grady in *The Emigrant* (1841) on the "ill wrought bridge[s]" and "public road[s]" of Lower Canada: "roads are things, in this wild clime unknown, / Where snow wrought highways must suffice for stone" (1847, 1859-60).

11. In his Foreword to part 2 of C. R. Young and J. H. Dales' *Engineering and Society with Special Reference to Canada* (1947), Harold Innis observes that, in contrast to their French predecessors, British engineers "concentrated on the problem of improvement of communications rather than defense" in the period surrounding the turn of the eighteenth into the nineteenth century, with particular emphasis on canals; "[t]he Royal Engineers built a canal between the Cascades and Coteau Landing between 1779 and 1783 to handle military stores. This was enlarged from 1801 to 1804 and seven locks . . . installed over a distance of nine miles. A road was developed across the Niagara peninsula, Yonge Street was extended north to Collingwood, and the North West Company built a small canal at Sault Ste. Marie (144-45). Innis also observes that the Rideau and Welland canals were built "[t]o offset the effect of the Erie Canal" (which, when completed in 1825, connected the Hudson River to Lake Erie) and notes that both were subsidized by the British government on account of their "military importance" (145, 150).

12. "As the Act of Union provided funds for the completion of the St. Lawrence canals" by 1850, observes Innis, "the British North America Act provided funds for construction of the Intercolonial Railway linking the system in Canada with that in the Maritimes and for extension to the West" (150).

13. See *Three Years in Canada*, 1:313-15 for MacTaggart's advocacy of other water-related schemes for the "improvement" of Quebec.

Works Cited

Bayley, Cornwall. *Canada. A Descriptive Poem, Written at Quebec, 1805.* Edited by D.M.R. Bentley. London: Canadian Poetry Press, 1990.

Bentley, D.M.R. Introduction. Pp. xi-xlviii in *Abram's Plains: A Poem.* By Thomas Cary. London: Canadian Poetry Press, 1986.

Burwell, Adam Hood. *Talbot Road: a Poem.* 1818. Edited by Michael Williams. London: Canadian Poetry Press, 1991.

Carver, Jonathan. *Travels through the Interior Parts of North America in the Years 1766, 1767, and 1768.* 1778. 3d. ed. 1781. 2 Vols. Minneapolis: Ross and Hianes, 1956.

Cary, Thomas. *Abram's Plains: a Poem.* 1789. Edited by D.M.R. Bentley. London: Canadian Poetry Press, 1986.

Certeau, Michel de. *The Practice of Everyday Life.* Translated by Steven F. Rendell. Berkeley: University of California Press, 1984.

Dean, William G. "Plate 24: British Garrisons to 1871." In *Historical Atlas of Canada: Volume II: the Land Transformed, 1800-1891.* Edited by R. Louis Gentilcore. Toronto: University of Toronto Press, 1993.

Doughty, Arthur George. Letter to the Rt. Hon. W.L. Mackenzie King. 12 July 1925. National Archives of Canada. RG 37, vol. 202 (Letters Sent 15 Jan. 1925 - 29 Sept. 1936). Ottawa. 137.

Emmerson, G.S "John MacTaggart." *Dictionary of Canadian Biography,* 6:480-82.

Innis, H.A. Foreword. Pp. 141-55 in *Engineering and Society with Special Reference to Canada.* By C. R. Young and J. H. Dales. Toronto: University of Toronto Press, 1947.

Lambert, John. *Travels through Canada, and the United States of North America, in the Years 1806, 1807, and 1808.* 1813. 3rd ed. London: Baldwin, Cradock, and Joy, 1816.

Lefebvre, Henri. *The Production of Space.* 1974. Trans. Donald Nicholson-Smith. Oxford: Blackwell, 1991.

Legget, Robert F. "First Bridge Over Ottawa River Proves to be 'Trussworthy.'" *Canadian Consulting Engineer* 21 (June 1979): 52-53, 59.

———. *John By, Lieutenant Colonel, Royal Engineers, 1779-1836, Builder the Rideau Canal, Founder of Ottawa.* Ottawa: Historical Society of Ottawa, 1982.

Mackay, J. *Quebec Hill; or, Canadian Scenery. A Poem. In Two Parts.* 1797. Edited by D.M.R. Bentley. London: Canadian Poetry Press, 1988.

MacTaggart, John. "The Engineer." Stewartry Museum. Environmental Health and Leisure Services Department. Stewartry District Council. Kirkcudbright, Scotland.

———. *Three Years in Canada: an Account of the Actual State of the Country in 1826-7-8.* 2 vols. London: Henry Colburn, 1829.

Miles, H.H. "Some Observations on Canadian Chorography and Topography, and on the Meritorious Services of the Late Jean Baptiste Duberger, Senr." Pp. 93-111 in *Transactions of the Literary and Historical Society of Quebec. Session of 1872-73.* NS Pt 10. Quebec: Middleton and Dawson, 1873.

Moodie, Susanna. *Roughing It in the Bush.* 1852. Afterword by Susan Glickman. New Canadian Library. Toronto: McClelland and Stewart, 1989.

Moore, Thomas. *Poetical Works.* Edited by A.D. Godley. London: Humphrey Melford, Oxford University Press, 1915.

Noppen, Luc, Claude Paulette, and Michel Tremblay. *Quebec: trots siecles d'architecture.* N.p.: Editions Libre Expression, 1979.

Porter, Whitworth. *History of the Corps Royal Engineers.* London: Longmans, Green, 1889.

Pothier, Bernard. "Jean-Baptiste Duberger." *Dictionary of Canadian Biography*, 6:223-24.

———. *The Quebec Model*. National Museum of Man Mercury Series: Canadian War Museum Paper 9. Ottawa: National Museums of Canada, 1978.

Ruddel, David T. *Quebec City, 1765-1832: the Evolution of a Colonial Town*. Mercury Series: History Division Papers 41. Ottawa: Canadian Museum of Civilization, n.d.

Robe, William. "Quebec." Lande Collection. MG 53 *189. National Archives of Canada. Ottawa.

Sinclair, David. Introduction. Pp. vi-xiii in *Nineteenth-Century Narrative Poems*. Edited by David Sinclair. New Canadian Library Original 8. Toronto: McClelland and Stewart, 1972.

Smiles, Samuel. *Lives of the Engineers, with an Account of Their Principal Works; Comprising also a History of Inland Communication in Britain*. 1861-62. Rev. ed. 5 Vols. London: J. Murray, 1874.

Smith, Michael. *A Geographical View of the Province of Upper Canada*. New York: Pelsue and Gould, 1813.

Stanley, George F.G. Introduction. Pp. 1-19 in *Mapping the Frontier: Charles Wilson's Diary of the Survey of the 49th Parallel, 1858-1862, while Secretary of the British Royal Commission*. Edited by George F.G. Stanley. Toronto: Macmillan, 1970.

Traill, Catharine Parr. *The Backwoods of Canada: Being Letters from the Wife of an Emigrant Officer, Illustrative of the Domestic Economy of British America*. 1836. Afterword by D. M. R. Bentley. New Canadian Library. Toronto: McClelland and Stewart, 1989.

Weld, Isaac. *Travels Through the States of North America, and the Provinces of Upper and Lower Canada, during the Years 1795, 1796, and 1797*. 1799. 4th ed. 1807. 2 Vols. New York: Johnson Reprint, 1968.

Wurtele, Fred C. "The English Cathedral of Quebec." *Transactions the Literary and Historical Society of Quebec* 20 (1891): 63-132.

Wynn, Graeme. "Forging a Canadian Nation." Pp. 373-409 in *North America: The Historical Geography of a Changing Continent*. Edited by Robert D. Mitchell and Paul A. Groves. Totowa, N.J.: Rowman and Littlefield, 1987.

Zeller, Suzanne. *Inventing Canada: Early Victorian Science and the Idea of a Transcontinental Nation*. Toronto: University of Toronto Press, 1987.

DETROIT - WINDSOR TO 1914

Daniel Jacobson
Michigan State University

*Not long before his death, Professor Jacobson presented this paper at a con-
ference on Canadian Studies held at Michigan State University. It was a
work-in-progress which was to become a comprehensive description and
analysis of the growth of Detroit and Windsor in their related biographies.
The reader might find the terms of reference and the preliminary charac-
terization of interest.*

A series of fine works on urban history and geography appeared in the 1980s.[1] Scholars reviewed the progress made and the
problems that remained in studying the urban community. As Erik
H. Monkkonen pointed out: "Neither the humanistic critique, the
statistical approach, nor the new urban history has provided a
lasting, dominant analytic paradigm. But from each approach we
can take something. From the statisticians, we can take seriously
the need to use large numerical overviews. And from the new urban historians, we can look for the impact of urban structures on
individuals."[2] There were those who thought it best to maintain
clear distinctions between urban history (urban life, people, and
institutions) and urban geography (patterns and distributions);[3]
there were others who thought that urban studies could be meaningful only through cross disciplinary research.[4] S. G. Checkland
pointed out five idioms as ways to proceed: (1) the city as a product of society; (2) the thematic aspect which emphasizes the work

of the disciplines and economic, social, governmental, spatial and perceptual themes; (3) the grand process agenda which attempts to conceptualize at least two conditions of society and the transition between the two as in changes from agricultural to industrial; (4) urban biography, an *histoire totale*, or a city existing in its own unique right; and (5) the family of cities, functioning under shared circumstances, where there are many commonalities as in a capital or private city, which makes comparisons possible.[5] At the same time Gilbert A. Stelter and Alan F. J. Artibise were raising other pertinent questions relating to the urban environment. "Who has the power? On whose behalf is it used? To what extent are the character and shape of cities a reflection of the power structure of the larger society?"[6]

This present paper lays out a profile of the Detroit, Michigan-Windsor, Ontario area, drawing much of its inspiration from Monkkonen. From Checkland's idioms it takes the idea of urban biography and the economic, governmental, spatial, and perceptual themes. It attempts to answer the types of questions asked by Stelter and Artibise. "Does the American-Canadian border make a difference?" "Who in the city of Detroit or Windsor and the Border Cities has the power to make decisions that affect urban development?" "Who is responsible for making the across-the-river connections viable?" The paper also draws upon the methodology of historical geography (the reconstruction and interpretation of past environments)[7] and urban historical geography (with emphasis upon the reconstruction of the morphology of the social environment).[8]

After a broad-based review of the origins and evolution of the respective communities, the study focuses on the morphology, demography, transportation and infrastructure of the Detroit-Windsor area in a specific year — 1914 — and the major events of that year: Ford's announcement of the five dollar work day, the coming of the Great War, and the incorporation of the "White Way" in Windsor, among others, and their effect on both site and community.

Finally, this study makes enthusiastic use of local histories, biographies, contemporary newspaper accounts, maps and photographs, city directories and reports of governmental agencies, business establishments and industrial firms.

Beginnings

Detroit-Windsor has evolved over the course of three hundred years. The area served in the seventeenth century as the seat of French control of the Great Lakes waterway and the Maumee-Wabash gateway to the south. English occupation and hegemony followed in the eighteenth century as did the Americans. Creation of the international boundary over time has served to separate the respective areas; it has also served to unite them, especially in times of crisis and tragedy.

The French were well aware of the waterways in the west: Lac Des Eaux de Mer (Lake St. Clair), the Detroit River, and Lake Erie. But not until 1701 did Sieur de Lamothe Cadillac establish Fort Pontchartrain on the north side of the Detroit River. Growth was slow but Indian camps began to augment the area's European population. On Chaussegros de Lery's map of 1754 a Pottowatamie village is shown west of the fort and Huron and Ottowa villages are depicted on the south shore; on the south shore, too, were the "Nouvelle habitation francaise . . .", the proprietors: Garvais, Marantete, Reaume, Pilette, Labutte, St. Louis and Bergeron (fig. 1).

English occupation of Detroit following the Seven Years' War tended to inhibit growth but did little to change the lives of the French of Indian settlers. John Montressor's map of 1763 does show the planted fields on both sides of the river (fig. 2). The English did not leave Detroit (following the Revolutionary War and the creation of the international boundary) until 1796, but with the abandonment they did establish Amherstburg (and Fort Malden) and Sandwich on the opposite side of the Detroit River. The former became a prime military installation, the latter a political community — the capital of the so-called Western District.[9]

War of 1812 and American Settlement

In 1805 Detroit (all save the fort) was destroyed by fire and a new and larger community, conforming in part to the Woodward Plan (north-south and east-west boulevards, 200 feet wide, intersecting circular plazas or circuses from which roads 120-feet wide would radiate, plus numerous lesser roads), was built to replace it.[10] But growth was slowed by Indian threats, the difficulties of travel over land and the Great Lakes, and the War of 1812. The international

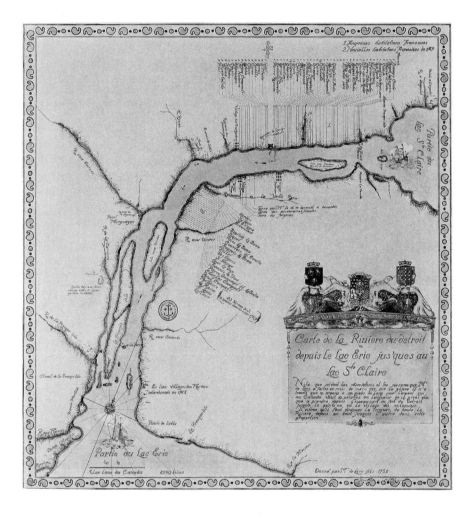

Figure 1. Chaussegros de Lery's map of 1754. (Courtesy of the
Burton Historical Collection, Detroit Public Library.)

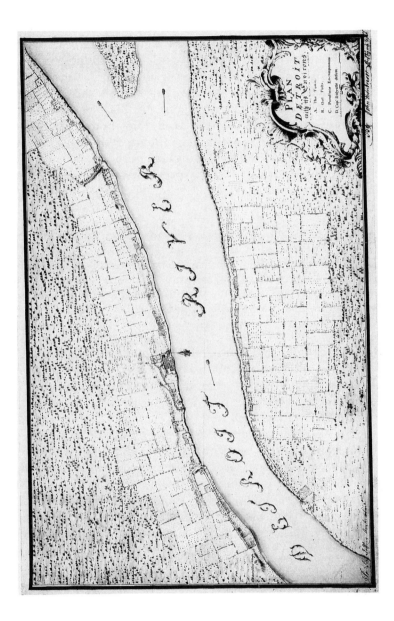

Figure 2. John Montressor's map of 1763. (Courtesy of the William
L. Clements Library.)

boundary helped, of course, to make the Detroit-Windsor area a battleground. General William Hull's American forces crossed the Detroit River but failed to take Fort Malden. Hull later retreated to Detroit and surrendered the community, then being bombarded from the Canadian shore, to British general Sir Isaac Brock. Detroit was not reoccupied by American troops until late September 1813.[11]

American settlers interested in land, jobs, and other opportunities began to move west in earnest following the war. Those who found their way to Detroit mingled with French Canadians, Indians, and the American military personnel who manned the fort. In 1827 Jefferson Avenue

> . . . was lined on both sides with low French houses, "whose unpainted fronts and moss covered roofs . . . looked as though they had braved the storms of the century." Here and there along the avenue a newly painted shop showed the presence of emigrants from the East. There were only two brick buildings on the street. Not a street had been paved or macadamized. Sidewalks were few. There were four churches, but not a public school.[12]

Visitors might view the Council House and the churchyard at St. Ann's and the old French ribbon farms. They might converse with Richard Cass, governor of the Michigan Territory, and Father Gabriel Richard, Vicar at St. Ann's, luminaries in the growing community of less than 1,500.

Fewer than 1,500 settlers in 1820, after 100 years of history! But soon the number would begin to rise with the establishment of the steam navigation on the Great Lakes, securing Indian lands by treaty in Michigan's interior, and the opening of the Erie Canal. Detroit's population, with New Englanders and New Yorkers among the majority of newcomers, increased to more than 2,000 in 1830, to nearly 7,000 in 1836, more than 9,000 in 1840, 21,000 in 1850 and well over 45,000 in 1860.[13]

The Ferry Becomes Windsor

Growth on the south shore could not, of course, match the American surge. Sandwich continued to be the center of settlement but The Ferry, directly across the river from Detroit, was also forming. Pierre St. Amour, who kept a small tavern there, and Francois Labalaine from the nearby Jannette Farm, ran log canoes, or ferries, to Detroit as early as the 1820s.[14]A scow, the *Olive*

Branch, was operating between the sites in 1825. The steam propelled *Argo No. 1,* built by Louis Davenport in Detroit, was in service in 1830 and the *United* followed in 1836. During the winter months communication across the river was maintained by sleigh. In 1830 James Dougall opened a general store at ferry terminus. It was he who changed the name of the community from The Ferry, or as some called it, South Detroit, to Windsor.[15]

Two observers of early Windsor have left these impressions of a frontier settlement. E.A. Teller described Windsor as a small village in 1837: ". . . Two large retail and wholesale stores are established here, and much wealth has been rapidly accumulated by the proprietors, in vending their merchandise to all classes in Michigan . . . who constantly during the spring and summer months, flock in crowds to these stores."[16] Mary Jameson was not quite as kind. It was a straggling place, she said, inhibited by an ignorant peasantry with ". . . all the symptoms of apathy, indolence, mistrust (and) hopelessness."[17] Aliens, forbidden to hold or transfer land by law, helped to keep Americans, for example, from moving to the opposite side of the river. The law was not abolished until 1853.[18]

Meanwhile Windsor had had *its* fire. On 16 April 1849, a pile of cedar posts resting on the wharf was ignited and stores and houses, the saloon and a nearby hotel were set ablaze. The local bucket brigade assisted by the Detroit Fire Department answered the call. Half of the community was apparently saved.[19] In 1851 Windsor could claim a population of 300. Yet in 1854 the growing community was incorporated as a village, population 1,000, and in 1858 as a town, population 2,000.[20]

The Great Western Railway

The growth of Windsor is attributed chiefly to the arrival of the Great Western Railway. Assisted by the Guarantee Act, which provided government support, and American stock purchases, the Great Western pushed west from Niagara Falls to London in 1853 and on to Windsor in 1854.[21] Windsorites were jubilant; Detroiters were enthusiastic.

In the afternoon the stores and business places of every kind were closed, and the river front was lined with people who gathered to see the incoming train to welcome the visitors from the neighboring province when the ferry should bring them over. At the foot of Woodward Avenue the throng was beyond all precedent. The train was to arrive at two o'clock, but it was nearly five o'clock before the whistle and the smoke of the locomotive gave notice to its approach. On reaching Windsor a salute was fired, the ferry soon brought the company to Detroit, and a processions moved from Campus Martius to the depot. . . .[22]

Arrival of the Great Western in Windsor sealed the growth of Sandwich and Amherstburg and doubtless assured the rise of Windsor.

Figure 3 indicates the disposition of the Great Western's holdings depot, roundhouse, engine house, wood house, platform, and wharf all on or near the waterfront north of Sandwich Street. Most of the community was built up between Park Street and Sandwich Street west of the Public Park and between Tuscarora Street and Sandwich Street east of the park. Lots were laid out south of Park Street on Bruce and Victoria Avenues, on Goyeau Street and south of Tuscarora Street on Mercer Street and Howard Avenue. But only on Goyeau did they extend to the village boundary at Tecumseh Road. The map also locates the community's town hall, bank, churches (Catholic and Methodist), and schools (Catholic and Protestant).

Hiram Walker and Walkerville

Hiram Walker, from Detroit, using provisions of the Reciprocity Treaty of 1854 (the free admission of grain, flour, and livestock) and taking advantage of the cheaper building materials, the less expensive real estate, and the relative absence of competition, began work on a distillery and flour mill on the south side of the river. In 1859 Walker set up his home, "The Cottage," on the riverbank. By 1866 Walkertown, the subsequent Walkerville, could be described as "a small village, situated on the riverside, about a mile above Windsor. It contains a distillery, carried on by Hiram Walker and Company, a hotel . . . , store, etc., and several tenements built by Walker and Co. for the convenience of their employees, which number from eighty to one hundred. . . ."[23]

In the very same year, 1866, Sandwich boasted a population of 1,000, Amherstburg 2,500, Windsor, 4,500; in the decade 1860–70 Detroit's population had risen from 45,619 to 79,577.[24]

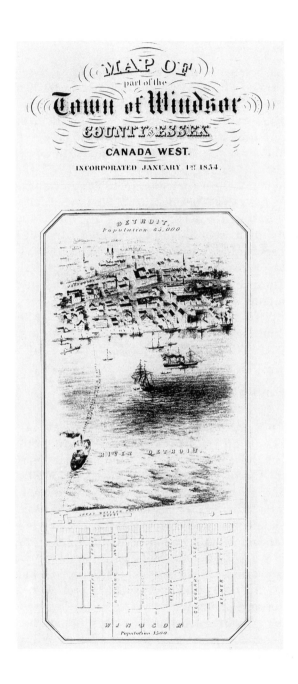

Figure 3. Great Western Railroad in Windsor, 1854. (Courtesy of the Municiple Archives - Windsor Public Library.)

The Slave Migration

The ethnic character of Detroit and the border had begun to change some years earlier. Africans fleeing slavery in the American South began to settle in upper Canada in the 1820s. Small communities were established at Amherstburg, Oro, and Wilberforce. A second wave appeared after passage of the Fugitive Slave Act (1850). Many moved to Windsor when employment opportunities with the Great Western Railway became available. In 1855 when Windsor had 1,400 residents, 259 were Africans; in 1859 in a population of 2,500, 700–800 were Africans. They lived on the eastern edge of the community, on McDougall, Assumption, Pitt, and Goyeau. They organized their own schools and churches. In 1867 there were barbers, grocers, laundry operators and hotel owners among them. William Lawson issued marriage licenses for the city and James and Robert Dunn owned Acme White Works, a varnishing manufacturing company on Goyeau.[25]

Immigrants from the British Isles, from the United States, and Canadians from eastern Canada, of course, continued to arrive in the border cities.

Street Railways and Electric Lights

On 20 July 1874 the horse-drawn street railway car replaced the omnibus, or stage, on Windsor's streets. "Starting out on Sandwich at Ferry Street the cars proceeded along upper Ferry to Chatham Street, west to Victoria Avenue, south to London Street, then west along London Street to Sandwich." A horse-drawn turntable reversed the car's direction at eastern terminus. A dozen years later (1886) the first electric streetcar system in North America (between Ferry and Sandwich and Peabody Bridge) was opened between Windsor and Walkerville. Because patronage was poor, however, the electric car was removed from service and the horse-drawn vehicle restored. By 1891, however, electric cars were operating between Windsor and Sandwich.

In 1887 the city streets began to be brightened by electric lights and on 1 November 1890, ". . . the citizens of Windsor witnessed for the first time their entire town brightly illuminated by the power of electricity." Homes, of course, continued, for the most part, to be illuminated by gas.[26]

Growth of Detroit

Detroit's growth can be attributed largely to manufacturing enterprise: wagons, carriages, ships and furniture-railroad cars, stoves, copper and brass products, iron and steel, pharmaceutical, paints and varnishes, shoes, chewing tobacco, and even ginger ale. The burgeoning manufactory called for and supported a burgeoning population. Immigrants poured into the city's port of entry on the east side, the Irish early on, followed by the Germans, the Jews, the Blacks, the Poles and others, each group living in their own neighborhoods. By 1880 the city had 1.5 miles from city hall, and by 1890 construction had already extended more than 2.5 miles from the city's center.[27]

With expansion Detroit was forced to meet growing problems in transportation, communication, energy and sanitation. Mayor Hazen S. Pingree, for example, found himself embroiled in controversies relating to streetcars, the municipal ownership of electric plants, and control over the telephones. There were constant problems with the water supply, the sewers, and the paving of the city's streets. The mayor was painfully aware that "... one half had to wait a long time for vital connections to the city's system of service."[28]

The Automobile

While Detroiters pondered the problems of the community's infrastructure, Charles B. King introduced a 4-cylinder gas-driven motor vehicle to the city's streets in 1894; Henry Ford followed with a 4-cylinder car, slung low, with large pneumatic tires in 1896; and Ransom E. Olds produced a 1-cylinder curved dash runabout in 1900 which he was manufacturing in a plant at Jefferson and Concord, where he employed 165 workers.

In 1903 Ford organized the Ford Motor Company and began to manufacture the Model A in a factory at Mack and Bellevue. When the plant proved too small Ford moved to new and larger quarters at Piquette and Beaubian; there the idea of the Model T was born. Still another move in 1909 took Ford to a newly designed plant (Albert Kahn, architect) at Woodward and Manchester, in suburban Highland Park. Meanwhile, Pierce, Packard, and others were also building cars in Detroit. The Dodge brother's (suppliers of automobile parts) built their new plant (Albert Kahn, architect) in

Hamtramck in 1910; two years later they were supplying Ford, among other things, with 180,000 transmission-axle sets. In Detroit the automobile industry was obviously well entrenched.[29]

Like their American counterparts Canadians were beginning to make automobiles. In 1893 Kickson's Carriage Works in Toronto produced an electric car; George F. Foss made a one cylinder gasoline car in Sherbrooke, Quebec in 1897; in 1899 the Good Brothers of Kitchener produced the LeRoy which was gasoline powered; thirty were built.[30] Other automobiles were also created and produced, but even a 35 percent tariff imposed on American imported vehicles could not save the local Canadian automobile industries.

In 1904 Gordon McGregor, manager of the Walkerville Wagon Works, whose company was losing money and manpower, visited with Henry Ford in Detroit. They talked about the tariff, the potential Canadian market, the possibilities of manufacturing parts in Canada, and questions pertaining to Canadian financing. McGregor invited Ford to inspect the probable plant site in the Walkerville-Windsor area.

The Walkerville Wagon Works assembly plant was a mess, its floor four-inches thick with paint drippings, its walls a crazy quilt of color from paint brush wipings. The only power machinery was a drill press, subsequently driven by the rear wheel of a Ford. The office staff was one stenographer and one bookkeeper. But in October, while the seventeen employees cheered, McGregor drove the first Model C down Sandwich Street.[31]

McGregor raised the money, of course and the Ford Motor Company of Canada, Ltd., was capitalized at $125,000. Ford would furnish the new company with all plans, drawings, specifications, and patents for "the sole and exclusive right to manufacture and sell its automobiles" in Canada and the British Empire. The plant began production in late 1904. Dodge Brothers, and other American companies, supplied the chassis and other parts. William Gray & Sons of Chatham, Ontario supplied the bodies and Chaplin Wheel Company, also of Chatham, some of the wheels. By 1 August 1905 Ford of Canada, moving ever so slowly, had assembled 117 cars, models C and B; in 1908 486 units were put together; with the switch to Model T, production increased to 2, 805 in 1911. A new expansion site was purchased in 1912. By 1913 the company was building its own motors and making plans for the manufacture of transmissions and other parts. And this corner of the world, just

west of Walkerville, and long known as Sandwich East, was re-
named Ford City.[32]

Windsor in 1914

Windsor had become a manufacturing community of nearly 25,000.
A lively business district had grown up at Sandwich and Ouellette
and extended on Ouellette to near Wyandotte. Residences, often
occupied by single families, filled the area to Tecumseh Road at the
city limits. Electrically operated streetcars carried passengers north
and out on Ouellette and Howard and east and west on Wyandotte
and London. The interurban Sandwich, Windsor and Amherstburg
Railway also crossed east-west near the waterfront, brought all of
the border cities together, and made connections with Tecumseh
and Amherstburg. Five major railroads—the Michigan Central,
Canadian Pacific, Pere Marquette, Wabash, and Grand Trunk (it
had taken over the Great Western in 1882)—served the community,
linking it with Toronto, Chicago and the world beyond. All were
connected with the Essex Terminal Railway which carried freight to
and from the city's growing factory districts.[33]

Michigan Central cars transported freight to Detroit via the
tunnel under the Detroit River, completed in 1910. The tunnel encouraged Michigan Central to lay up its ferries—*Transport, Transfer
II,* and *Detroit*—which were sold to Wabash Railway in 1912. Despite the tunnel, however, the ferries operating between the foot of
Ouellette and Woodward, continued to carry a massive volume of
freight and passengers in 1914. Ferry boats—the *Pleasure, Promise,*
and *Britannia* among them—were arriving at the slips every twelve
minutes, or five boats each hour, carrying as many as 6,000 people
on any given day.[34]

The city's streets, laid down years before with flag or flagstone,
had been macadamized, or after the installation of the sewers, re-
surfaced with asphalt. In 1914 the *Detroit News,* commenting editorially on the best pavement results, pointed out: "Experience has
shown that asphalt block gives the best services and is necessary
for streets on which there is heavy traffic, while concrete, preferably with tar surfacing, is well adopted for residential streets. . . ."[35]
The editorial concluded that in Windsor the street railways were a
menace to the durability of the pavement and that water and im-
proper drainage were enemies.

The opening of Windsor's Industrial Exposition, watched over
by the Daughter of the Empire, featured a glittering "White Way."

In mid-February the cedar poles on which the nitrogen-filled tung-sten lamps would be mounted began to arrive. By May the hydro transmission line between St. Thomas and Windsor was nearly completed. In September the arc lamps were placed on the poles of Ouellette from Wyandotte to the ferry.[36]

> The completion of the longest high power electric transmission line in the world and fulfillment of a promise made some years ago by Sir Adam Black that the entire of Ontario would be supplied with electrical power from the great falls at Niagara is to be realized tonight at 8 o'clock at the opening of the Windsor Industrial Exposition. . . .

Thousands of people lined Windsor's streets to catch sight of the street illumination, ". . . the equal of which had never before been witnessed in Canada."[37] A button was pressed and Windsor's principal streets were immediately lit up. In less than a month hydro power would be available in Windsor's residential area, and there was talk of exporting it to Detroit.

The activity in the factory districts was astonishing. In one, the Swedish Crucible Steel Company had begun work on the plant's foundations and Detroit Steel Products Company and the Vincent Steel Process Company were building; in the other district Ontario Steel Products was beginning in development.[38] For more than three years Windsor had been averaging at least one new industry per month.

> Everybody in Windsor knows that special legislation was granted to us, which brought about the factory site scheme. Instead of granting large bo-nuses in cash to induce industries to locate here, Windsor took the lead and launched a new plan, that of buying land well selected for the purpose, with proper railway facilities and of offering this land to manufactures at cost price, instead of a cash bonus.[39]

There was no favoritism. All firms were treated alike. If a com-pany could show that it employed twenty-five or more hands it could claim tax exemptions, free water and electricity for ten years. There were many takers. Encouraged to pass the new industrial by-laws guaranteeing the expenditure of $200,000 on new factory buildings and equipment, Windsorites responded with an overwhelming and positive ten to one vote. Manufacturing, after all, was their bread and butter.[40]

There was increasing industrial activity in the other border cities as well. In Ford City, Ford Motor Company erected large additions to its plant "giving them a four-story factory, 705 feet long and 73 feet wide along the Detroit River. . . ."[41] At the height of the season Ford was shipping 85 cars per day and employing 1,500 hands.[42] The company expected to produce some 20,000 vehicles during the 1914 production year. Assembly was undertaken at the new site of the United States Steel plan at Ojibway where a mile and three quarters of paved street was laid across the property. There was also growing industrial activity in the Sandwich factory district and in Walkerville with the population having climbed to over 4,700.[43]

The diversity of religious affiliation had also been registered. There was still a large French Catholic minority of close to 3,000 but the English Catholics outnumbered them with well over 4,400. There were large congregations of Episcopalians (over 3,700) and Presbyterians (over 2,500) and a Baptist congregation that numbered nearly 1,000. There were about 800 Colored Methodists and nearly 250 Colored Baptists, more than 400 Jews, and lesser numbers of Lutherans, Mormons, Confucianists, Plymouth Brethren, Congregationalists and Christian Scientists.[44] The burgeoning manufactories had brought numerous central and eastern Europeans to the border cities.

Such growth and expansion in the border cities, however, brought an array of modern urban problems as well, most prominently the forty tons of garbage strewn over Windsor's alleys and the "dump" site proposed on Langlois, where three dozen people lived.[45] The Essex County Medical Society recommended the use of Walkerville's incinerator, despite the cost, until Windsor could build its own, at a site in the factory districts.[46] There was the threat of tuberculosis. In January alone 207 new cases were reported on the other side of the river.[47] There was concern about the water supply and industrial pollution and the growing number of deaths from typhoid:

> . . . one could take a drink from a faucet one minute and the water might be free from pollution but in the very next minute the water might be grossly impure, through ships passing by and dumping garbage and excrete in the river near the intake. . . .[48]

There were also the problems of the poor and the unemployed. On Marion Avenue Alderman George Parent, ". . . found men out of work, signs of destitution and deplorable sanitary condition."[49] One boarding house had thirty renters in it. They had run up a bill of $1,200 in one of the stores and the proprietor refused to "stand" the men any longer.[50] An editorial in the *Evening Record* spoke of "The Slum Problem" and the danger of "human stable."[51] Alderman Parent promised to help.

There was the problem of the income tax. "All nonresidents of the country, if they be earning or drawing an income or salary in the United States, whether it be a telephone operator receiving $5 a week or a person receiving $50 a week, must file a state of income."[52] Since about half of the working population of the border cities worked in Detroit they were subject to the American income tax law. There was also a Canadian tax. Thus a Windsorite, for example, earning $1,200 a year might have to contribute about $21 to American and Canadian governments.[53]

Windsor's mayor, the Honorable Henry Clay, had one particular problem with which *he* was concerned: the municipal ownership of the street railways. Clay's enthusiasm for municipal ownership of the street car lines was contested, however, by the Detroit United Railway Company (DUR) which operated the Sandwich Windsor and Amherstburg interurban, and the city's lines. The DUR, anticipating revenue increases, wanted permission to run tracks on Ferry Street from Sandwich to Chatham to Bruce and beyond; it wanted to build a loop at Ferry and Victoria to connect Sandwich and London; it wanted to double track London from Bruce to the city limits, except for the bridge over the Canadian Pacific Railway tracks. Permission for the DUR to proceed was granted by the city council.[54]

Residents were appalled—especially by the possibility of the Ferry loop. They claimed that property values along the route would decline and that Chatham would probably be blocked.

The avenue is blind, ending at Chatham Street in a number of residences. To make the turn, which would be a short one, the cars would have to keep pretty close to the east curb. Upon rounding the corner the east curb on the corner of Victoria and Chatham would have to be cut short. This would mean that the space between Victoria and Ferry avenues on Chatham Street would be made dangerous to all traffic.[55]

Agitation against the loop continued to mount, but the DUR proceeded with plans to lay the track, despite the mayor's opposition and his threat to use force if need be. The local newspaper commented editorially: "The street railway company is trying 'safety first' by tearing up Ferry Avenue before the council has an opportunity to rescind permission to lay the loop tracks."[56]

The agitation continued as the DUR tore up the pavement at Chatham and Ferry and piled ties high at Ferry and Sandwich. An injunction served on the company from Toronto, ". . . restraining the Canadian end of the DUR from proceeding with the work on building the loop line on Ferry Avenue . . ."[57] made it appear that the loop was a gone goose. The sharply divided city council passed a bylaw which permitted the DUR to go on with its work but it was soon discovered that the bylaw was prepared in the offices of the DUR. Mayor Clay, and those who supported him, were absolutely indignant. Work on the loop line was stopped. The police were called out to support the mayor's order. "While I am reluctant to disregard the wishes of the council, I cannot permit this work to continue without proper authority from the rate payers."[58]

An editorial in the *Evening Record* exhorted the citizens to put their best foot forward: "Windsor is getting to be a fine looking town. It is much more tidy and neat than it used to be. The authorities can't do it all. Much depends on individual efforts by the citizenry. Take pride in the appearance of your town and strangers will do the same."[59]

Detroit in 1914

In 1914 there were more than 600,000 people within the corporate limits of Detroit in an area of 41.76 square miles. "A casual survey of the new office buildings, hotels, stores, commercial plants, apartment houses, and private residences that are springing up day after day offers the best evidence of the rapid and prosperous growth of Detroit."[60] The city was crisscrossed by nearly 800 miles of street railway; 64,000 of its residences and 24,000 of its stores, offices, and factories were owned by its occupants, thereby leading all the cities in the United States of more than 500,000 population in home ownership. Woodward Avenue stretched from the Detroit River north to Palmer Park. It was paved with brick to Atwater, with cedar to Jefferson Avenue, with asphalt over its remainder.

The city was a burgeoning manufactory. Four stove plants made 1,500 stoves a day. Other plants made paints and varnishes, pharmaceutical products, marine motors, ships and overalls, freight cars, malleable iron, brass and bronze goods, cigars, and a host of other items. In 1914, Detroit, not unexpectedly was primarily the "Auto City of the World" It manufactured 68 percent of the 350,000 cars made in the United States. It was the world leader in the manufacture of auto accessories and parts. One of its firms made over 3.5 million door locks, another more than 2 million spark plugs, still another, 750,000 hinges. The Detroit City Directory for 1914 lists 43 automobile manufacturers, including Ford, Hupp, Studebaker and Winton.[61]

At Highland Park, Ford's original Albert Kahn-designed plant stood four stories high, was 860-feet long and 75-feet deep. Ford ". . . was counting on a highly systematized and organized work process with maximum utilization of gravity for transport of raw materials, parts and sub-assemblies—hence the necessity for a multistory scheme. . . ."[62] Introduction of the moving assembly lines for magnetos, engines and transmissions in 1913 and chassis in early 1914 seemed clearly to outmode the multistory building. Yet Edward Gray designed a new 6-story unit for Ford directly across John R. Street in that year. "Thousands of holes were cut through the floors so that the parts that stared in the rough on the top floor gravitated down, through chutes, conveyors, or tubes and finally became a finished article on the ground floor."[63]

Better light, a cleaner floor, fewer columns and more even temperatures were enhanced the morale of the staff. Julian Street, a journalist who visited the machine shop at Highland Park in 1914, was captivated by its "efficiency:"

> Of course there was order in that place; of course there was system-relentless system-terrible "efficiency"—but to my mind, unaccustomed to such things, the whole room, with its interminable aisles, its whirling shafts and wheels, its forest of roof-supporting posts and flapping, flying, leather hafting, its endless rows of writhing machinery, its shrieking, hammering, and clatter, its smell of oil, its autumn haze of smoke, its savage looking foreign population—to my mind it expressed but one thing, and that thing was delirium.[64]

In 1909 Henry Ford announced that he would build only the Model T. One historian has since noted that "with its 13 1/2 inch axle clearance, the better to survive America's atrocious roads, this black funny-looking body swooping up and backward over the rear axle, and its other lack of adornment, except for the brass radiator, head, slide, and tall lights, the simplicity of the Model T was like the bikini beside an old-time poplin bathing costume. . . ."[65]

Americans fell in love with the "Tin Lizzie." Production increased dramatically and the price for the vehicle dropped accordingly. In 1909, 13,840 cars came off the line; each sold for $950. In 1914, 230,788 were made; each sold for only $490.[66]

The Eight-Hour, Five-Dollar Day

On Monday, 5 January 1914 the front page of *Detroit News* featured the following headline: WORKERS GET $10,000,000 OF FORD'S PROFITS THIS YEAR; 26,500 WILL SHARE. The rewards were intended apparently for all of Ford's male employees over twenty-two years of age; the females were not included. Ford would expect, of course, that all would perform well on the job, and make a commitment to the community.

> The laborer who sweeps the floor will receive $5 a day, or $30 a week, for the minimum wage will be increased from the $2.34 now prevailing to $5, the addition being in the form of dividends from the amount that would otherwise go to the seven stockholders of the company. The increase really amounts to more than this, for the working day has been cut from nine hours to eight.[67]

News of an eight-hour, five-dollar, profit-sharing day fell on the other American automobile manufacturers, the public, and the financial world in general like a bomb. Every daily newspaper in the country and thousands in the world carried the story. Henry Ford's name was common currency. He was, the papers indicated, creating a new American revolution. And Detroit was its mecca. "Detroit became in 1914 what California had been in 1849, the end of the rainbow."[68] The day after the announcement 10,000 job-seekers congregated near the doors of the Ford plant. The following morning a similar number of potential workers were turned away with the fire hose. Those seeking employment continued to march on Highland Park, while the employees themselves basked in their newfound earnings. More than fifty employees were married during the opening weeks of the profit-sharing scheme; employees were saving more and beginning to pay their bills.[69]

In the border cities the Ford profit sharing plan was hailed with somewhat less enthusiasm.

The position of the Canadian branch is in a much different position to that of the American concern in that the firm over the river has been paying immense dividends right along, while the Canadian branch declared no dividend last year. This may result in the workers at the factory above Walkerville being eliminated from the profit-sharing scheme inaugurated by Mr. Ford.[70]

Not until over a year later, 21 April 1915 was Gordon McGregor able to tell his employees that the Ford Motor Company of Canada, Ltd. had achieved a four-dollar day for eight hours of work.[71]

Detroit-Windsor Connections

The year had virtually begun with the announcement of the five dollar day. The repercussions in the Windsor area have been noted. In the months that followed, other events would point up the significance of the Detroit-Windsor connection. Early in February the *Promise* was caught in an ice-jam in mid-river; Windsorites on board were late for the noonday meal.[72] By the end of March, 1,300 immigrants had been admitted to Canada through the port of Windsor; over 1,000 had been rejected; in April alone there were 800 admissions, among them 200 Canadians returning to permanent residence. Thirty families moved into Essex County to farm.[73]

In the same month Detroit women, from various parts of the city, flocked to Windsor hoping to buy butter and eggs cheap. The tariff had been lifted! Essex County farmers were selling butter for thirty-five cents a pound; eggs were selling for twenty-four cents a dozen.[74] When members of the royal family, the Duke of Conneaught and his daughter, the Princess Patricia, visited Windsor in May, the city hall was freshly painted and some streets were specially paved. Representatives from all the border cities were in the welcoming committee: the mayor of Detroit, the American consul, and other prominent Detroiters among them.[75]

When stores in Detroit started to close early on Saturday, there was a great increase in business on the other side of the river, merchants said by 30 percent.[76] When the *Empress of Ireland*, a Canadian Pacific Railway vessel, was rammed and ripped from the middle to the stern in dense fog in the Gulf of St. Lawrence and sank with eight Windsorites aboard, the *Detroit News* commiserated, saying that Windsor lies ". . . in the valley of the shadow of death."[77] To commemorate the anniversary of the Treaty of Ghent and the celebration of peace between the United States and Canada, plans were afoot to build a tunnel between Detroit and Windsor. One engineer wrote:

> I will contract to build the smaller tunnel under the river, per design, from the foot of Woodward Avenue, Detroit to the Windsor shore, assuming the distance to be 2,500 linear feet for $2,900,000. I will contract for the larger tunnel, as per design, for the sum of $3,500,000. Time for construction, two years.[78]

But neither of Duncan McBean's plans materialized; nor did the water gates or towers oft-mentioned by others. Arrangements were made, however, for Thanksgiving services in the churches and for peace programs in the schools for celebration in 1915.[79]
    Meanwhile that July:

> Hundreds of Detroiters are today celebrating the Fourth of July on Canadian soil. Every boat landing at the Windsor ferry this morning carried crowds of Americans who are seeking rest and shade along the Canadian river front. Many of the roadhouses were over crowded long before noon.[80]

Although there is no law calling for it United States tourists floated flags of both countries. It is estimated that 250 automobiles crossed the river during that day.[81]

Canada at War

At July's end the world was plunged into a state of war. Austria declared war on Serbia. Germany prepared to declare war on Russia. The British stripped its fleet for action in the North Sea. After the British war declaration Canada followed suit. In Windsor and the border cities young men began to flock to the colors. Capt. G.H. Wilkinson of E Company 21st Fusilliers, ". . . never saw so many men anxious to go to the front. . . ."[82] And the women, too, ". . . with serious and earnest determination, sought ways to assist the Empire in her crucial hour."[83] Americans were caught up in the fervor. A dozen ferried over to "war-mad Windsor" and ". . . announced that they would stay until the call to arms was made and then enlist."[84]

Austrians and Hungarians living in Detroit but working in Windsor's factories were expected to lose their jobs, nearly 2,000 workers in all.[85] Those engaged in road building and receiving pay in Windsor would be watched. And Windsor's mayor, ". . . taking no chances of damage by hot-headed and reckless German sympathizers across the boarder,"[86] put the city's waterworks under guard. Wartime frenzy had seized the city.

By mid-August the first volunteers, members of the 14th field ambulance, marched to the Canadian Pacific Railway station to catch their train and depart for Sarnia and the east.[87] Other contingents followed as hundreds gathered to see the troops off. At months end hundreds of Windsor's volunteers were under canvas at the Valcartier, Quebec training camp. Thirty-two thousand men in ". . . six thousand tents shining under the autumn sun. An inspiring spectacle. . . ."[88]

Canadian troops were conveyed for further training to Aldershot and Salisbury Plains in southeast England in September. By November the first Canadian units were already in action in France. Windsorites gathered again at the Canadian Pacific Railway stations to send other recruits to Val Cartier. Near month's end it was reported that Frank W. Wade had died of battle wounds in a French hospital.[89] He was the first Windsorite to die in World War I.[90]

At the end of the year, Oscar B. Marx, mayor of Detroit and Fred L. Howell (who had replaced Windsor's Mayor Clay in July), exchanged seasons greetings. Mayor Howell wrote, "We look forward to the coming year with a hope of firm belief that the future years will bring, if possible, even more cordial relations between us. . . ."[91]

Notes

1. Derek Fraser and Anthony Sutcliffe, eds., *The Pursuit of Urban History* (London: Edward Arnold, 1983); Howard Gillette Jr. and Zane L.Miller, *American Urbanism* (New York: Greenwood Press, 1987); Kenneth T. Jackson, *Crabgrass Frontier: The Suburbanization of the United States* (New York: Oxford University Press, 1985); Eric H. Monkkonen, *American Becomes Urban* (Berkeley: University of California Press, 1988); Gilbert A. Stelter and Alan F. J. Artibise, *Power and Place: Canadian Urban Development in the North American Context* (Vancouver: University of British Columbia Press, 1986); Jon C. Teaford, *The Twentieth Century American City* (Baltimore: Johns Hopkins University Press, 1986).

2. Monkkonen, *America Becomes Urban*, 30.

3. Dietrich Deneke and Gareth Shaw, eds., *Urban Historical Geography* (New York: Cambridge University Press, 1988), 16.

4. Theodore Hershberg, "The Future of Urban History," in Fraser and Suttcliffe, eds.

5. S. G. Checkland, "An Urban History Horoscope," in Fraser and Suttcliffe, eds.

6. Stelter and Artibise, 1.

7. Deneke and Shaw, 14.

8. Ibid.,12.

9. Leo Johnson, "The Settlement of Western District, 1749–1850," in *Aspects of Nineteenth Century Ontario*, ed. F. H. Armstrong, H. A. Stevenson and J. D. Wilson (Toronto: University of Toronto Press, 1974), 19.

10. Clarence M. Burton, *The Building of Detroit* (Detroit: C. M. Burton, 1912), 24.

11. Sidney Glazer, *Detroit: A Study in Urban Development* (New York: Bookman Associates, Inc.,1965), 22.

12. Almon E. Parkins, *The Historical Geography of Detroit* (Port Washington: Kennicat Press, 1970), 178.

13. Ibid., 170.

14. F. J. Holton, D. H. Bedford, and Francis Cleary, "History of the Windsor and Detroit Ferries," *Ontario History* 16 (1918): 40.

15. Frederick H. Armstrong, "James Dougall and the Founding of Windsor, Ontario," *Ontario History* 76 (1984): 52.

16. Ibid., 54.

17. Martin J. Havran, "Windsor-Its First Hundred Years," *Ontario History* 46 (1954): 182.

18. Ibid.

19. Ibid.

20. Francis Cleary, "Notes on the Early History of the County of Essex," *Ontario History* 6 (1905): 182.

21. Russell Smith, "The Early Years of the Great Western Railway, 1833–1857," *Ontario History* 60 (1968): 210–11, 219.

22. James J. Talman, "The Development of the Railway Network of Southwestern Ontario to 1876," *Canadian Historical Association* (1953): 55, 57.

23. Ronald G.Hoskins, "Hiram Walker: A Man of Two Countries," *Detroit Perspective* 2 (1975): 224.

24. *Essex County Sketches*, 8; Burton, 44.

25. Jason H. Silverman, *Unwelcome Guests: Canada West's Response to American Fugitive Slaves, 1780–1865* (Millwood: Associated Faculty Press, 1985), 21; Daniel G. Hill, *The Freedom Seekers* (Agincourt, Ont.: The Book Society of Canada, Ltd., 1981), 52–53; Charlotte B. Perry, *The History of the Coloured Canadian in Windsor, Ontario: 1867–1967*. (Windsor: Summer Printing and Publishing Co., 1967), 19.

26. Martin J. Havran, "The Growth of Windsor, Ontario, 1845–1900" (Master's thesis, Wayne State University, 1953), 17–51.

27. Parkins, 301.

28. Melvin G.Holli, *Reform in Detroit* (New York: Oxford University Press, 1969), 49–50, 98–100, 123–24.

29. Helen E. Keep and M. Agnes Burton, *Guide to Detroit* (Detroit: The Detroit News Co., 1916), 35–36; Merrill Denison, *The Power to Go* (Garden City: Doubleday & Co., Inc.), 141, 144.

30. Grant Hildebrand, *Designing for Industry: The Architecture of Albert Kahn* (Cambridge: MIT Press, 1974), 44; *The Evening Record*, 4 July 1914.

31. Mira Wilkins and Frank E. Hill, *American Business Abroad: Ford on Six Continents* (Detroit: Wayne State University Press, 1964), 14.

32. Robert Collins, *A Great Way to Go* (Toronto: The Ryerson Press, 1969), 47;Wilkins and Hill, 18; *Vernon's City of Windsor, Sandwich and Walkerville (Including Ford City) Street, Alphabetical Business and Miscellaneous Directory* (Hamilton: Henry Vernon & Sons Publisher, 1914), 20

33. Collins, 47; Robert Markovich, "A Theoretic Study of the Windsor Transportation Network" (Master's thesis, University of Windsor, 1968), 64; Wilkins and Hill, 42; *Windsor, Walkerville, Ford, Sandwich, Ojibway: 1913* (Windsor, Ont.: *The Evening Record*, 1914), 61.

34. Ibid., 93; George W. Hilton, *The Great Lakes Car Ferries* (Berkeley: Howell-North, 1962), 33–34.

35. *Detroit News*, 17 May 1914, 5.

36. *Evening Record*, 18 February 1914, 1; 30 May 1914, 2; 8 September 1914, 3.

37. *Evening Record*, 12 September 1914, 3.

38. Idem, 14 September 1914, 1.

39. Idem, 7 January 1914, 4.

40. Idem, 24 June 1914, 1.

41. Idem, 4 March 1914, 1.

42. Idem, 8 April 1914, 4.

43. Idem, 18 May 1914, 1.

44. Idem, 11 June 1914, l.

45. Idem, 9 January 1914, 1

46. Idem, 2 March 1914, 1.

47. Idem, 9 March 1914, 1.

48. *Detroit News*, 4 February 1914, 1.

49. *Evening Record*, 17 January 1914, 1.

50. Idem, 19 January 1914, l.

51. Idem, 20 January 1914, 1.

52. Idem, 2 June 1914, 4.

53. *Detroit News*, 23 March 1914, 1.

54. *Evening Record*, 13 January 1914, 4.

55. Idem, 13 March 1914, 1.

56. Ibid.

57. *Evening Record*, 8 April 1914, 1.

58. Idem, 29 April 1914, 1

59. Idem, 30 April 1914, 1.

60. Idem, 30 May 1914, 4.

61. *Detroit City Directory, 1914* (Detroit: R. L. Polk & Co.,1914), 7–31.

62. *The Legacy of Albert Kahn* (Detroit: The Detroit Institute of Arts, 1970), 12.

63. Hildebrand, 45.

64. Julian Street, "Detroit the Dynamic," *Collier's*, 4 July 1914, 24.

65. Denison, 146.

66. David Hounshell, *From the American System to Mass Production: The Development of Manufacturing Technology in the United States* (Baltimore: Johns Hopkins University Press, 1984), 224.

67. *Detroit News*, 5 January 1914, 1, 5.

68. David L. Lewis, *The Public Image of Henry Ford* (Detroit: Wayne State University Press, 1976), 72.

69. *Detroit Tribune*, 1 February 1914, 1.

70. *Evening Record*, 8 January 1914, 8

71. Collins, 55.

72. *Detroit News*, 12 February 1914, 1.

73. *Detroit Tribune*, 3 May 1914, 14.·

74. Idem, 12 April 1914, 16.

75. Idem, 3 May 1914, 14

76. *Evening Record*, 7 May 1914, 1.

77. *Detroit News*, 30 May 1914, 2.

78. *Evening Record*, 17 June 1914, 4.

79. Idem, 18 June 1914, 4.

80. *Detroit News*, 4 July 1914, 9.

81. *Evening Record*, 6 July 1914, 1.

82. *Detroit Times*, 2 August 1914, 1.

83. *Evening Record*, 11 August 1914, 1.

84. *Detroit News*, 5 August 1914, 1.

85. Ibid., 15.

86. *Evening Record*, 12 August 1914, 1.

87. Idem, 18 August 1914, 1

88. Newton MacTavish, "The Cynic at Valcartier," *The New Canadian Magazine*, 44 (1914): 7.

89. *Detroit News*, 1 December 1914, 1.

90. Idem, 23 December 1914, 17.

91. *Evening Record*, 8 January 1914, 1.

GOVERNMENT AND GOVERNANCE

THE FAILURE OF CANADIAN POLITICAL LEADERSHIP?

Gordon Stewart
Michigan State University

A case can be made that the historical record of Canadian political leaders is a dismal one. In the 140 years since Canadian confederation was established in 1867, numerous attempts to find a constitutional framework acceptable to all Canadians have failed. No other modern, industrialized, urbanized, high-per-capita income country has such a record of futility in such a fundamental aspect of national life. The 1992 referendum was the most ambitious attempt so far to address this basic feature of Canada. It was comprehensive in nature, addressing not only the ancient vexation of Quebec's place in Canada but other central issues that were raised during the ten years of constitutional debate that followed the patriation of the British North America Act in 1982. The Charlottetown Accord on which the referendum turned proposed to recognize Quebec as a distinct society thus providing a legal setting within which Quebec could continue its efforts to preserve its language and culture within Canada and Anglophone North America; it proposed a wide-ranging recognition of the autonomy of aboriginal peoples; and it tried to encompass reforms of the Senate and the working of Parliament in order to give some of Canada's regions more recognition and greater influence.

The overwhelming defeat of the referendum which had been drafted with well-orchestrated fanfare in Charlottetown (site of the first agreements on the 1867 British North America Act) seemed a confirmatory sign of the ineptness of political leadership. This is especially so since post-referendum polls showed that a common discontent among voters across the country was a distrust of the politicians who had devised the scheme. There were, of course, a range of other factors at work to explain the failure of the referendum. Inside Quebec, polls found that voters thought Robert Bourassa had made too many concessions, including Quebec's historical weight in the Senate. Outside Quebec, the "no" voters thought Quebec had won too much, including a permanent fixed number of seats in the Commons irrespective of future demographic trends which would likely reduce the percentage of Quebec's population in Canada. Some voters in the west were fearful that the aboriginal clauses would give too much power to Native peoples. In the end, the only group in Canada that gave unequivocal support was in fact the aboriginal peoples who believed correctly that they had finally secured territorial recognition and legal rights denied to them since the period of conquest and the absorption and marginalization of the nineteenth and twentieth centuries. Yet behind this array of explanations for the failure of the referendum there was one common thread — dissatisfaction with the political leaders who devised this ungainly solution. As *Maclean's* remarked in its post-mortem editorial "the referendum campaign stands as the most sweeping rebuff to elected politicians in the country's 125 years."[1]

The constitutional debacle can be seen as a consequence of the poverty of thinking by the nation's political leaders. There was a good deal of criticism, for example, that throughout the decade of constitutional debate the political leaders had proceeded by closed door meetings. This created a culture of deal-making which ensured that any product of those meetings would seem complex and expedient rather than uplifting and appealing to Canadian people. Negotiations between the prime minister and the provincial premiers (the "first ministers" as the Guide to the Meech Lake Constitutional Accord calls them) were the locus for decision-making on constitutional issues in the 1980s. In a 1989 survey of public opinion Thomas Coucherne, Director of the School of Policy Studies at Queen's University, pointed out that during this decade of fundamental discussion about the future of Canada, the federal Parliament in Ottawa and the provincial legislatures played a small role. The prime minister, the provincial premiers and their advisors largely usurped the policy-making functions of elected representatives in the legislatures.[2] There was a sense that the politicians were simply not up to the occasion, perhaps not even aware of the occasion. To be sure, in the latter stages of the decade of debate an attempt was made to open up the process and given Canadian people from Halifax to Vancouver the opportunity to participate in framing a new constitution by means of Joe Clark's forums across Canada. The entire decade of constitutional-mongering, however, was characterized by politicians and their advisors trying to work out solutions in camera.

The frustration this caused is apparent in remarks made by Jack Granatstein of York University, author of many books on Canada and her international relations – and, it is worth adding, no meek defender of Canadian nationalism:

> What makes all this insufferable is that these measures are proposed directly in the face of the expressed wishes of the people. The Spicer Commission's report made crystal clear that Canadians want a strong central government; every opinion poll since Spicer has said the same. No matter, our federal and provincial negotiators, existing in a dream world of their own making, know better. So much for the openness and responsiveness of this process, put in place to correct the perceived flaws of the closed-door bargaining that gave us the Meech Lake Accord.[3]

In Granatstein's view Brian Mulroney's actions throughout all this may well have been informed by rather narrow and personal partisan goals. While conceding that the prime minister genuinely wished to find a solution which would satisfy Quebec, Granatstein thinks that purely political motives led Mulroney to push things too far.

> He also aimed at solidifying the Progressive Conservative party's hold in Quebec, at entrenching his own position at its head, and in eradicating the image and memory of Pierre Trudeau in the province. Those latter reasons while politically potent were more than slightly self-serving. No one . . . should accept Mulroney's endlessly repeated claims of virtue on constitutional questions at face value.[4]

In his intriguingly and tellingly titled *One Eyed Kings: Promise and Illusion in Canadian Politics*, Ron Graham offered a similar appraisal of Mulroney, remarking that he did not think Mulroney "sought office for any other reason beyond his own need for glory" and that Mulroney's "approach to policy is too partisan and event-driven. . . ."[5] Even within the system itself candid observers were troubled by this phenomenon. Canada's ambassador to the United

States Allen Gottleib, remarked in an interview on 7 November 1993 that people in Canada were "alienated from politicians."[6]

The Granatstein and Graham critiques, the Gottleib observation, the post-referendum polling results of Maclean's present an unflattering view of Canadian political leaders—their ideas, their motives and the procedures they chose to use. The indictment is that they are self-serving, unwilling to open up the debate, a prey to special interests and lacking the vision to present a fresh perspective that might develop creative concepts of Canadian federalism and nationalism. It is fair to note at this point that political leaders in other democracies have suffered in recent times from similar criticisms and that confidence in political leadership in Germany, France, Italy, Britain, and the United States is at a low ebb. The case in Canada seems more serious because the doubts are not centered on issues of economic policy, corruption, law and order however but on the very existence of the state itself. The issue in Canada seems terminal rather than transitory. If agreement cannot be secured now, if 125 years of political experience are inadequate for addressing these issues, what hope is there for the future of Canada?

The inadequate performance of political leaders in 1992 seems to fit a pattern that has been evident since Canadian confederation in 1867. At no point in modern Canadian history has a prime minister been able to articulate an attractive vision of Canada that has appealed to Quebec and Canadians in the different regions. In so far as prime ministers have tackled the problems of Canadian diversity, they have done so by compromise and expediency. Indeed, one of the hallmarks of Canadian political culture has been this genius for compromise which, it is argued, has led to the survival of Canada and given it a useful international role as a facilitator of understanding. The downside is that this political tradition, as was evident between 1982 and 1992, is unlikely to find creative solutions that will capture the imagination and push thinking to a level where permanent constitutional answers might be found.

The culture of compromise certainly has its merits. Inside Canada, the tensions between Quebec and English Canada, as well as the tensions between regions have historically been contained by careful allotment of cabinet posts in Ottawa, deployment of federal patronage and contracts and other such accommodations among regional, provincial and federal elites. The process is not unique to Canada and is characteristic of other democracies with linguistically segmented societies. The Dutch scholar Arend Lijphart has developed a theory about "elite accommodation" as the foundation for stability in such polities as Holland, Belgium, and Canada.[7] It is too easy for academics to deplore this way of conducting business which may well be an indispensable means of keeping intact countries that are difficult to govern because of linguistic divisions. The strength, ingenuity and success of the tradition must be recognized, but in the wake of the 1992 debacle perhaps it is worth asking whether these features of Canadian political culture have run their course and are no longer as fruitful in outcomes as they once were.

The issues at stake here can be illustrated by looking at the records of Canada's most successful political leaders and the ways in which those records have fallen short. To begin with the most renowned of all, John A. Macdonald, it is clear that he simply hoped that in the long run the French problem in Canada would go away. He thought time would solve all. While he accepted the absolute necessity of collaboration with French Canadian leaders to run Canadian governments—indeed, his entire career was built on that successful collaboration—he viewed the duality of Canada as a passing phenomenon that might last as long as a hundred years but would eventually yield to the assimilationist forces of Anglophone North America. Macdonald was the major figure behind the success of the confederation scheme in 1867 and was prime minister for twenty of the first twenty-four years of the new confederation. Throughout that time he worked with politicians from Quebec (George Etienne Cartier before Confederation and Hector Louis Langevin thereafter) to keep French and English in harness at the national level. Through these leaders, French Canadians secured access to cabinet offices, federal posts, contracts, and a range of other opportunities and could join with English Canadians in thinking that the federal system had payoffs that benefited their economy and society. Macdonald appreciated the French Canadian political support as the key to keeping him in power for so many years. He described the French Canadians as his "sheet anchor" and he acted on that reality by attending to their concerns as far as he could without alienating too many voters in English Canada. His career was characterized by ingenious balancing acts. He refused to prevent the execution of Louis Riel because he knew the majority of Ontarians wanted his blood, but shortly afterward he refused to disallow the Jesuits Estates Act of the Quebec Legislature which that same majority detested as papal intervention in Canadian affairs because he understood the need to re-establish his standing with Quebec voters let down by the Riel decision.

His approach worked. The new nation held together. Despite discontent over various issues (such as the Riel execution), Quebec accepted the federal state of Canada. While this success must be noted, it is also worth observing that MacDonald left no constitutional legacy, either in terms of structure or of rhetoric, that has been of any help in the modern debate. The British North America Act itself is a telling example in this context. The sections dealing with the two languages are not featured as core elements but are dealt with in section 133 under the heading "miscellaneous provisions." There has always been a debate about what Macdonald had in mind in 1867. At one end of the spectrum are those who see him simply as a politician trying to get a piece of legislation through; at the other end are those who see Macdonald working alongside Cartier to create a beginning moment of Canadian political culture in which French and English Canadians viewed themselves as two founding peoples. Whatever section of the spectrum one concentrates on, it is difficult to point to any declaration or speech by Macdonald that might be use in the present debate. It is true that Manitoba entered confederation as a bilingual province in 1870 but it did so not because Macdonald envisaged a bicultural Canada from coast to coast but because he was forced into the solution by the first Metis rebellion. When the Manitoba legislature did away with the rights of its Francophone minority in 1890, Macdonald was not energetic in fighting for their restoration. Such an arrangement in Manitoba had never been part of a national vision for Macdonald.[8]

Macdonald's successors continued this pattern of balancing and compromise in the interests of national unity. Wilfrid Laurier, the first French Canadian prime minister (in office from 1896 to 1911), raised the art to an even higher level in the sense that he presented leadership by compromise as the glorious and quintessential attribute of Canadian political leaders. During the 1896 election campaign he reminded Canadians of Aesop's fable about the struggle of the wind and the sun to determine who was stronger. The more the wind blew and tried to force the man to take off his coat the tighter the coat was held; but the sun's warmth encouraged the coat to come off. So it was with leadership in Canada — the sunny ways to compromise could achieve much more than the futile attempts to force recognition of rights. In keeping with this philosophy, Laurier was prepared to negotiate a solution in Manitoba which watered down the terms of the 1870 Manitoba Act and the 1867 British North America Act which had provided rights and assurances to the Francophone minority in the west. When Alberta and Saskatchewan entered confederation in 1906, Laurier did not fight for the retention of language rights for the French speaking groups in those new provinces.

Laurier's great challenge came from the revitalized imperialism which swept across Britain and its settlement colonies in the two decades before the Great War. Most English Canadians wished Canada to play a more active role in the empire; most French Canadians while remaining loyal to the colonial state in North America, disapproved of an active role for Canada in British imperial expansion. Laurier steered his way through these shoals with great skill. His government introduced a new intermediate tariff which gave preference to British imports over those from nonempire countries, thus showing he was willing to support closer empire economic ties. He turned up at Queen Victoria's diamond jubilee celebrations in London in 1897 and cut a fine figure as a colorful and grateful colonial statesman dedicated to the greatest empire the world had seen. When the South African war broke out in 1899, he refused to send official Canadian contingents but did allow the raising of volunteer units which the government would send to South Africa to serve under British command. When naval rivalry between Britain and Germany heated up after 1900, Laurier declined to provide Canadian money for a more powerful Royal Navy (as Canadian imperialists wished) but he did promise to fund a small Canadian navy that would be available to the empire in the event of war. This solution was derided by nationalists in Quebec (led by Laurier's erstwhile colleague Henri Bourassa) as simply covert concurrence in the jingoism of English Canada.

Buffeted by these winds of French Canadian nationalism and English Canadian imperialism, Laurier, even more than Macdonald, raised the art of compromise to the point where it became the hallmark of successful leadership. His efforts were often criticized from opposite perspectives in Quebec and Ontario and he could sound somewhat plaintive at times about the lack of understanding accorded to his tacking course, but he did articulate a philosophy of compromise which had been instinctual and rhetorically terse in the case of Macdonald. As he went down to defeat in the 1911 election (in which his opponents depicted him as having sold out the empire and, through the reciprocal trade agreement, opened Canada to annexation by the United States), Laurier gave eloquent voice to his credo. "I am branded in Quebec as a traitor to the French," he declared, "and in Ontario as a traitor to the

English. In Quebec I am branded as a Jingo, and in Ontario as a Separatist. In Quebec I am attached as an Imperialist, and in Ontario as an anti-Imperialist. I am neither. I am a Canadian. Canada has been the inspiration of my life. I have before me as a pillar of fire by night and as a pillar of cloud by day a policy of true Canadianism, of moderation, of conciliation. I have followed it consistently since 1896, and I now appeal with confidence to the whole Canadian people to uphold me in this policy of sound Canadianism which makes for the greatness of our country and of the Empire."[9]

Laurier lost the election, which suggests that his attempt to define a Canadianism that transcended current preoccupations with empire in English Canada and with cultural Catholic nationalism in Quebec was not appreciated by contemporaries no matter how much it appealed to subsequent generations of academic historians down to the 1960s. Laurier's paean to moderation and compromise in spite of his electoral failure in 1911 became the standard course for his successors although they were not quite so eloquent in their description of it. This was certainly true for William Lyon MacKenzie King, Canada's prime minister for most of the 1920s, 1930s, and 1940s. His was more of a cheeseparing approach than Laurier's . Frank Scott, poet, legal philosopher, cofounder of the Co-operative Commonwealth Federation and political gadfly in Quebec, said of him: "he did nothing by halves that he could do by quarters."[10]

Mackenzie King's main achievement was to restructure the relationship with Britain in ways that defused the imperial controversy in Canada. Along with other colonial prime ministers such as Jan Smuts of South Africa, he worked with the imperial government to redefine empire as commonwealth. By 1927 Canada had its first direct diplomatic representation in Washington at its own embassy and by 1931 Britain formally recognized the complete autonomy of the dominions in foreign affairs. Throughout the interwar years Mackenzie King sought better ties with the United States as a sign that Canada had a new sense of its North American priorities in external relations rather than the old Atlantic and imperial ones. This helped in Quebec where such a North American outlook was taken for granted. As Henri Bourassa observed, French Canadians were "American by ethnical temperament" — meaning geographically American.[11] Mackenzie King's course and methods ensured that when World War II broke out, Canada made her own separate declaration of war on Germany in contrast to 1914 when it entered automatically as a colony of Britain. When the prospect of a French-English split over conscription loomed, King, recalled the crisis in 1917 when Quebec had been alienated from the rest of Canada and adopted an ambivalent stance ("conscription if necessary but not necessarily conscription"); with the intervention of other factors he succeeded in avoiding a repetition of the 1917 crisis.[12]

In recent times the one prime minister who seemed to be an exception to this pattern of keeping peace by accommodation was Pierre Trudeau. His active policy of seeking to strengthen bilingualism in Ottawa and across the country appears to have been an attempt to address the concerns of Quebecois by actual structural change which dealt with their fundamental complaints about their place in Canada. However, the more Trudeau's leadership on this matter is seen in its historical perspective the less worthy it actually is as an exercise in disinterested statesmanship seeking a solution based on a new definition of what Canada is about. In retrospect his emphasis on bilingualism at the federal structures were no longer center stage. After the 1960s the key question in Quebec was how Canada's constitutional and political system could be altered to allow Quebec to cultivate and defend its Francophone culture. In particular, the question became one of ensuring that Quebec could deploy language legislation that would protect its distinct society.[13] Quebecois were no longer concerned as they had been in the days of Henri Bourassa with Francophone minority rights outside of Quebec or even with the significance of bilingual federalism throughout Canada. Far from taking this seismic shift into account and trying to incorporate it into a new constitutional arrangement, Trudeau's policies were designed to destroy modern Quebec nationalism as it had emerged after the 1960s.[14]

Trudeau's view of Quebec nationalism had been formed during the struggle against Maurice Duplessis's corrupt Catholic nationalism as articulated through the machine of the Union National from the 1930s through the 1950s. Moreover, Trudeau believed that ethnically based nationalism in general was a nineteenth-century phenomenon that was the unhealthy product of particular historical conditions in Europe and which was bound to disappear from the world state. The upsurge of the parti quebecois and more generally the sharpened demand (which cut across party lines inside Quebec) to defend the French language in the province were taken by Trudeau to be latterday manifestations of this old fashioned nationalism rather than contemporary forces reflecting actual social and cultural goals in Quebec that had to be reckoned with. His policy of federal bilingualism was designed to undermine the new nationalism in Quebec, reconcile Quebecois to the existing constitutional structures, and so turn the province away from separatist thinking.

His actions during the so-called October crisis in 1970 were a powerful illustration of this dynamic. There is no evidence that a revolutionary situation existed in Quebec but Trudeau appeared solemnly on television to declare that there was indeed such a threat and that the War Measures Act, which had not been invoked since its passage during World War I, was necessary to save the country. The disproportion between the rhetoric and the reality suggested to nationalist critics inside Quebec that Trudeau was intent on destroying the new nationalism by linking it with state-threatening terrorism in order to eliminate his political rivals from the Quebec and Canadian landscape.[15] In much the same way that Granatstein has detected in Mulroney's case a desire to shore up his political position in Quebec, so Trudeau's approach to the Quebec problem was affected by his goal of weakening his Quebec critics. It is essential to appreciate that the reaction against Trudeau's view cut across a wide spectrum of opinion in Quebec and was not confined to more radical nationalist circles. The federal government policies under Trudeau were designed to extend Ottawa's powers and to constrain and even roll back provincial power.[16] This direction threatened to weaken further Quebec's ability to mold its society and culture. Trudeau's entire approach undermined the possibility of a strong province which most Quebecois regarded as critical if they were to remain part of Canada.

It is telling in this context that it was Trudeau who as prime minister was responsible for the patriation of the British North America Act in 1982 without securing conditions that would have reassured Quebec that the province would not be subject to the English Canadian majority on basic matters such as language rights, and community rights as distinct from individual rights. Trudeau, in short, was intent on undermining Quebec nationalism rather than seeking a constitutional environment within which Canadian and Quebec nationalism could coexist. The entire decade of debate begun in 1982 came about because of this failure at the outset to get Quebec's acquiescence to the terms of patriation. Because of Trudeau's history on these matters, the patriation (with its accompanying Charter of Rights) was viewed in Quebec as a device to thwart Quebec's ability to protect its special culture within Quebec itself. As Christian Defour put it in his essay "Le defi quebecois," ". . . la societe quebecoise est depuis 1982 en competition avec une vision constitutionnalisee du Canada qui ne lui est pas compatible."[17] Thus even Trudeau's exceptionalism turns out upon closer scrutiny not to be a radical break from to the pattern. Like all national leaders since 1867, he failed to place the constitutional debate beyond the level of political maneuvering.

The commonalities in this pattern from Macdonald to Trudeau and Mulroney suggest that there are some deep structures in Canadian political culture. To be sure, each of these leaders was working within particular historical conditions which led him to chart his own course to preserve political stability and hold the country together, but the parallels in spite of the variety of conditions are striking. One line of explanation for these common responses that is illuminating concerns the origins of Canadian politics. The political culture of contemporary Canada has been molded by many economic, social, institutional, and international factors that have only made their presence felt in recent decades but there are some orientations that were formed at the point of origin and still make their mark on the Canadian political landscape. A good example of this kind of phenomenon comes from the field of American politics. During the colonial period there was a constant struggle for power between the British-appointed governors and the local colonial legislatures. Because the governors did not possess the income and patronage deployed by the Crown's ministers in Britain, they were not able to build up sufficient influence to manage the colonial assemblies as the executive managed Parliament in Britain. For their part the colonial assemblies watched carefully for opportunities to assert their powers. Thus in contrast to eighteenth-century Britain where executive and legislative spheres were intertwined, in the American colonies there were separate spheres for the executive and legislative functions. Long before the explicit written imprimatur was placed on this separation during the revolutionary struggle and its attendant constitution making, American politics had been characterized by a separation of the powers. In short, actual conditions in colonial politics had established a particular orientation which left a permanent mark on the American political landscape.

Certain consequences stemming from the actual working of politics prior to Confederation left permanent marks on Canadian political culture in a manner similar to the separation of the powers feature in U.S. politics. Those that concern us here include the tendency of Canadian political leaders to use executive power rather than democratic consultation to address constitutional issues and their penchant for using patronage deployment in support of policy initiatives. During the struggle for local control of colonial government between 1790 and the 1840s political leaders mobilized their popular support by promising that once the narrow, British-supported ruling groups had been displaced, the reformers would take over and staff the public service with like-minded individuals. Since the American option of fighting a war for independence was a nonstarter in Canada, the reform impulse centered on getting the patriots into power. Once in office the new regimes needed to distribute patronage to their supporters throughout the constituencies in order to make sure the old ways had been buried and that local Canadian control had indeed been established. Patronage was the only way of securing local control if a revolutionary break from Britain was not an option. These political developments were underway before the concept of a neutral public service was in place and even before there was movement to articulate and defend such a concept. Thus the public service became the arena in which parties shored up their strength and extended their reach into society. The forces seemed so natural that Macdonald could declare openly (in a manner that no contemporary British or American politician could have done) that "in the distribution of government patronage we carry out the true constitutional principle that whenever an office is vacant it belongs to the party supporting the government."[18]

Because of these origins the Canadian parties were not well prepared to deal with issues of principle as they arose in various periods of tension between English and French Canadians. The preferred method was to defuse the tension by turning to more cabinet positions for the aggrieved group and prescribing a range of patronage medicine that would soothe the patient.[19] Political leaders were most successful when they were able to keep the big, divisive issues between the two cultures at the margins. Within this culture it never occurred to political leaders, for example, that the federal public service might have been used as an arena for experiment in connection with the dual nature of Canada. Some contemporaries did indeed see these possibilities and remarked upon the obtuseness of politicians in not seizing them. In 1877 William LeSueur, speaking before a Parliamentary Select Committee on the federal public service, pointed out that in a service where two languages are used it is obviously unfair that a man who brings to the Service a knowledge of both, and whose knowledge of both is made use of by the Department in which he serves, should derive no advantage whatsoever from the fact. Such, however, is the fact. In the Department in which I serve a man who knows both French and English is made to do work requiring a knowledge of both those languages and do it for his seniors. A senior clerk may send to a junior clerk that portion of his work which requires knowledge of a second language and the junior gets nothing at all in the way of promotion for this special qualification.[20]

The failure of Canadian political leaders to respond to this possible line of development is an example of how the origins of Canadian politics gave a certain cast to the way in which Canadian leaders thought about Canada that blinkered them to more creative structural solutions which might have prepared the ground for more fruitful outcomes in the twentieth century.

The question that naturally arises is why Canada has survived so long if these disadvantageous features existed within the political culture. The answer lies at two levels. First, as suggested previously in spite of the critique that can be made of Canadian political leaders, they were successful in terms of their own times. For every William LeSeuer there were nine Ontarians and Quebecois who were perfectly happy with the way in which cabinet ministers dispensed patronage. Indeed, deployment of patronage in this systematic and comprehensive manner was a shared value between English and French Canadians and contributed in a major way to the loyalty of both groups to the Canadian colonial state. The methods of Macdonald, Laurier, and Mackenzie King worked and kept Canada intact. Second, for much of the nineteenth century, and arguably down to the 1960s, Canadians of both language groups shared the assumption that it was important to keep Canada intact to prevent too much Americanization. Recent work on the history of national identity has drawn attention to the importance of the "other" in providing common ground for such an identity. In her account of the origins of modern British nationalism, Linda Colley has shown how the disaggregated Scottish, Welsh, and English regional identities were fused into a British one in the heat of the world wide struggle, including several wars, against France between 1688 and 1815.[21] In the case of Canada, in contrast to this pattern, most English and French Canadians had only a fragile basis for a common sense of nationalism. Many of the historical experiences which forge a national identity have worked in the opposite direction in Canadian history. Wars, for example, have often been unifying forces but Canadians were divided by the Boer War in South Africa, by the Great War, and again in World War II as the two major ethnic groups disagreed about where Canada's national interest lay in these imperial and European conflicts. There was no common attachment to a flag or to the 1867 Parliamentary legislation which provided only a serviceable rather than an inspiring "constitution" which all Canadians could regard with reverence. Canadian history itself was told in two versions.

The single most important historical force holding the country together in the nineteenth century was created by the view of the United States as the "other" against which definitions of Canadianism were invented and cherished. English Canadians had memories of the revolution and the war of 1812 as influenced by loyalist mythology while the French Canadians feared absorption into a secular leveling republic Consequently, both saw the colonial state of Canada as an entity worth preserving. As Jacques Monet pointed out in his study of Quebec in the 1840s, the Quebec people were ready to defend the British colonial state of Canada to the last cannon shot.[22] While this fear of the United States lessened in the later decades of the nineteenth century, it remained the case that the more conservative political culture in Canada saw benefits in marking out a different course in North America from that of the United States.

These factors made Canadian political leaders successful in holding the country together after confederation in 1867. They worked within the political assumptions of their day, they addressed issues by a range of compromise techniques, and they held a common view that the struggle to keep Canada separate from American influence and control was a worthwhile national goal. French and English Canadians shared these views in spite of tensions and periodic crises over language issues, the west, the empire, and federal-provincial relations. Identification of these forces at work in Canadian history enables us to appreciate the type of political leadership that became characteristic in Canada. Once that understanding is in place, the crude condemnation of Canadian leaders as failed constitution makers can be put in a fairer perspective. What remains, however, is the indictment that these political traditions that have held the country together for so many years have a downside to them which makes political leaders curiously leaden-footed when it comes to devising contemporary solutions that would inspire Canadians to think afresh about the future of their country. The political traditions of Canada have made the national parties and the national leaders dinosaurs—lots of weight and reach in society but small amounts of intellectual flexibility that would enable them to come up with new approaches to a new environment. In 1968 Pierre Trudeau thought that Canada's constitutional problems would be solved because "we have politicians who we hope will get better and better all the time."[23] The record since then suggests that the old patterns have not changed.

The new environment has developed over many years but the main features have become most apparent since the 1960s. The contemporary secularized Quebec nationalism that emerged in that decade no longer saw the need to keep up a united Canada in face of perceived threats of Americanization. On the contrary, it was the continued existence of the unreformed Canadian system and the possible assimilative consequences of the patriation of the constitution in 1982 which threatened to undermine the Francophone culture. Above all, most Quebecois saw the urgent necessity for extraordinary power at the provincial level to protect and promote the French language inside Quebec. They insisted on recognition of the concept later summed up at Meech Lake in the phrase "distinct society" so that they would have a constitutional basis upon which to justify language legislation. Moreover, as Canada (including Quebec) found in the post-1945 era that its economy was becoming more and more bound with that of the United States, the old argument that the Canadian east-west economy (begun with Macdonald's national policy in 1878) was the best option for economic growth made increasingly little sense. Attempts by Ottawa in the 1960s, 1970s, and 1980s to seek a so-called third option by increasing trade with Japan and the European Community did not alter the fundamental linkage of the Canadian to the United States economy. The signing of the Free Trade Agreement in 1988 was the culminating moment. With prospective access to a freer North American market (subsequently enlarged by the North American Free Trade Agreement which included Mexico as well as the United States), there was less need for the traditional federal political structure of Canada within which provinces and regions could pursue economic growth. Thus, in the new context of international economic forces and the modern nationalism shared by most Quebecois, the historical pattern of Canadian political leadership seemed to have ground to a failure in 1992. Conditions had changed so that the traditional methods of behind-the-scenes mediation, elite accommodation, and deployment of patronage no longer worked. Even worse, such features of the system were viewed (as revealed by the Maclean's poll) as harmful.

But my title has a question mark. Perhaps Canadian politics, and its leaders, far from being inept, are in fact remarkably appropriate for the world of the late twentieth century. The root of the criticism regarding the futility of constitution-making in Canada rests on the assumption that the nation state is a necessary, desirable, and permanent feature of the landscape and that Canadian political leaders since 1867 have failed because they have been unable to construct a Canadian nation-state. Current developments around the world call the assumptions underlying the critique into question. The internationalization of the economy in the late twentieth century has meant that many countries no longer control their economic destiny in the way that was once considered the sine qua non of statehood. The ways in which European states are giving up aspects of sovereignty in order to create better economic conditions in Europe are powerful signs of the receding importance of nineteenth-century concepts of national sovereignty. Moreover, those national sovereignties that seemed so deep-rooted in the nineteenth century are turning out to be creations of their times rather than permanent historical phenomena. In current scholarship nations are treated as imagined communities, invented associations which are studied in a skeptical rather than a celebratory mode. Historians examine how traditions are invented to sustain a particular nationalist value system, how historical myths and fictions have been deployed to convey a version of history that underlies what purports to be an actual reality of national identity. As David Cannadine points out:

> This skepticism has been much underscored by recent events in Europe, as old and not-so-old nations have disintegrated before our very eyes, and as the Brussels bureaucracy, the Hague judiciary and the open market erode what remains of national sovereignty, with the result that the classic late-nineteenth-century nation-state seems to be passing into history, if not into oblivion.[24]

National identity is, in short, contingent, relational, and oppositional rather than immutable — it is an outcome of internal circumstance and prevailing international order of things. The ways in which British national identity is eroding in the face of changed international circumstances — the loss of empire, the need for the European market — comprise a particularly telling case because

British nationalism has been such a powerful force on the modern world state. As J. G. A. Pocock observed in a recent wide-ranging thinkpiece on history and sovereignty: "In both Europe before and after 1989, and in the Pacific region as viewed from the southern hemisphere, can it be said that what is going on is the emancipation from state sovereignty of the global operation of Community, but in the Pacific region not institutionalized but let rip."[25] If this internationalizing of the economy is indeed to be a major characteristic of world history for the next several decades then the old need for viable, unitary states is weakened. In this context the inability of Canadian leaders to achieve agreement that will invent Canada anew is irrelevant. The forces that will determine how well people in Quebec and the other Provinces of Canada will live will not be determined by the continuance of a traditional Canadian state but by the ability of Canadian leaders to negotiate effectively in the new hemispheric and international economic order. In this setting, the federal government in Ottawa can function as a kind of holding operation, negotiating optimal terms for Canada's participation in the North American and world economies while simply keeping in place a tenuous domestic stability which never reaches an ultimate solution.

The case can be taken even further to argue that the very qualities in Canadian leadership which I took to task in this paper are qualities which will wear well in the post-modern world. Ottawa has lost a great deal of its ability to control the Canadian economy (as has the government in London, the British economy). The trade flows and investment patterns are so powerful that the Canadian government can adjust direction here, add an emphasis there, but cannot change the fundamental direction of the Canadian ship as it navigates the rapids. Canadian leaders can try to understand the forces at work and mediate as far as their influence goes to ameliorate the negative impacts upon Canada. Since 1867, Canadian leaders have been unable to define a solution to Canada's regional divisions and the perennial problem of Quebec. What they have done is mediate discourses. They have set up innumerable ingenious forums where Quebec nationalists, federalists, regionalists and aboriginal spokespeople can present their perspectives. Leadership takes place at the point of intersection of all these discourses about history and the future and consists chiefly in keeping the dialogue in motion as a kind of permanently active public discursive safety net which makes enough people think that there is a framework within which the country continues to articulate itself. This discourse keeps Canada politically operational. And perhaps that is all that leadership can achieve. The historical traditions of Canadian leaders have prepared them well for this role. Academic conferences are hailing Canada already as the first post-modern state for precisely this reason.[26]

In the end, of course it will not be academics who shape the future. In the pleasant settings of academic meetings, the positive attributes of the post modern state (such as mediating the discourses developed by nationalist, regional ,and ethnic demands thus providing the illusion of a center, the illusion of a state) will be admired. But the big question, notwithstanding the ideological and economic explanations for the fading away of the nation state, is whether such an outcome will be welcomed by the peoples of Canada. If there is an economic payoff, perhaps the question can be left unanswered; but if there is not, if the international economy continues to struggle, then the demand for stronger states might take on a new lease. The proposition that nationalism is a spent force in world history (as Trudeau thought) is certainly being called into question in eastern Europe, Russia, the Middle East, and parts of Asia. If the world system underpinned by the General Agreement on Tariffs and Trade (GATT) and good working relations between the emerging trade blocs in Europe, North America, and Asia assures general economic well-being, the style of Canadian political leadership will fit the bill nicely. If the world reverts to a jungle of competing nation-states, each seeking to control its own economic destiny, then the inability of Canadian leaders to forge a strong federal Canadian state within which Quebec can live will begin to matter.

Notes

1. *Maclean's*, 2 November 1992, 12. During an interview on 7 November 1992 in the *New York Times* Ambassador Gottleib said that Canadians were "alienated from politicians."

2. Nart Habugabm "Shaping the Future," *Maclean's*, 3 July 1989, 58–59.

3. J. L. Granatstein, "The Great Canadian Crap Shoot," in *Canada: The State of the Federation*, ed. Douglas Brown and Robert Young (Toronto, 1992), 110.

4. Ibid.

5. Ron Graham, *One Eyed Kings. Promise and Illusion in Canadian Politics* (Toronto, 1986), 435–36. It is worth pointing out in defense of Mulroney that he understood Quebec's exclusion from the patriation of the BNA Act was a constitutional problem that required attention and could not simply be ignored. His act of opening up negotiations was therefore an act of statesmanship whatever other motivations can be identified.

6. *New York Times*, 7 November 1992.

7. Arend Lijphart, *Democracy in Plural Societies: A Comparative Explanation* (New Haven, 1977). Application of Lijphart's approach to the Canadian case is best appreciated through the work of Kenneth Macrae in his two books: *Conflict and Compromise in Multilingual Societies* (Waterloo, Ont., 1983) and *Consociational Democracy: Political Accommodation in Segmented Societies* (Toronto, 1974).

8. Macdonald's career, his impact on Canadian political culture and his view of the British North America Act can be assessed in a range of books and articles. The most sympathetic portrayal is Donald G. Creighton's two volume biography *The Young Politician, The Old Chieftain* (Toronto, 1952, 1955). The issues raised in his paper are dealt with at greater length in Gordon T. Steward, *The Origins of Canadian Politics* (Vancouver, 1986) and "John A. Macdonald's Greatest Triumph," *Canadian Historical Review* 63 (1982): 3–33. See also Peter B. Waite's *Macdonald, His Life and Times* (Toronto, 1975) and the same author's summary of current thinking on Macdonald in *Dictionary of Canadian Biography*, 12:590–612.

9. J. M. Bliss, *Canadian History in Documents* (Toronto, 1966), 220. Laurier's legacy is suggested by the title of Barbara Robertson's biography *Laurier: The*

. *Great Conciliator* (Toronto, 1971). Other standard interpretations are John W. Dafoe, *Laurier: A Study in Canadian Politics* (1922; reprint, Toronto, 1963) and Joseph Schull, *Laurier: The First Canadian* (New York, 1965).

10. F.R. Scott. "WLMK," in *The Blasted Pine. An Anthology of Satire, Invective and Disrespectful Verse Chiefly by Canadian Writers*, ed. A. J. M. Smith (Toronto, 1967). The last verses of Scott's poem read:

> He seemed to be in the centre
> Because we had no centre,
> No vision
> To pierce the smoke-screen of his politics
>
> Truly he will be remembered
> Wherever men honour ingenuity
> Ambiguity, inactivity, and political longevity
>
> Let us raise a temple
> To the cult of mediocrity,
> Do nothing by halves
> Which can be done by quarters

11. Henri Bourassa, "The French-Canadian in the British Empire," *The Monthly Review* 9 (October 1902): 53-68 quoted in Carl Berger, ed., *Imperialism and Nationalism 1884–1914: A Conflict in Canadian Thought* (Toronto, 1969), 73.

12. The best overview of the Mackenzie King period is Robert Bothwell, Ian Drummond, and John English, *Canada 1900–1945* (Toronto, 1987). The World War II conscription issue is analyzed on pages 331–35. The standard scholarly biography is H. Blair Neatby, *William Lyon Mackenzie King* (1958; reprint, Toronto, 1976) and a breathless, popular one is Bruce Hutchinson, *The Incredible Canadian: A Candid Portrait of William Lyon Mackenzie King* (New York, 1953).

13. The change came during the Quiet Revolution of the 1960s when nationalists feared that if current trends continued Quebec would gradually become more and more Anglophone, especially in the business world and the workplace, unless measures were taken to make French by law the working language of the province. A flavor of the times can be gained from Raymond Barbeau's *Le Quebec bientot unilingue?* (Montreal, 1965). An informative survey of the evolution of nationalist ideology and politics since the 1960s is provided in Alain Gagnon, (Scarborough, Ont., 1990).

14. Trudeau's career is treated in Walter Stewart, *Shrug, Trudeau in Power* (Toronto, 1971), Richard J. Gwyn, *The Northern Magus. Pierre Trudeau and Canadians* (Toronto, 1980) and Stephen Clarkson, *Trudeau and our Times* (Toronto, 1990). His ideas on Canadian nationalism are dealt with in James Laxer, *The Liberal Idea of Canada. Pierre Trudeau and the Question of Canada's Survival* (Toronto, 1977) and the fault lines that developed between him and Quebec nationalist in the 1960s are described in Gerard Pelletier's *Years of Impotence 1950–1966* (Toronto, 1984).

15. Dan Danields, ed., *Quebec, Canada and the October Crisis* (Montreal, 1973) provides a critique from the left. Jean Provencher, *La Grande Peur d'Octobre '70* (Montreal, 1974) gives a good sense of the atmosphere at the time. A characteristically balanced assessment is given in Robert Bothwell, Ian Drummond, and John English, *Canada Since 1945: Power, Politics and Provincialism* (Toronto, 1981), 392–94 where they point out that Trudeau took pains to acknowledge the legitimacy of the parti quebecois and distinguish it from the terrorists who had kidnapped Laporte and Cross.

16. David Milne, *Tug of War. Ottawa and the Provinces under Trudeau and Mulroney* (Toronto, 1986), 2.

17. Christian Defour, *Le defi quebecois* (Montreal, 1989), 13.

18. Stewart, "John A. Macdonald's Greatest Triumph," 21; Norman Ward, "Responsible Government," *Journal of Canadian Studies* 14 (1979): 3; Alain-G Gagnon, ed., *Democracy with Justice* (Ottawa, 1992), 157–73.

19. Jeffrey Simpson, *The Spoils of Power* (Toronto, 1988) written by the national political correspondent of the *Globe & Mail* is a comprehensive examination of the role of patronage in Canadian politics. Ralph Heintzman, "The Political Culture of Quebec 1840–1960," *Canadian Journal of Political Science* 16 (1983): 3–59 makes the case that "Quebec's traditional political culture was shaped by the dialectic of patronage. Economic need encouraged Quebecois to exploit the political process for advancement. The result was the preoccupation of the political process with patronage."

20. Notes on Civil Service Reform by William Dawson LeSueur, Select Committee on the Present Condition of the Civil Service, *Canada. House of Commons. Journals* 9 (1877): appendix 7. For LeSueur's place in late nineteenth-century Canadian culture see A. B. McKillop, *A Critical Spirit* (Toronto, 1977).

21. Linda Colley, *Britons. Forging the Nation 1707–1837* (New Haven, 1992), passim. The conceptual starting point for Colley is taken from Benedict Anderson,

Imagined Communities: Reflections on the Origins and Spread of Nationalism (1991 edition).

22. Jacques Monet, *The Last Cannon Shot: A Study of French Canadian Nationalism 1837–1850* (Toronto, 1969).

23. Pierre Trudeau, *Conversations with Canadians* (Toronto, 1972), 210.

24. David Cannadine, "Penguin Island Story," *Times Literary Supplement*, 12 March 1993; T. O. Ranger, ed., *The Invention of Tradition* (Cambridge, 1983). Max Beloff in the *TLS* of 26 March 1993 points out that Cannadine makes some factual blunders in this statement. There is the Court of the European Communities at Luxembourg which, some might argue, does intervene against old definitions of national sovereignty but the International Court of Justice at the Hague has not usually interfered with national sovereignty. On the contrary, its very existence is based on the notion of national states operating in the context of international law. The criticism does not, however, undermine the point being made about the transformation in the concepts of and workings of national sovereignty in late twentieth century Europe.

25. J. G. A. Pocock, "History and Sovereignty: The Historiographical Response to Europeanisation in Two British Cultures," *Journal of British Studies* 31(1992): 388.

26. The 19th annual conference of The British Association of Canadian Studies has for its theme "Canada: The First Postmodern State?"

Acknowledgment is made to Robert H. Babcock, who published an earlier version of Professor Stewart's essay in his *Canadian-American Public Policy*.

THE GOVERNANCE OF THE SHARED GREAT LAKES BASIN ECOSYSTEM

Henry A. Regier
University of Toronto

Introduction

Humans have done many things and learned many lessons over the past two centuries in this Great Lakes case history. Many opportunities were grasped—often in ways that created eventual disadvantages almost as great as the original benefits. Long ago benefits and drawbacks could be kept separate in space and time and between different groups of people, but those times are past. People are only beginning to learn how to cope and to create within an awareness of ecosystemic limits and connectedness. The governance structures and processes on balance still reflect the earlier presupposition of nonlinkage—a presupposition that became a disabling norm.

The adjective *binational* is often attached to the concept of *governance* of the Great Lakes. What is formally binational, i.e., between the formal institutions of the nationstates of the United States and Canada, makes up only a small fraction of Great Lakes governance. The formally binational part, though important, is often exaggerated, especially in scholarly works on this subject.

A number of Indian tribes as "nations" are now reasserting some measure of "sovereignty" over parts of the shared Basin. Their claims to preeminent rights and responsibilities for some features of large geographic parts of the interconnected shared ecosystem are no longer ignored, though they are being contested step

109

by step. The financial benefits to the Indians from casinos and "free trade" may help to offset losses of benefits from treaty rights that have been denied them unlawfully, though a number of wrongs may not make a right.

Quebec, with a large measure of sovereignty with respect to ecosystemic phenomena, is beginning to act more responsibly with respect to ecological realities in the St. Lawrence River valley. When it has achieved high credibility in its own ecosystemic husbandry within Quebec, it will likely make stronger demands for reductions of harmful influences that flow down the Great Lakes chain and down the St. Lawrence River.

Transnationally the Great Lakes are coming to be appreciated as part of a global heritage. In the 1987 *Report of the World Commission on Environment and Development, the Brundtland Report,* academician N. N. Moiseev remarked: "Some unique objects like . . . the Great Lakes of . . . North America are part of the global patrimony. They are some of the absolute values our planet possesses and their significance transcends national boundaries" (285).

A number of coastal wetlands, all of Lake Superior, and some terrestrial features such as the Niagara Escarpment of Southern Ontario now have Biosphere Reserve status under UNESCO auspices. Increasingly, those who govern the region will be expected to render an account of the state of this basin, through some global governance institution, to the people of the world. Governments are already rendering prototypical accounts, such as the "Rio Plus Five" documentation, following five years after the global agreements on sustainability, biodiversity, and climate change at the 1992 UN Conference on Environment and Development in Rio de Janeiro.

At subnational levels of governance, there are many transjurisdictional arrangements within and between sovereign jurisdictions. There are no formal or informal attempts to keep track of them all. The few political scientists who appear to comprehend this evolutionary emergence of governance have not yet described or explained it, except very generally. So it is left to the nonexpert to address the question, as attempted in what follows here.

Basinwide Ecosystemic Problems: The Record

Starting two centuries ago, Americans and Canadians have cooperated on numerous opportunities and shared many problems. Indians have been involved collaboratively in many of these ventures, but their roles remain largely unreported. In the Great Lakes Basin, renewable resources such as forests, furbearers, fish and waterfowl were seldom exploited in an entirely separate manner in different jurisdictions; people of the First Nations were often involved with Americans and Canadians in the exploitation. Transportation infrastructure cut through and across different jurisdictions, especially the canals for ship transport. Heavy industry, manufacturing, and utilities also were organized in a regional context. The exploitation of commercial, industrial, and settlement opportunities was usually abusive in an ecological sense. For basin-level effects, the *shared culture* of commercial and industrial progress in the Great Lakes Basin may be held accountable primarily, with differences between Americans and Canadians as a second-order consideration. Quebecois downstream along the St. Lawrence River were generally as abusive as the other Canadians and the Americans. People of the First Nations were generally not as abusive ecologically, except when they became integrated into a culture of commercial progress, as with the fur industry.

Partly Solved Ecosystemic Problems of the Past

The sketches that follow are not comprehensive but provide glimpses of some of the problems that have plagued the Great Lakes Basin in the past, some of the solutions and, for some of the more difficult problems, ongoing attempts to mitigate them.

Raw organic wastes with human and other feces were dumped untreated into water, thereby contaminating domestic water supplies and causing outbreaks of dangerous diseases. Collection of most such wastes in sewers and treatment of most of the effluent with chlorine reduced the risk of transmission of such pathogens. The risk remains, however, especially at beaches in and near cities where some sewage still escapes treatment and flows into the waters.

Plant nutrients, especially phosphates, entered waters through sewer effluents and runoff from urban and agricultural areas. The resulting blooms of algae of various kinds—filamentous, colonial, unicellular—fouled beaches and contributed to reductions and extinctions of valued deepwater fish species. Loadings of phosphates were reduced through improvements in sewage treatment plants, reduction in the use of phosphates in detergents, and better land-use practices. The timing and extent of efforts to reduce phosphate loadings varied among state and provincial jurisdictions. Generally, within a jurisdiction, the first kind of limitation applied had the politically weakest group of antagonists. Unacceptably high loadings still persist in some areas. Chemicals that replaced phosphates in detergents are still under scrutiny.

Overfishing was already occurring more than a century ago, we note with hindsight, in Lake Ontario as a whole, in parts of the other lakes and connecting rivers, and even with a few lake trout stocks in Lake Superior. In fact some of it was deliberate, such as attempts to eliminate the large sturgeon which were destroying fishing gear and were relatively worthless in the market in early times. Beginning a century ago, there have been attempts to create a treaty to curtail overfishing by using standard regulations across all the waters of all the lakes. These attempts failed, partially because they were perceived by some American states as an attempt by the U.S. federal government to usurp control of state fishery responsibilities. Overfishing was eventually curtailed, in part by substituting less exploitive angler fisheries for commercial net fisheries. Different jurisdictions solved the overfishing problem through different kinds of policy mechanisms. Lack of uniformity of regulations among jurisdictions was problematic for some sports fishers but did not prevent resolution of interjurisdictional allocational problems. These problems were eased by the Great Lakes Fishery Convention in 1955.

Persistent pesticides came to be recognized in part because of the scientific research done on birds at Michigan State University, and on lake trout in New York State. The consequences of bioaccumulation of DDT were invoked as a likely cause of reproductive failure of lake trout in Lake Michigan. Unacceptably high concentrations of DDT in large salmon prevented the sale of surplus spawners of the spawning runs and thus created a problem with dead salmon in streams. Numerous species of birds with feeding relationships to fish suffered from the persistent poisons. Persistent pesticides were gradually and progressively banned within each jurisdiction of the basin, with no explicit strategy of formal coordination. One of the last legitimate uses of DDT involved tobacco farms; some loading into the lakes through atmospheric routes from elsewhere is still occurring.

The sea lamprey likely entered the lakes through invasion via ship canals and some may have been introduced through the release of larval lamprey from bait buckets. Larval lamprey were still used as bait in some New York waters and perhaps elsewhere in the basin in the 1950s. Collaboration between Canada and the

United States led to a series of methods of partial control of sea lamprey. The most cost-effective method has been a chemical lampricide which the lamprey control agents use somewhat to their own embarrassment since they decry the use of toxic chemicals generally in these waters. One of the lampricides, TFM, comes from the manufacturers mixed together with some inadvertent contaminants. Some of the latter are now of concern because of possible adverse effects on species other than lamprey. In some waters in the Great Lakes system, notably the St. Mary's River, no existing method of lamprey control is cost-effective, though some methods currently under development may prove to be applicable. Reduction of the intensity of sea lamprey predation together with elimination of overfishing has led to a partial recovery of lake trout and lake whitefish in Lake Superior and in some other waters. The Great Lakes Fishery Commission had been given executive responsibility in 1955 to control sea lamprey, but it took several decades for the commission to institute a formally coordinated control program transcending the binational border.

Other non-native fish introduced long ago also became pests, at least for some decades, most notably the alewife and rainbow smelt. These thrived in larger waters that had become moderately enriched or eutrophic. Commercial fisheries were developed in several parts of the Great Lakes for these prolific, low-valued species and overfishing of smelt may have occurred occasionally in Lake Erie.

Small kokanee salmon were introduced by Ontario in hopes that they would create self-reproducing stocks that would competitively suppress alewife and smelt. Large coho and chinook salmon were introduced by Michigan, with reproduction ensured through hatchery technology; these were potential predators on the "weedy" species. Thus salmonids were introduced to combat some of the effects of eutrophication and of prior overfishing of lake trout, as well as to provide angling and fishing opportunities. The Ontario introductions were ultimately unsuccessful, but Michigan's hatchery-based efforts succeeded and soon Ontario and the other American states then followed Michigan's example.

The salmon, and the rebounding native lake trout, helped to reduce the abundance of alewife and smelt and may have contributed to the reversal as well as mitigation of eutrophication. Salmon provided highly popular angling opportunities. But the large salmon were plagued with unacceptably high levels of persistent pesticides, as mentioned earlier, as well as hazardous contaminants.

Their contamination made them highly unpopular with people who feared that the inevitable ingestion of the contaminated flesh — despite warnings to anglers through widely distributed health advisories — would lead to permanent impairment of human consumers and especially their offspring. Some of these justifiably concerned people have judged Pacific salmon to be an undesirable exotic, on balance, and are also unfavorably disposed toward the native lake trout because of their contamination. Fisheries respond by suggesting that without the valued fish that become contaminated, the Great Lakes might be relegated to a role of assimilating and eventually inactivating contaminants from valued chemical industries.

Because of the variable climate in the Great Lakes, a series of years may be wetter than normal and another series may be drier than normal. Such series do not appear in a predictable manner. The four connecting rivers between the lakes, not counting the Straits of Mackinac, are too small in cross-section to drain excess waters rapidly through the chain of lakes, thus lake levels may rise notably above long-term norms during a period of wet years. But the rivers' outflows are deep enough to drain away water continuously even during extended periods of drought, thus leading to low-water intervals. State, provincial, and municipal governments failed to educate the citizenry about the unpredictable but inevitable rising and falling of lake levels. These governments also failed to introduce planning and regulatory methods to protect ignorant citizens from the consequences of these phenomena, e.g., by zoning areas at risk from high water as inappropriate for permanent structural development. As a result, people created structures near the water's edge when water levels were low and then suffered severe harm when water levels rose again. It is now widely recognized, after several binational studies of this general subject in recent decades, that lake levels and river flows cannot be controlled simultaneously and any effective control of levels or flows would benefit relatively few people at great expense to many others. Belatedly, lower levels of government are taking their own precautionary responsibilities more seriously.

The coastal zone and especially coastal wetlands as ecosystems have been drastically altered, frequently degraded, and sometimes completely destroyed in much of the southern half of the basin. These systems together served as a massive "ecotone" or ecological intergrade between the land and the water, to the benefit of both the terrestrial and aquatic ecological systems of the basin. Debasement of such an ecotone leads to the isolation of land and water and to the impoverishment of both the terrestrial and aquatic systems. Coastal wetlands are dependent on water fluctuations of a number of different periodicities, including the longer-term fluctuations sketched in the preceding paragraph. Thus people interested in preserving wetlands have countered some of the political efforts of riparian owners in the area of controlling lake levels. Political problems related to levels and flows have been more intense in American than in Canadian jurisdictions, in part because zoning is politically less acceptable in the United States.

Hazardous industrial contaminants—including chlorinated hydrocarbons with biological and ecological behaviors like those of some persistent pesticides—have caused even greater concern than the persistent pesticides. As with the latter, the disastrous effects of some contaminants on a variety of birds, reptiles, fish, and wild mammals are graphically evident in anatomical deformities. But the effects on humans, as with the pesticides, are not as graphic and may not yet have been discovered in full. To prevent all such hazardous contaminants from entering the environment, indoors or outdoors, is now shared policy and is being implemented, ever so gradually. What to do about contaminants already in the environment is currently under political debate. To some it seems obvious that all but a small fraction of the contaminants already in the environment are not retrievable technically, let alone economically. The key issue politically is where to draw the line between what is retrievable and destructible and what must be left to de-toxify under natural influences. The political process appears to be deadlocked on the issue of where to draw that line between what is retrievable and what is not. Remediation of contaminated sediments in local hot spots is continuing on a quasi-experimental basis and knowledge is accumulating that will help with the formulation of such policy. The issue of creating adequate safeguards for humans while the irretrievable contaminants are still active in the environment is not being addressed comprehensively. Fully addressing this issue might involve tacit acceptance of contamination as a necessary evil which is feared by anticontaminant activists.

With respect to the release of substances into the environment, the relevant rights are coming under increasingly strict scrutiny. Any right to release hazardous toxic substances is becoming strongly constrained under a policy of "zero discharge." Arrogated rights to many kinds of environmental use are being rejected more often. Legitimate rights must have appropriate responsibilities explicitly and closely linked to them, with the onus on the participant to demonstrate adequate responsibility. Such reforms will presumably continue, toward a goal of sustainable development.

This section has outlined examples of ecosystemic problems recognized in the past and now partly resolved. None has been fully resolved, nor even resolved to the extent generally considered to be acceptable. All the ecosystem problems can be blamed on the American-Canadian culture of the basin, and the partial corrections have occurred through cooperation, some of it formal and some of it informal. As a whole, Americans have caused much more ecological harm to the Great Lakes than have Canadians, but on an average per-capita basis the differences are not great. Equity with respect to "pollution rights" is often reckoned on a per-capita basis internationally, especially if such reckoning favors the stronger nation. Implicitly, phosphate loadings are allocated on a per-capita basis while hydroelectric use of water and harvest of fish are on a per-jurisdiction basis.

Largely Unsolved Ecosystemic Problems of the Present

New exotic species keep appearing in the basin. Some are microorganisms pathogenic on fish which enter the basin through importation of eggs and brood stock of fish for rearing in hatcheries followed by release of young into the basin's waters. Quite stringent quarantine methods are now in place in an attempt to reduce this risk but importation and release of live fish and eggs are difficult to control and thus the quarantine program, in effect, is voluntary.

Other exotics, notably the zebra mussel, have entered the lakes through release of ballast water from oceangoing vessels. Throughout the 1980s, vessel owners, the shipping lobby, and the government agencies serving those interests strongly resisted concerted efforts to reduce the risk of such releases. A legacy of the explicit deregulatory policy of the two federal governments in that decade is the current infestation of zebra mussels and other pests, such as the river ruffe, now expanding into Great Lakes waters. Perhaps the only effective solution to the continuing ballast water problem will be to prevent oceangoing vessels from entering the Great Lakes. Vessel owners and their captains may be the last of the breed of environmentally irresponsible autocrats, which once were so common in industry and commerce.

Pollution by organic wastes and enrichment by plant nutrients can be controlled only if the necessary sewage collection and treatment infrastructure is sufficiently large and is functioning properly. In numerous older urban areas around the Great Lakes the sewage infrastructure is too small, is aging, uses dated technology, and is breaking down more frequently. If such infrastructure is not rehabilitated or replaced, pollution and enrichment will again intensify beyond current levels which are not yet acceptably low near many urban areas. Such infrastructural renewal must be accompanied by reductions in loading of water and wastes into sewers, which can be done cost-effectively.

Ecosystemic Problems Not Yet Generally Recognized

The combined infrastructure for heating and cooling the downtown cores of large cities appears to be aging and obsolescent, in Toronto and some other Great Lakes cities. One problem stems from the necessity to phase out chlorofluorocarbons (CFCs) as coolants in refrigeration, because of the role of leaked CFCs in destroying the atmospheric shield against ultraviolet radiation. Another challenge is the need to become more energy-efficient, and thus reduce the demands on electricity generated through use of fossil fuel or radioactive materials, both of which produce wastes that are environmentally unacceptable. New physical technology of various types offers better combined heating and cooling infrastructure at less than half of the current energy costs. Behavioral changes to induce men to dress sensibly in summer and women to dress sensibly in winter would permit further efficiencies. In addition, there may be a cost-effective role for cold deep lake water to absorb some of the excess heat with relatively large flows in midsummer and small flows in midwinter. The warmed water could perhaps be used to feed the commercial and domestic water system of the city or to rehabilitate degraded streams and wetlands in the city. If numerous urban areas were to use deep lake water for urban cooling, and if that water were not then used to displace earlier withdrawals for water works purposes, then the depth of the warm surface layer in offshore waters would be increased in summer and the temperature of some inshore waters would be cooled. Whether the overall ecological effects locally would be beneficial or detrimental is not immediately clear; any reduction in use of CFCs, fossil fuels, and uranium would have regional and global environmental benefits.

The perennial issue of prospective water diversions into and out of the basin will presumably reoccur. The key issue may be whether the U.S. Congress will continue to be accessible for large funds in support of water-related megaprojects in the southern Great Plains. The huge fiscal deficits in Canada and the US may forestall new megaprojects, to the advantage of environmental interests. Presidential vetoes of relevant line items in the US federal budget would also help.

Climate change due to buildup of heat-trap gases in the atmosphere may be under way and may not be reversible for at least a number of decades. Numerous consequences, mostly adverse to present users of the Great Lakes aquatic system, are being explored by researchers. The currently foreseeable direct effects of climate change may exacerbate numerous kinds of adverse consequences of those human influences on the Great Lakes that are only partly resolved at present. A precautionary no-regrets policy to prepare for any climate warming would be to work toward more complete correction of present ecological abuses, both in terrestrial and aquatic parts of the basin.

Whether because of better climate due to climate change, relatively better economic circumstances, or because of the inexorable growth of human numbers, many people may migrate into the Great Lakes Basin in the next few decades. Again the main consequence may be exacerbation of currently unresolved problems. And again a no-regrets policy would be to expedite environmental reform so that, on average, humans place fewer and smaller demands on the natural parts of our shared ecosystem. If people today were to reduce the current adverse impact per-capita by half, in order to permit some further rehabilitation, then a doubling of the human population would keep the negative impact at its current overall level. It would be better to reduce the per-capita impact by two-thirds if a doubling of population is expected.

Interjurisdictional Agreements Relevant to the Great Lakes Basin Ecosystem

Joint uses of the Great Lakes are administered with respect to interjurisdictional agreements that vary in scope from global to local. The most formally binding agreements currently are the treaties between entities with preeminent claims to geographic parts of the basin — between Canada and the United States and between each of these nations and a number of Indian nations.

In both Canada and the United States, a number of treaties with Indian tribes were not honored fully, if at all, by Americans and Canadians. These injustices are being corrected, belatedly, and the corrections in turn lead to some injustices to the Whites of the relevant locale which then need to be mitigated. Although making amends will not be painless, it will most likely be far less intense than the pain suffered unjustly by Indians over the many decades.

The Boundary Waters Treaty of 1909 between the United States and Canada applies to the Great Lakes and other waters. The terms of the treaty are sufficiently comprehensive to include more matters than the water quality and water quantity issues that are generally referred to it, i.e., the Great Lakes Water Quality Agreement of 1972 and 1978, as amended notably in 1987, is an elaboration of the terse terms of the Boundary Waters Treaty. The levels of Lakes Superior and Ontario and the air quality at the southern end of Lake Huron are managed jointly under this treaty.

The Great Lakes Fishery Convention of 1955 provided the legal basis for joint efforts by Canada and the United States to control the exotic sea lamprey. This convention also authorized joint research and coordinative activities to facilitate equitable sharing of the fishery resources at overall levels of maximum sustainable yield. Some First Nations tribes have become involved in negotiating allocation of yield between their jurisdictions and others within a lake. Under the facilitative auspices of the Great Lakes Fishery Commission, the federal, state, and provincial agencies with responsibilities for fisheries devised a Strategic Great Lakes Fishery Management Plan of 1981. Some Indian jurisdictions have endorsed the plan, after the fact. With respect to fisheries, this plan plays a role that is similar to those of the Great Lakes Water Quality Agreements under the Boundary Waters Treaty.

Migratory songbirds were protected and waterfowl kills were controlled cooperatively under the Migratory Birds Treaty of 1917. Indian nations were not signatory to this treaty, but they have usually honored its general intent, perhaps because it is not inconsistent with their own traditions.

Two regional federal commissions within the United States, often with informal Canadian involvement, have played strong roles in the Great Lakes Basin: the Great Lakes Commission (GLC) since about 1955 and the Great Lakes Basin Commission (GLBC) from 1957 to 1981. The latter, a river basin commission in the American mold, facilitated regional information sharing and comprehensive integrated planning. The GLC initially served the interests of ship transportation and related facilities and industry; since the termination of GLBC the GLC has continued some of the activities of GLBC with some support from private foundations. In recent years

GLC has facilitated the emergence of the Great Lakes Association of Mayors, which meets annually, and also the creation by cooperating stakeholders of a Great Lakes/St. Lawrence River Basin Ecosystem Charter.

The American Great Lakes states, with the subsequent involvement of the provinces of Ontario and Quebec, developed two agreements in the mid-1980s: the first was on sharing water quantities in the Great Lakes Charter of 1985; and the second was on protecting and remediating water quality under the Great Lakes Toxics Substances Control Agreement of 1986. These interjurisdictional efforts were partly in response to the diminishing commitment to Great Lakes issues within the federal administrations, starting in the late 1970s.

There are as yet few formal links between Great Lakes jurisdictions and the developing global agreements, such as those formalized to some extent at the U.N. Conference on Environment and Development (UNCED), in Rio de Janiero in June 1992. The Biosphere Reserve initiative, part of the UNESCO's Man and the Biosphere Program dating from the early 1970s, is being applied in the Great Lakes Basin. This initiative may be a vanguard for basin efforts generally consistent with the Biodiversity Convention of UNCED in 1992. Informal collaboration by American and Canadian researchers on likely effects of climatic change in the basin may be a precursor to more formal basin-level involvement in the global climate change convention of UNCED.

Since the mid-1970s, the geographic scope of activities under most of the agreements outlined above has extended downstream from the Great Lakes for various distances down the St. Lawrence River. As is the case with "states rights" in the United States, precisely where the formal limits on "sovereignty," with respect to various ecosystemic features, lie between the jurisdictions of Canada and Quebec has been in continuing informal dispute. The gradual withdrawal of commitment on various ecosystemic issues in the Great Lakes by the Canadian federal government and the strengthening of the role of Ontario may lead to comparable levels of de facto sovereignty on ecosystemic issues in Ontario and Quebec. "Extra-constitutional" state-provincial agreements in the Great Lakes-St. Lawrence River Basin may then become stronger and may achieve effective preeminence over the "constitutional" Boundary Waters Treaty and the Great Lakes Fishery Convention. Put another way, as citizens' interests in and commitments to the nation-state wane, its treaties may come to be superseded by other kinds of agreements. Such a process appears to be under way in the United States and Canada while the opposite may be true within the Indian nations. But the latter type of nation may be preadapted to fit the emerging Canadian and American conventions if they continue toward "bioregionalism."

Transjurisdictional Governance: Formal and Informal

The various interjurisdictional agreements in the Great Lakes are basically of a "framework type." They contain terse, general statements of issues, expectations, and intentions, and specify the form of a joint organization to work toward realization of these intentions.

The interjurisdictional organization put in charge of a particular agreement is provided with an initial set of formally negotiated responsibilities. But the terms are not fully precise and are subject to periodic reinterpretation by the parties to the agreement and by the agreement's administrative organization. There is a general tendency for an interjurisdictional organization to expand its activities gradually and incrementally. Depending on the swings of the politics of federal, state, and provincial administrations, the formal parties may condone or even foster expansion or may act to trim back some unwanted adventitious activities.

Both the International Joint Commission (IJC) with responsibilities under the Boundary Water Treaty, and the Great Lakes Fishery Commission (GLFC) under the Great Lakes Fishery Convention, report to the executive level of the federal governments and have formal mandates to convene public hearings in Canada and in the United States. This has interesting implications with respect to sovereignty on ecosystemic features. Citizens with interests in Great Lakes issues have found the public hearings very useful for participating in basinwide governance. The public hearings under IJC auspices have attracted more public involvement and press attention than those of GLFC.

Generally the IJC is more politicized than the GLFC or the regional and state-provincial commissions, at least in recent years. Appointment to the IJC has become part of the patronage system for retired legislators and political workers loyal to the federal administration in power. Idealistic observers ("IJC groupies") and politically tolerant activists try to ignore the politicization and tend to act on the hope that partisan biases are not excessive.

GLFC commissioners generally include senior administrators of fishery agencies at federal, state, and provincial levels plus some nongovernmental experts. The fishery administrators are influenced by party politics, but tend to play at bureaucratic politics more than party politics. Commissioners of the regional and state-provincial commissions are generally senior officials in their jurisdictional bureaucracies, and tend to behave more like fishery commissioners than IJC commissioners.

Both the IJC and GLFC have secretariats for the Great Lakes and a variety of boards, committees, study task forces, groups of advisors, etc. There has never been an attempt to describe fully and explain in detail the "actor system" organized around one of these commissions. They are relatively open, self-organizing political systems. Though the formally constituted and federally appointed commissioners play central roles of facilitation, legitimation, and funding, each commission consists of a family of elements, some of which could be reconstituted somewhat and organized to take interjurisdictional leadership if the federal commissions were to be reduced greatly in effectiveness.

Some elements of the IJC and GLFC families overlap and are strongly interactive at the working level. At the commission level, IJC commissioners and their senior staff may see themselves as operating at a higher political level than the GLFC and the other commissions. IJC receptions tend to be in rather plush settings compared to GLFC receptions. Formal meetings between IJC and GLFC commissioners may degenerate into a quasi-hearing process in which IJC commissioners expect to be briefed on technical fishery issues but do not expect to offer information to the GLFC commissioners.

During the 1980s the public hearings of the IJC were exploited effectively by environmental activists of nongovernmental organizations. The commissioners found themselves caught between strong proenvironmental pressure from the public and the press and concerted efforts by the federal administrations to reduce commitment and to devolve responsibility for local and regional environmental issues to lower levels of governments. One governmental response was to diminish the role of IJC Great Lakes Boards and the regional office, thus effectively weakening the Great Lakes staff function of IJC. Part of this was justified by a decision by the federal parties to report on compliance to the Great Lakes Water Quality Agreement directly to the commission rather than indirectly through board reports which had created difficulties in accountability for agency administrators.

A consortium of environmental nongovernmental organizations, Great Lakes United (GLU), was created in 1981. It was originally proposed as an American consortium to act as a regional lobby in Washington. An unlikely tentative alliance of Michigan outdoorsmen and New York radical activists was replaced by a basinwide consortium of antipollution, biological-conservation, and nature-preservation organizations. The participating American organizations have had difficulties relating to the international dimensions of GLU. Since many American activists make the tacit assumption that Washington is the primary locus of effective power on environmental issues, within the Great Lakes Basin, and even globally, the ultimate strategy of GLU has been to lobby in Washington.

One of the most effective governance procedures is occurring locally under the stewardship of hundreds of groups of informed and committed volunteers and usually linked to some appropriate level of government. These groups are increasingly taking the lead in nature and especially wetland preservation and coastal zone husbandry. Governance institutions, formal and informal, in the St. Lawrence River part of the basin have come to resemble what has evolved in the Great Lakes part of the basin.

Indian nations now have some involvement in the various formal and informal aspects of governance. But the magnitude and complexity of the governance phenomenon is such that the few people of the First Nations who are expert in such matters have had to limit their involvement to only a few of the key governance activities of special interest to them, such as fisheries exploitation and effects of contaminants on human health.

Industrial, commercial, and business interests of various kinds have Great Lakes regional organizations or fora. Most have some involvement in environmental issues. Until recently most of these organizations resisted environmental reforms, but that has been changing recently. Now that reforms are inevitable, it makes good business sense to be leading rather than following. Great Lakes enterprises are beginning to fund research and information activities relevant to clean and green technology.

Many of the research and scholarly activities directly relevant to innovation in Great Lakes Basin governance have been funded by private foundations. Academics and not-for-profit private researchers have been the beneficiaries of such funds. The more costly rigorous science on natural features of the Great Lakes Basin has been funded primarily by governments directly or through granting agencies for university-based research. Practical application of scientific understanding has been assisted strongly through "references" and other joint interjurisdictional efforts under IJC and GLFC auspices, funded directly by the two federal parties. Until recently industry and commerce have funded research mainly to combat what they perceived to be inappropriate environmental reform; this is now changing. Thus funds from different sources have been applied in different but generally complementary ways.

The New Realities

The 1960s brought a major multipronged reform toward *integrity* in North America and elsewhere in the West. The state of cultural *disintegrity* — sustained by an international state of war or cold war, by racial discrimination, by gender inequities, and by massive environmental abuse — needed to be addressed. Political processes of several compatible types were initiated toward such reform. The notion of integrity — of healthy, robust self-organizing capabilities to result in a more desirable and sustainable culture and nature — was central, if implicit, in this broad reform.

Thus racial *integration* in the schools and in the cities was undertaken. Women as the disadvantaged gender became more fully integrated in the professions and in organizational leadership. Within the cultural-natural ecosystems the integrity of nature was protected more fully and disintegrated features of ecosystems began to be rehabilitated. Part of the solution to the Cold War was to link healthy self-organizing institutions across the frontier, notably science, and to assist self-organizing market and democratic processes in groups of countries where centralized command and control processes were impoverishing those nations culturally, environmentally, and economically. Cooperation between the open self-organizing institutions — science, the market, democracy — of the different states is intended to undercut the proclivities to injustices within and conflict between closed, controlled nation states.

Winds of reform blowing in the direction of integrity were blowing strongly in the 1960s and early 1970s. But then the direction of the winds changed, in the late 1970s, with a kind of counter-reformation. For some years it appeared that the earlier reform campaign would be defeated, but such has not been the case. Instead, it may be that the 1980s have contributed to the overall reform by clarifying the excessive abuses that accompany both the free enterprise and welfare state conventions.

The 1990s may be less war-oriented and more integrity-oriented than has been seen for a long time. This provides an opportunity for some modest celebration and then to face the reality that the disintegrative consequences of many bad features of the twentieth century still need to be met and resolved. This is a challenge for decades to come, presumably for the entire twenty-first century. Perhaps what is most worth celebrating is that people are no longer blocked from addressing directly the disintegrative features of the Western culture. A bioregional culture may be forming.

Fortunately for those in the Great Lakes Basin, the frontiers were demilitarized about 150 years ago. Self-organizing social institutions have generally been evolving toward integrity in all the political jurisdictions at all levels in the basin. These open systems include science, democracy, the market and, most important, the natural parts of the Great Lakes and St. Lawrence River Basin ecosystem. The natural part of the basin system has always ignored the interjurisdictional boundaries. The various cultural open systems have been interdigitating and anastomosing gradually, system by system, over the decades.

Perhaps we should perceive the natural-cultural basin as a case study of the "new realities," as Peter Drucker calls our current mindset and aspirations in his 1989 book with that title. There may be no transnational bioregion in the world which has progressed as far as the basin within these "new realities."

Present Opportunities

It may be that many opinion leaders active in the Great Lakes Basin now share the general mindset and hopes sketched above. Several times during the past decade Charles Ross, once the American dean of the IJC commissioners when that was not a patronage post, recommended the creation of a democratic representative assembly for the Great Lakes Basin. The public hearings convened formally under the auspices of the International Joint Commission and the Great Lakes Fishery Commission may be steps in this direction. The U.S. National Research Council (NRC) and the Royal Society of Canada (RSC) sponsored a joint nongovernmental review in 1984-85 of the state of science relevant to the 1978 Great Lakes Water Quality Agreement. Great Lakes United, the nongovernmental consortium of citizen groups, conducted basinwide hearings in 1986-87 concerning the 1978 agreement. The mayors are meeting annually in open sessions. Numerous sectors of the basin's economy have organized regular coordinating meetings and cooperative action. The time may be ready to organize and convene a representative assembly, initially at least on an informal basis constitutionally.

Elizabeth Brown-Weiss, as a member of the 1984–85 NRC-RSC Review, recommended the institution of an environmental ombudsman on a basinwide basis. In 1989 the Rawson Academy of Ottawa convened a basinwide activity to propose an Ecosystem Charter for the Great Lakes. With the leadership of the Great Lakes Commission, such an Ecosystem Charter emerged in 1994 and has been endorsed by numerous agencies and individuals.

Many people have been working hard in the Great Lakes Basin toward the reforms sketched in this paper. The time may be right to attempt some necessary institutionalization of the largely informal efforts to date. The Indian nations would presumably contribute in an important way to the new institutional structures and processes. Any such consolidation of reform should be preparatory for further urgent efforts; we are far from ready for what is coming regionally and globally — climate change, ultraviolet radiation, demographic migrations, global trade integration.

If the Great Lakes-St. Lawrence River Basin case study is to evolve rapidly and serve as an exemplar elsewhere, it will need to recruit members of a new generation. This could be an interesting challenge to colleges and universities as well as to nongovernmental organizations.

Acknowledgments

Much of the work reflected in this paper has been funded by private foundations active in the Great Lakes Basin, notably the American and Canadian Donner Foundations, the Joyce Foundation and, earlier, the Max Bell Foundation. The Donner Canadian Foundation provided support for this paper. I acknowledge help from Bruce Bandurski, Lee Botts, Lynton Caldwell, Marc Clemens, Glenda Daniels, Michael Donahue, George Francis, Andrew Hamilton, Bud Harris, John Jackson, Nathalie La Violette, Sally Lerner, Paul Muldoon, Don Munton, Ron Shimizu, and Phil Weller.

Bibliography

Berkes, F. 1989. *Common Property Resources: Ecology and Community-Based Sustainable Development*, London: Belhaven Press.

Caldwell, L.K., ed. 1988. *Perspectives on Ecosystem Management for the Great Lakes*. Albany: State University of New York Press.

———.1990. *Between Two Worlds: Science, the Environmental Movement and Policy Change*. Cambridge, U. K.: Cambridge University Press.

Christie, W.J., M. Becker, J.W. Cowden, and J.R. Vallentyne. 1986. "Managing the Great Lakes Basin as a Home." *Journal of Great Lakes Research* 12(1): 2–17.

Colborn, T.E., A. Davidson, S.N. Green, R.A. Hodge, C.I. Jackson, and R.A. Liroff. 1990. *Great Lakes, Great Legacy?* Washington, D.C.: The Conservation Foundation and Ottawa, The Institute for Research on Public Policy.

Daniels, G., and D. Misener, eds. 1984. *Decisions for the Great Lakes*. Calument, Ind.: Purdue University Press.

Drucker, P.F. 1989. *The New Realities*. New York: Harper & Row.

———. 1993a. *The Ecological Vision*. New Brunswick: Transaction.

———. 1993b. *Post-Capitalist Society*. New York: HarperCollins.

Edwards, C.J., and H.A. Regier, eds. 1990. *The Ecosystem Approach to the Integrity of the Great Lakes in Turbulent Times*. Ann Arbor, Mich.: Great Lakes Fishery Commission Special Publication.

Great Lakes Commission. 1994. *Ecosystem Charter for the Great Lakes-St. Lawrence Basin*. Ann Arbor, Mich.: The Great Lakes Commission.

Hartig, J.H., and M.A. Zarull. 1992. *Under RAPs: Toward Grassroots Ecological Democracy in the Great Lakes Basin*. Ann Arbor: University of Michigan Press.

Haug, P.T., B.L. Bandurski, and A.L. Hamilton, eds. 1986. *Toward a Transboundary Monitoring Method: a Continuing Binational Exploration*. 2 Vols. Washington and Ottawa: International Joint Commission.

Hickcox, D.H., ed. 1988. *The Great Lakes: Living with North America's Inland Waters*. Bethesda, Md.: American Water Resources Association.

La Violette, N. 1993. "A comparison of Great Lakes Remedial Action Plans and St. Lawrence River Restoration Plans." *Journal of Great Lakes Research* 19(2): 389–99.

Lerner, S., ed. 1992. *Environmental Stewardship: Studies in Active Earthkeeping*. Waterloo, Ontario: University of Waterloo, Department of Geography Publications Series.

Manno, J. 1993. "Advocacy and Diplomacy in the Great Lakes: A Case History of Non-governmental-organization Participation in

Negotiating the Great Lakes Water Quality Agreement." *Buffalo Environmental Law Journal* 1(1): 1–61.

Muldoon, P.R., with D.A. Scriven and J.M. Olson. 1986. *Cross-Border Litigation: Environmental Rights in the Great Lakes Ecosystem.* Toronto: Carswell.

National Research Council of the United States and The Royal Society of Canada (NRC/RSC). 1985. *The Great Lakes Water Quality Agreement: An Evolving Instrument for Ecosystem Management.* Washington: National Academy Press.

Ostrom, E. 1990. *Governing the Commons: the Evolution of Institutions for Collective Action.* Cambridge, U. K., Cambridge University Press.

Pinkerton, E., ed. 1989. *Co-operative Management of Local Fisheries: New Directions for Improved Management and Community Development.* Vancouver: University of British Columbia Press.

Prince, H.H., and F.M. D'Itri. 1985. *Coastal Wetlands.* Chelsea, Mich.: Lewis Publications.

Rawson Academy of Aquatic Sciences (RAAS). 1989. *Towards an Ecosystem Charter for the Great Lakes-St. Lawrence.* Ottawa: Rawson Academy of Aquatic Sciences. Occasional Paper No. 1.

Regier, H.A. 1992. "Ecosystem Integrity in the Great Lakes Basin: An Historical Sketch of Ideas and Actions." *Journal of Aquatic Ecosystem Health* 1: 25–37.

Satz, R.N. 1991. *Chippewa Treaty Rights.* Wisconsin Academy of Sciences, Arts and Letters. Volume 79, no. 1.

Schmidtke, N.W., ed. 1988. *Toxic Contamination in Large Lakes. Proceedings of the World Conference on Large Lakes, Mackinac, Michigan. 1986.* 4 Vols. Chelsea, Mich.: Lewis Publications.

Tarlock, A.D., and S.L. Deutsch, eds. 1989. "Symposium on Prevention of Groundwater Contamination in the Great Lakes Region." *Chicago: Chicago-Kent Law Review* 65(2): 345–554.

World Commission on Environmental Development (WCED). 1987. *Our Common Future: Report of the World Commission on Environment and Development,* G.H. Brundtland, Chair. Oxford: Oxford University Press.

Weller, P. 1990. *Freshwater Seas: Saving the Great Lakes.* Toronto: Between the Lines Press.

Westra, L. 1994. *An Environmental Proposal for Ethics: the Principle of Integrity.* Lanham, Md.: Rowman & Littlefield.

Whillans, T.H., spec. ed. 1986. "Saving the Great Lakes." *Alternatives* 13(3): 1–70.

———., spec. ed. 1987. "The Great Lakes." *Seasons* 37(3): 17–57.

Woodley, S., J.J. Kay, and G.R. Francis, eds. 1993. *Ecological Integrity and the Management of Ecosystems*. Delray Beach, Fl.: St. Lucie Press.

QUEBEC! QUEBEC!

THE CHALLENGE OF QUEBEC: CULTURAL IDENTITY AND ECONOMIC INTEGRATION

Louis Balthazar
Université Laval

In the fall of 1988, two major developments contributed to widening the gap of misunderstanding between French-speaking Quebecers and the rest of Canada. One may even consider this period as a watershed in the long and painful process that led to the rejection of the Meech Lake constitutional agreements by a majority of informed English-speaking Canadians. This rejection is still considered as an affront by many Quebecers and is one of the main reasons that 49.4 percent voted Yes in the 1995 Quebec referendum on sovereignty.

First, in the November 1988 federal election, Quebecers voted overwhelmingly for the Progressive Conservative Party, led by Brian Mulroney. Since the contemplated Free Trade Agreement (FTA) with the United States was at the heart of the campaign, this vote may be considered a confirmation of the endorsement of FTA by both major provincial parties in Quebec. For the many Canadian elites who were strongly opposed to the deal for nationalist reasons, the Quebec attitude indicated a lack of Canadian patriotism on the part of French-speaking Quebecers, a breach in Canadian solidarity, and an absence of empathy for the cause of Canadian culture that was perceived as being seriously threatened by FTA. Especially for those English-speaking Canadians who had been devoted to the promotion of bilingualism and to a better understanding of Quebec since the early days of the Royal Commission on Bilingualism and Biculturalism in the 1960s, the Quebec stance in favor of tighter integration with the United States was seen as a "betrayal."

Hardly a month later, the government of Quebec committed another act of "betrayal." After the Supreme Court of Canada had ruled against maintaining the 1977 provision of the Quebec Charter of the French Language requiring French-only commercial signs, Premier Bourassa invoked the Canadian Constitution's "notwithstanding clause" to exempt his government from observing the Court's judgment. Bill 178 was rushed through Quebec's National Assembly, softening some aspects of the linguistic legislation, but keeping the ban on outdoor commercial signs in a language other than French. Bourassa thought he was acting on behalf of public opinion in Quebec. In the rest of Canada, as well as among the English-speaking population of Quebec, Bill 178 was an intolerable violation of rights. Oddly enough, there was more outcry over this bill than there had been in the previous eleven years when the French-only rule for commercial signs was always in effect. Bill 178 was considered even more restrictive than Bill 101, even though it was not. While Quebecers had been perceived as being naively exposed to American domination with their approval of FTA, they were now labeled overly protective with their insistence on maintaining the integrity of the Charter of the French Language.[1]

These two positions may be intimately related to one another. From a Quebec perspective, it makes great sense to insist on protecting identity through linguistic legislation and, at the same time, to open up to the neighboring country. Whatever the merits of Bill 178 and FTA (a case could be made against both concrete policies), the protection of cultural identity and promotion of economic integration are two mutually compatible goals. Both are essential parts of a contemporary Quebec strategy. This article intends to illustrate the complementarity of these two trends which constitute a real challenge for Quebec as well as for Canada.

I

The affirmation of identity, especially when it takes the form of nationalism, is often considered the great danger of our time. Some would even recommend the containment of nationalism as a doctrine worthy of succeeding the containment of Communism. Nobody denies the perverse consequences of phenomena such as "ethnic cleansing," ethnic fanaticism, or racism. But there are calls for a balance between extreme integration and extreme diversity. Jacques Attali, former president of the European Bank for Reconstruction and Development, is one of those who would not wage an all-out war against any form of nationalism. He is much more cautious:

> The pressing and very practical challenge at this moment in history is to rebuild nations without stirring up xenophobia, to promote nationalism without provoking chauvinism, and to unify Europe while allowing diversity.[2]

We may go a step further and make the point that cultural security is a necessary condition of openness. It is certainly true, at the individual level, that when a person feels secure about his or her identity, he or she is more likely to enter into healthy and beneficial relations with others. Insecurity and frustration almost invariably generate dysfunctional behavior. Why would it not be the same for groups, peoples, or nations? Is it not a worthwhile goal for humanity to strike a balance between cultural diversity and the sharing of the world's riches?

French-speaking Quebecers would like to keep their "distinct society" as well as their Canadian citizenship and their North American ethos and economic freedom. They would like to use their specificity as a launching pad for their integration within the global environment. "The mixture of distinctiveness and similarity that has come to characterize Quebec society remains its best entry point into the new global order."[3] As long as distinctiveness is accompanied by similarities, autonomy and the affirmation of identity should not be seen as contrary to integration. In other words, it would be incorrect to assume that greater autonomy produces less integration. Some degree of autonomy may be conducive to integration.

Of course, this is true for Canada as a whole, as well as for Quebec. To the extent that the northern country develops its own identity and manifests its differences, its similarities and sharing with the United States will be acceptable. The problem has been Canada's greater concern with its cohesion than with its specificity. A one and indivisible Canada, ruled by a Charter of Rights and Freedoms and subject to the process of judicial review, has come to offer an image that is not much different from that of the United States.[4] This image would come even closer to being a replica of that of its neighbor if the concept of the equality of all provinces ever leads Canadians to adopt a Senate on the American model.

One of the ironies of the contemporary situation is that Quebec has become the best defender of the British Parliamentary system in Canada. Quebec has also advocated an orientation for Canada that would make it look quite different from the United States. Nothing was less American than the Meech Lake agreement but it is unlikely that such agreement will ever be considered again. In fact, any constitutional reform based on the symmetry of all provinces is more likely to fail than to succeed. It is obvious that the smaller Canadian provinces (Saskatchewan, Manitoba, and the Maritime) are in favor of more centralization and a stronger national government than Quebec could ever accept. Quebecers actually seem allergic to the very concept of a Canadian *nation*. They are quite willing to live in a Canada that is not a homogeneous nation-state, as was the case in previous years.[5] Consequently, the only solution to the Canadian conundrum would be to let English-speaking provinces (at least the smaller ones) endow their central government with strong powers while Quebec (and perhaps B.C., Alberta, and Ontario) enjoys a larger measure of autonomy. This would not make Canada easy to govern. But is governing Canada that easy right now? Such a plan would reduce the tension within Canada and, since it would make Canada quite different from the United States, might make it more open to a certain degree of integration with its neighbor. Quebec, being more secure with respect to its autonomy, would be more likely to reinforce its ties with the rest of Canada.[6]

Let us not deny, however, that some types of autonomous assertions are inward-looking and may run contrary to the dynamism of integration. It is therefore important to address the following question: what kind of identity is a boost for larger communities? And what kind of integration is possible without abolishing diversity and identity?

II

There is no doubt that some forms of affirmation and promotion of identity have been deleterious and sometimes extremely harmful to the well-being of peoples ; some nationalisms have tended toward exclusivism and toward the destruction of other forms of identity around them. To express an allegiance to one's group while promoting the hate of others is certainly not an effective way to bring about peace and participation in a larger whole.

Such behavior occurs when collective identity is conceived as an absolute phenomenon, at the expense of individual rights. The affirmation of collective identity is not conducive to any real security for its adherents if it is not first and foremost contingent upon the well-being of the individuals who compose the group.

Identity may also be dangerous if it is deprived of any flexibility, of any possibility of evolution or change. One example is an identity based strictly on ethnicity. One cannot change one's ethnic origin and ethnicity is usually determined by birth. It is possible to promote an ethnic identity while respecting others and even making room for interethnic relations, but ethnicity often tends to be exclusive. Furthermore, its fixed nature does not allow population exchange or social dynamism.

Another form of identity that may produce intolerance and social conflict is one based on religion. Religious allegiance is not necessarily related to exclusivism and some religions actually promote toleration and universal brotherhood. It is the link between civic life and religious adherence that may be perverse. Alliance between church and state has frequently produced intolerance.

Throughout history, French Canadians, not unlike nineteenth-century nationalities in central Europe, have manifested some form of traditional nationalism that could include elements of the aforementioned types of identity. To be a French Canadian was often more or less equivalent to belonging to an ethnic group. It was not impossible to *become* a French Canadian, but is was rare. Although some Europeans were integrated into the French Canadian community, it remained rather homogeneous. It is important to note, however, that marriages between Amerindians and French Canadians were numerous. In addition, it was almost unthinkable between 1840 and 1950 to belong to French Canada without professing the Roman Catholic faith. Since it was proclaimed that language was "guardian of the faith" by the clerical authorities who were very powerful in Quebec during that period, the Catholic religion seemed to be an essential component of French Canadian identity.

The Quiet Revolution, which took place in the 1960s as a result of post World War II's important socio-economic transformation, has radically altered this conception of identity. Most Quebec institutions were secularized amazingly fast. While religious authorities have remained an important voice in the province of Quebec, and many Quebecers are still Catholic at heart, if not in practice, it would be inconceivable now to say that French Canada will be Catholic or just won't exist, as could still be said in the early sixties. The Quiet Revolution was also the time when French-speaking Quebecers changed their names. French Canadians became Québécois. This could only correspond to a profound change of identity. More or less explicitly, Quebec Francophones came to realize that only on the territory of the province of Quebec did they constitute a critical mass, sufficient to create a network of communications and institutions that would allow them to develop and modernize their society while maintaining their specific culture. When traditional forms of allegiance to the region, the parish or the large family began to disappear, language acquired a new relevance. Language was no longer guardian of the faith but the expression of a specific culture.

A problem for French Canadians during this time was the rapidly declining birth rate. From 1965 to 1970, it went from 3 to 2.5. As a consequence, the "revenge of the cradles" could no longer be the main instrument of community maintenance and perpetuation. This led Quebec elites to turn their attention to immigration. What has been normal before—the integration of most immigrants into the English-speaking community—became unacceptable. They suddenly realized that if the newcomers continued to swell the number of Anglophones in Montréal, the metropolis would soon have a majority of English-speaking people. Therefore something had to be done to ensure the integration of most migrant peoples into the French-speaking majority. Something had to be done, also, to reverse the quasicolonial situation of a small community of Anglophones, most of whom had not learned the language of the majority and had made downtown Montreal look almost as English as any other North American city.

According to the new way of thinking, therefore, Quebec as a whole should become French-speaking and should reflect the identity of its Francophone majority. Thenceforth, a new definition of "Quebecer" would slowly arise: someone who would agree to live in a particular French-speaking society and pay heed to its government, whatever one's ethnic origin, religion, or even main spoken language. As this definition was assimilated by the population, French-speaking Quebecers would move from an ethnic conception of their identity to a civic one. The Quebec culture was becoming more dynamic and likely to evolve considerably along pluralistic and multiethnic lines.

Such a profound change, however, did not reach the consciousness of the majority of French-speaking Quebecers for quite some time. Even if they called themselves Québécois (which is a territorial and civic appellation), many continued to think of themselves as French Canadians (that is, in an ethnic way). Even to this day, while the evolution toward pluralism has become irreversible, ethnic consciousness has not completely disappeared.[7]

The linguistic legislation that was a response to the desire for change among the population contributed greatly to the acceleration of the process toward a new consciousness. Bill 22 in 1974, which made French the official language of Quebec, and Bill 101 in 1977, which proclaimed the Charter of the French Language, brought about a new concept of citizenship in Quebec. The charter, in particular, represented a strong move toward making the French language the common idiom of public life. French was not only the native language of the French-Canadian majority. It became the main language of communication for all Quebec citizens. Anglophone institutions were maintained, such as a complete education network. But newcomers were called to adopt the French language. Only French public schools were opened to incoming immigrants. Private firms were also urged to conduct their domestic operations, and address their employees and customers in French.

The charter was radical enough to be considered the moral equivalent of political independence. According to some observers, it deterred many Quebecers from responding to the call for sovereignty-association in 1980. It could even be said that, in itself, had it not been so frequently and so successfully challenged in the Courts, the charter would have made Quebecers better and more contented Canadians. By removing their deep-seated linguistic unsecurity and granting them a solid civic type identity, it allowed them to share more confidently with others.[8]

It became more and more difficult and, for that matter, totally illogical, for French-speaking Quebecers to consider Anglophones and immigrants as alien, while their government's law required the latter to be integrated into Quebec's French-language society. The children of immigrants were, in fact, integrated in large proportions as they flocked to French-speaking public schools. Twenty years after the charter's implementation, Quebecers' identity appears more visibly than ever as pluralistic and multiethnic, at least in the city of Montreal, and also, to a certain extent, in other areas. It is true that a high proportion of those labeled as members of cultural communities are still using English more often than French. But the real effect of the Charter of the French Language will not be felt until a whole generation of immigrants has been subject to it, especially through the school system.

One problem that slows down the integration of immigrants is the very high concentration of newcomers in the city of Montreal. French-speaking Quebecers by birth have moved in great numbers to the suburbs surrounding the metropolis. As a consequence, in the city of Montreal proper, there are practically too many immigrants for the number of Quebec-born people responsible for their integration. In some schools, for instance, the majority of students were not born in Quebec, which is certainly not an ideal condition for integration. This has produced the anomalous situation of young people speaking English as soon as they leave the classroom.

Quebec is not exempt from racism but, by and large, it is no more racist than other Canadian provinces or the United States. To account for the relative uneasiness that has prevailed over the transformation of Quebec identity, one must remember that this has occurred within the span of one generation. No wonder French-speaking Quebecers have been at times rather clumsy in their attitudes toward minorities.

There is a tendency among Francophones to consider Anglophones a powerful majority, although the Quebec English-speaking community has come to perceive itself as an unfortunate minority. It is doubtful that Anglo-Quebecers are as miserable as they sometimes pretend to be, for they still benefit from their own school system, which they control themselves (a far better situation than that of most Francophones outside Quebec) ; they enjoy all possible civic freedoms ; and they benefit from various high-quality social and educational services. Both Francophones and Anglophones are slow to share a collective identity, but it is encouraging to note that this is no longer the case among a growing number of young people.

A large number of Quebecers of diverse ethnic origins fully accept the new civic society or, at least, are sympathetic to the goals of a majority of French-speaking Quebecers. This does not mean, of course, that they favor sovereignty. But the Quebec government has been somewhat hesitant as to which policy to adopt. Some of its members have expressed a willingness to welcome immigrants in a way that maintains a distance between native Quebecers and newcomers. For instance, some Quebec government officials have talked about "the contribution of cultural communities" to the mainstream Quebec culture. Representatives of those communities have stated demands for the recognition and preservation of their identity of origin. While there is no reason not to allow immigrants to keep part of their traditions, most of them would be satisfied just to be recognized as full-fledged Quebecers (and Canadians, of course). In January 1996, the Bouchard government dropped the label of "cultural communities" and boldly created a new department, "Relations with Citizens," thus showing its intention to emphasize the equality of all.

Given a sound immigration policy that provides for a certain selection process for immigrants (apart from the case of refugees) and according to which preference would be granted to those who show more potential for a smooth integration, the Quebec population would not only grow, but it would also be enriched by its ethnic variety. Great civilizations (the United States and France being our chosen points of reference) have shown that multiethnicity contributes to the positive evolution of societies. There is no reason to assume that Quebec could not remain French-speaking and unique while undergoing a dynamic evolution. Tomorrow's Quebec may be quite different from what it is today and, at the same time, remain a distinct society offering specific features of its own. It is important for the Quebec government to enjoy just enough autonomy to be able to steer the course of this evolution. It must, in particular, keep minimum control over its immigration, even though this jurisdiction is still, not sanctioned by the Canadian Constitution.

The aboriginal population of Québec merits special consideration. Contrary to the immigrants, the Amerindians and Inuit are natives of the land and trace their origins back to the pre colonial era. Their insistence on keeping their own identity has been largely recognized by the government of Quebec. French Canadians have always been more accommodating toward Amerindians and Inuit than their Canadian neighbors. The Western Metis were half-French, half-Indian. Louis Riel was celebrated as a brother in Quebec and, as noted above, intermarriage was frequent between the two communities. Unfortunate mistakes and the fuzzy nature of jurisdictions, especially for the Kanesatake Mohawks, have somewhat blurred this tradition. A great deal of misinformation setting up Quebecers and aboriginals as enemies, and misguided attitudes on the part of some native leaders as well as Quebec officials, have contributed to the deterioration of the rapport between Quebecers and their native population. If an agreement was once signed between the James Bay Crees and the government of Quebec, however, and celebrated as a breakthrough,[9] there is no reason that there could not be a similar accord in the future. The aboriginal population could enjoy as much self-government as Quebec, if it so desired. This could also occur within a sovereign Quebec, although most natives have expressed their preference for staying in Canada.

In principle, therefore, if not always in fact, the Quebec identity has rid itself of its ethnic characteristics. It has become a civic identity based on individual freedom, flexibility, and openness to all. There is always the danger, however, that ethnicity could reappear. According to many Quebecers and among the most articulate analysts of the contemporary situation, this danger is related to certain conceptions of Canada that are still alive.[10] If, for instance, Quebec is just a province like any other with more French Canadians in its population than elsewhere, we may be led to consider those French Canadians as just one component of the Canadian ethnic mosaic. In such a situation, French-speaking Quebecers are caught between two alternatives. Either they give up on preserving their special identity and become Canadians like all others, or they keep on fighting for their cause but remain prisoners of the trappings of ethnicity.

In this respect, the Charlottetown constitutional agreements (rejected in the October 1992 referendum) implied a dubious status for French-speaking Quebecers. The province of Quebec was given a number of seats equal to that of all other provinces in a new Senate. But it was compensated for with a guarantee of 25 percent of the seats in the House of Commons, a privilege Quebec never requested. Moreover, there was a provision requiring a double majority in the Senate for certain votes pertaining to culture or language. For a bill to become law in these matters, both Francophone and Anglophone Senators would have had to concur. The definition of such attributes remained vague and was bound to be ambiguous. Who is a Francophone? Who is an Anglophone? While it is easy and clear to define a Quebecer as someone living in the territory of Quebec and committed to the duties of citizenship under the aegis of the Quebec government, the definition of a French-speaking Canadian would more likely lend itself to considerations as nebulous as those related to ethnic belonging. As long as French-speaking Quebecers see themselves as an ethnic group fighting for recognition, they are not very likely to accept the process of continental integration. Being on the defensive, they tend to consider integration as a threat to their identity. On the contrary, if their identity is secured by a civic society and takes a pluralistic and multiethnic form, they can contemplate integration as a process of enrichment and fruitful relations.

Unfortunately the Chrétien government, elected in 1993 without the support of French-speaking Quebecers, did not move an inch toward addressing the status of Quebec as a distinct global society of its own until the fateful referendum of 1995. The inaction of the Canadian government may be the main reason for the high vote in favor of sovereignty-partnership. The country had to come to the brink before Chrétien began to move in the direction of constitutional change.

Despite the strong sovereignty movement, and perhaps along with it, Quebecers are more and more outward-looking. Let us see how integrationist trends have developed in the last thirty-odd years.

III

During the Quiet Revolution of the 1960s, the Quebec government and, to some extent, the Quebec population, manifested a rekindled interest in international relations. A new link was created with France and some other countries. The United States was another object of renewed discovery, as the New York bureau was elevated to the rank of "délégation générale" and new missions were opened in several American cities. This rediscovery took on new and unprecedented dimensions in the seventies.

For a long time, Quebecers have felt very close to the United States. Many of them migrated south in the late nineteenth century and up to the First World War. At that time, American capital came north to Quebec and provided thousands of jobs. Quebecers were also attracted by American products and particularly by American mass culture. The Quebec elites, however, were not in favor of this Americanization of the French Canadian population. First, the clerical authorities preached resistance to American "materialism" without much success, especially among the lesser educated. Later, as a secular elite gradually replaced the religious one, a certain anti-Americanism became fashionable among those who modeled themselves after European culture. There was a time when it could be said that Quebec had its head in Europe and its body in America. Educated people had turned their attention to France while the masses enjoyed American cinema, music, and sports.

By the mid-seventies, a considerable number of Quebec elites in universities, government, the media, and the artistic community were taking a new look at the United States. Some intellectuals were talking about their "américanité," still others became conscious of a spiritual affinity between Quebec and the United States. The Quebec government, especially under René Lévesque, a great admirer of American culture, became more interested than ever in reinforcing connections with the United States and in building a new image of Quebec among American elites.

Quebec had always maintained close economic ties with the United States, although on a smaller scale than Ontario, which is anchored in the Great Lakes area. This dependency on the American economy was considered a blessing by many in Quebec, even in government circles, so much so that Quebec officials were calling for more investment from the south at the very moment the Canadian federal government was trying to restrict and regulate the flow of American capital.

American capital had contributed to Quebec's state building with the nationalization of hydroelectric power in 1962 and the huge James Bay development in the 1970s. A delicate balance was sought between the imperatives of Quebec's identity and the American economic connection. This balance was not always reached. There were also times when American economic elites worried about the direction of Quebec nationalism and times when Quebecers had to resist American pressures, such as in the film industry.

By and large, however, Quebec was able to maintain its cultural identity and also some amount of economic specificity because of its particular institutions, which included Hydro-Quebec, the Quebec Deposit and Investment Fund ("Caisse de dépôt et de placement"), the Desjardins cooperative movement and others considered as "variants of German-style corporatism,"[11] in spite of American skepticism toward such interventions from the state or collective organizations into the economy. It remains to be seen how long these institutions can survive in the context of NAFTA. Should Quebec become independent, American pressure might cause them to be restricted as a precondition of Quebec's readmission into the free trade zone.

Culturally speaking, at a time when English-speaking Canadians lament the threat to their culture brought about by FTA and NAFTA, Quebecers are becoming more autonomous. Between 1985 and 1990, according to Statistics Canada, the rate of attraction to American television programs in Quebec declined by 12 percent. In 1990, while 76 percent of English-speaking Canadians were watching United States productions, this was true of only 33 percent of Quebecers. Moreover, in 1991, the top ten programs on the ratings list in Quebec were indigenous productions.[12] Thus, integration with the United States did not go so far as to seriously erode Quebec cultural activities. Quebecers were enthused with the United States, sought out the American market, welcomed American investment, and traveled south in great numbers, but they remained themselves and continued to support their own cultural productions.

One may wonder why Quebecers are so eager to integrate with the United States and yet so reluctant to share more with other Canadians. Why not become more integrated with the rest of Canada? The fact is that Quebecers tend to be more suspicious of "Canadianism," at least of a certain conception of Canadian unity, than they are of the United States. This may at times constitute a grave mistake, but it is very understandable. The United States does not constitute a political threat, nor even a cultural one. No American institution would invalidate Quebec laws (as the Supreme Court of Canada may do with its interpretation of the 1982 Constitution and of the Charter of Rights and Freedoms), no American institution claims to be competent in matters pertaining to Quebec culture, and no one, in the United States, thus far has proposed that Quebecers be part of the one and indivisible American nation.

Quebecers are very willing to remain Canadians, as public opinion polls constantly indicate. But they insist on not losing their specific identity in the process. In fact, it is more than possible for Quebecers to be more closely integrated with Canada than with the United States. Even those who favor political sovereignty propose to keep an economic and even a political union with the rest of Canada. Therefore, if barriers or customs offices are ever erected on the Trans-Canada highway, it certainly will not be as a result of Quebecers' will.

The Quebec government still adheres to a firm policy of putting down all barriers to interprovincial trade in Canada. Free trade with other Canadian provinces is certainly desired at least as much, if not more, than free trade with the United States. The vast majority in Quebec favor a high degree of economic cooperation among all Canadian actors. If North America includes Mexico, in addition to the United States, it certainly includes Canada first, in the Quebec perspective.

Conclusion

Perhaps the challenge of reconciling integration with the preservation of identity will not be met. But many signs seem to point to the fact that just enough identity, understood in a civic sense, is not an obstacle but a vehicle for integration. By maintaining their cultural identity, Quebecers may bring a valuable contribution to an integrated North America. This will not be easy but it is possible.

If Canadians would agree to let Quebecers fashion their society in a distinct way, it might help the Canadian political entity to be quite distinct from the United States. Then Canada as a whole could become a more valuable partner, be more secure about its identity and distinctiveness and, as a consequence, more open to integration.

Notes

1. After five years, according to the "notwithstanding clause" of the Constitution, Bill 178 had to be revised. It was thus superseded, in 1993, by Bill 86 that maintained some restrictions in advertisement but complied by the Court's ruling. Bilingual signs are now legal.

2. Jacques Attali, "To Save Russia, The G-7 Must Become the G-8," Los Angeles Times Syndicate, *The News*, Mexico, 43, no. 225 (21 March 1993): 11.

3. Daniel Latouche, "Québec, See Under Canada: Québec Nationalism in the New Global Age," in *Québec State and Society*, 2d ed., ed. Alain-G. Gagnon (Toronto: Nelson Canada, 1993), 53.

4. See Seymour Martin Lipset, *Continental Divide* (New York: Routledge, 1990), 225.

5. See David V.J. Bell, *The Roots of Disunity* (Toronto: Oxford University Press, 1992).

6. This argument was well made by Kenneth McRoberts. See *Canada Watch* (Toronto: Robarts Center of Canadian Studies, York University, November 1993), 1.

7. It has somewhat revealed itself during the referendum campaign of 1995. Premier Jacques Parizeau's unfortunate speech acknowledging defeat on the night of the voting, deploring "some ethnic votes" against his project, did much to

resurrect the old image of ethnic nationalism. Had the "yes" won, however, Parizeau's prepared speech would have been one of generous inclusion.

8.   See J.A. Laponce, *Languages and Their Territories* (Toronto: University of Toronto Press, 1991); "Reducing the Tensions From Language Contacts," in *Language and State, Cowansville*, ed. David Schneiderman (Québec: Les Éditions Yvon Blais Inc., 1991), 173–79. Linguistic security did not play the same role in 1995 as in the 1980 referendum perhaps because it had been weakened.

9.   Cree Grand Chief Billy Diamond declared in 1983: "The Agreement itself is the first modern comprehensive land claims agreement. More importantly, our people were very involved in the elaboration of the Agreement. . . . To this date, it remains a unique agreement in North American relations between the Indians and the white man. Moreover, the Cree people consider that the agreement has met the test of time. . . . The James Bay and Northern Quebec Agreement is, in many respects, our charter of rights." Quoted by Mr. John Ciaccia, Minister of International Affairs in the Government of Quebec, in a speech delivered to the Association for Canadian Studies in the United States, Boston, Mass., 22 November 1991.

10.   See Jean Larose, *La petite noirceur* (Montréal: Boréal, 1987), 50; Martin Masse, "Pour l'indépendance, contre le nationalisme," *Le Devoir*, Montréal, 26 June 1992, B-8.

11.   Alain Noël, "Politics in a High-Unemployment Society," in Gagnon, 443.

12.   *Le Devoir*, 4 March 1993, A-4.

SOCIAL, POLITICAL, AND LINGUISTIC SUBVERSION IN QUEBEC FILMS OF THE 1980S

Henry Garrity
Bowling Green State University

In his 1990 book, *Cinéma de l'imaginaire québécois*, Heinz Weinmann divides Quebec's film history into two distinct periods: (1) Denys Arcand's *Jésus de Montréal*; and (2) all that led up to it. Weinmann's psychosocial thesis posits that important Quebecois films reflect the French-Canadian "roman familial," the communal vision of the family betrayed, first by the defeats of 1760 and 1837, second by the abandonment of national traditions in the 1960s and 1970s and, last, by the defeat of the referendum in 1980.[1]

In examining such films as *La petite Aurore, Tit-Coq, Mon Oncle Antoine, Les bons débarras, Un Zoo la nuit,* and *Le Déclin de l'empire américain*, Weinmann traces a transition from an individual to a collective vision of society. He sets *Jésus de Montréal* apart from the rest as the expression of a moral renaissance, a hint that restoring the faith of French Canadians in themselves and, by extension, in their society, requires a return to the fundamental values which protected French culture and language through 200 years of subjugation.

Un Zoo la nuit, Pouvoir intime, Le Déclin de l'empire américain, and *Jésus de Montréal* are all post-Quiet Revolution and postreferendum, and suggest conflicting attitudes, social and cinematic. If "revolutionary" cinema, quiet or otherwise, existed before the referendum, it was surely manifest in such films as Gilles Groux's *Le Chat dans le sac* (1964), Claude Jutras's *A tout prendre* (1963), Michel Brault's *Les Ordres* (1974), and Denys Arcand's *On est au coton* (1970). These were films that challenged accepted cinematic forms and traditional social values. As political statements, each has a subtext of individual freedom and expression—the primacy of the individual over the collective.

For *Jésus de Montréal*, Weinmann proposes a vocation of social integration, a way of saving the Quebec social fiber:

> *Jésus de Montréal*, parmi ses multiples mérites, est la première oeuvre québécoise d'envergure qui s'emploie à changer l'image de l'Autre, de l'Etranger en se basant sur le message révolutionnaire d'Amour, de don de Soi de Jésus. Le défi d'Arcand est de taille: après avoir évacué le religieux de sa conscience lors de la Révolution tranquille, le Québec peut-il réactualiser à Montréal, dans tout le pays, la parole du Christ, parole qui avait déjà animé sa première fondation hospitalière Ville-Marie?[2]

Albeit true that the idealism of Montreal's Christ decries the hedonistic selfishness of the dead-end, do-nothing philosophy of the university professors portrayed in *Le Déclin de l'empire américain*, while expelling the idolaters of mammon from the flesh-pots of television commercials, the film deals with the sin of greed that Arcand has already treated in at least one early film: *Réjeanne Padovani*. Perhaps, then, *Jésus de Montréal*, less divorced from what precedes it than Weinmann believes, represents a chapter in a tale of societal activity that goes beyond the films of Arcand and that links it with such other films as Yves Simoneau's *Pouvoir intime* and Jean-Claude Lauzon's *Un Zoo la nuit*. The link is subversion: sometimes serious, at times sardonic, often ironic, but always reflective of modern reality in Quebec.

In the context of these films, subversion is meant as any image, spoken or visual, which, while representing a traditional icon of political, moral, or social value, tends to undermine the icon, calling into question its traditionally accepted value. In each of these films, too, the mechanism for subverting the icon is the conflict between the superior molar organizing authority and the molecular, inferior subgroup which refuses to adhere to the value structure of the superior group, representing authority in its many forms. As described by Deleuze/Guattari: "I am not your kind. I belong to an inferior class. What matters is to break down the wall. I may take flight, but all the while I am fleeing, I will be looking for a weapon."[3] In the following discussion, subversion is seen in two guises: sociopolitical and linguistic.

To examine the subverted social and political icons, it may be instructive to begin with Heinz Weinmann's "roman familial." In speaking of *Jésus*, Weinmann makes the following observation:

Les personnages de *Jésus de Montréal* sont des adultes émancipés qui n'ont plus besoin de la famille ni comme refuge ni comme protection. Ils reflètent ainsi largement les tendances démographiques d'un Québec qui désaffecte de plus en plus la famille traditionnelle.[4]

It is certainly in the work of Denys Arcand that the dissolution of the family nucleus is the most evident, but in this regard, *Jésus* differs little from its predecessors in the Arcand canon. In *Le Déclin* few in the Yuppie-like university crowd are even married. The only marriage portrayed is held together by lies and deception — the tumens-comme-tu respires (you lie as easily as you breathe) syndrome — a mask for infidelity. As for the often referred-to traditional value of the large Quebecois family, there is only one child on screen in either *Jésus* or *Le Déclin*, although references are made to others. The dynamic in *Le Déclin* is that of the individual, not the familial or communal. Besides the unmarried university professors, there are two loners: the homosexual and the archetypal, macho, anti-intellectual whose monosyllabic responses and beer drinking mock the pseudo-intellectual chatter and pseudo-sophisticated wine sipping of the others. Finally, there is the one married couple whose solidarity is continually subverted, spiritually by Rémy's memories of past infidelities, physically by Remy's continuous sexual relationships with their friends, and finally by the couple's joint participation in sex parties.

The family of Daniel Coulombe who portrays Arcand's *Jésus de Montréal* is not the Holy Family of the Bible, the model for all family relationships sanctioned by the Catholic Church. The very notion of the biblical paradigm is subverted by the narrative inclusion of ancient texts questioning the Virgin Birth and even the marital status of Mary and Joseph. Daniel's "family" is recruited from among the unmarried, principally actors, whose careers in the theater distance them from traditional family values — the image of mother, father, and children.

The figure of the dysfunctional family plays an integral part in Yves Simoneau's *Pouvoir intime*. Like Jésus in Arcand's film, Theo (God) recruits his "family" from among outsiders to the traditional family icon: in this case the criminal class. Theo, the gang leader and only father, has a biological son, but the father/son relationship has become estranged as a result of Theo's absence, his incarceration in prison. Even the memory of the absent (deceased) mother, the traditional glue of the Quebecois family, can no longer keep the center together.

Simoneau's father/son relationship seems the mirror image of Jean-Claude Lauzon's in *Un Zoo la nuit*, where the dysfunctional relationship is caused by the son's (Marcel's) imprisonment and where the absent mother returns really and/or symbolically in one of the final sequences to aid the reunion of son and father which occurs only because of the father's impending death. In another mirroring of *Un Zoo*, the parent/child union in *Pouvoir intime* takes place only because of the son's death.

A second great icon of post-Duplessis society in Quebec is the State replacing the Church as the means for advancing society's goals. Arcand's discredited Church, symbolized by its clerics, and his State, subverted by its faith in commerce, are at the center of the sociopolitical message of *Jésus de Montréal*. The priest who calls upon Daniel Coulombe to update the Passion play on Mount Royal has a mistress whom he will not avow publicly for fear of losing his pension or of being exiled to the Western prairies to finish his days in an unimportant and uncultivated parish. Arcand portrays a Catholic hierarchy intent on obfuscating the scientific and archaeological research in the Middle East, especially those studies of the Dead Sea scrolls which call into question the traditional Christian view of the life and nature of Christ and the Holy Family. A sequence in a dubbing studio at the NFB sets the Big Bang theory in opposition to the creationist dogma of the Church, subverting traditional faith and certainty in the Church's teaching, which characterized Quebecois values for centuries, by suggesting a scientific alternative.

In the final scene of *Pouvoir intime*'s tale of robbery and treachery, Simoneau focuses his critical lens on the Church. His is not a vision of the splendid decor of Montreal's Oratoire Saint Joseph or Notre Dame but, instead, the image of an abandoned, fire-ravaged structure. Isolated in the countryside, silhouetted against verdant Quebec farmland, the icon would, at first, appear to be the traditional one often represented in mythic views of Quebec country life. But the burned-out building, emptied of its religious trappings and unused for services, is a subverted image of a derelict church in which a new couple, a homosexual man and androgynous woman, meet to divide the spoils of the robbery, the central action of the film. The empty shell of the church indexes the meaninglessness of the symbol as an organizing structure in society, and thus takes its place along with the ineffectual State, the government of social programs, which replaced the Church as the icon of Quebecois' faith in the two decades following the October crisis.

In Lauzon's *Un Zoo la nuit*, the State as represented by authority, by law and order, is subverted through the corruption of traditional icons of authority (the police) and the breakdown of the family. The corruption of authority begins with the venality of the police. The prison, metaphor for the State's protective security, becomes the scene of insecurity, a homosexual rape arranged by corrupt police interested in obtaining illegal drug money owed them by the film's hero/inmate. The police are abetted by a prison guard who unlocks the cell of the assailant and admits him into the cell of the victim, Marcel. The corruptors, George and Charlie, are past masters at violence of all sorts, particularly the sadistic. They threaten Marcel with killing his father and girlfriend unless he returns his cache of drugs and the hundreds of thousands of dollars made from their illegal traffic.

Corruption in *Un Zoo la nuit* goes beyond venality to vice. Lauzon seems also to subvert the Hollywood image of the police tandem, the two-man team of the traditional buddy picture, of which *Lethal Weapon* and *Lethal Weapon II* are recent examples. Charlie runs the drug operation; George, his homosexual partner, propositions Marcel in a restaurant men's room, takes pleasure in slashing Marcel's face in an alley, and meets his own end, seduced by Marcel's prison friend who uses George's sexual predilection against him.

Simoneau's *Pouvoir intime* establishes hierarchy of traditional icons: the State, the capitalist system, the criminal gang, the family, the Church, and the couple only to subvert each image by methodically showing the reverse reality of the icon. The government is corrupt, financial security compromised by greed, the family broken, the Church in ruins, and the traditional couple a failure. Jean-Claude Lauzon makes no less powerful a political commentary on modern Quebec than either Simoneau or Arcand. The director depicts a violent urban setting, its streets devoid of inhabitants, the hero alone.

The subverted icon of Simoneau's State, the corrupt head of security for the minister of defense, is evoked in *Pouvoir intime*'s initial sequence. He represents the top of a vertical, terrorizing, power order which will prevail throughout the film until it, too, is subverted. Government cannot be trusted and those in power do not trust it themselves. "A friend is more grateful than a government," says the head of security.

Perhaps, above all, there is the pursuit of money as security against a hostile social environment. Through money, everyone is corrupted. In *Jésus de Montréal*, the Church wants to modernize the Passion play to attract a greater audience, the electronic media need to sell their air time, and show-business lawyers want to make a buck commercializing any phenomenon because such opportunities do not last long. Young actors, men and women, are persuaded that their bodies are commodities to be sold, at any price, to the makers of TV commercials.

The subversive agents of all of these films are outsiders to the traditional values of the society. Their opposition to accepted values implies a binary structure which is indeed apparent in each diegesis. As university professors, the men in *Le Déclin* are portrayed as unproductive, contributing either nothing or nothing of value to the universal body of knowledge. The women academics, if more productive intellectually than the men, live nonetheless as pointless an existence as their male counterparts. Other academic women are in subservient professional roles because they do not hold doctorates, the sine qua non of university survival—the degree ridiculed, incidentally, by the men who hold it. They all live on the fringes of normal society as they live on the fringes of the American empire. They represent a peripheral group, like other groups and individuals in all films discussed here.

Le Déclin opposes men and women and subverts the traditional role of each. In the first half of this binary-structured scenario, the men, waiting at home for the women, are at work in the kitchen, traditional domain of the female. As they wait, they gossip and prepare the meal for the women who will return when they finish their day's work. The women, by the same token, are occupied at traditionally considered male activities: they are working out at the gym, ogling semidressed men while commenting on their bodies. Separate, each group denigrates the intellectual, social, and sexual prowess of the other. Together, they are still separate, a collection of rootless individuals careening from one sexual adventure to the next, affairs legitimized because they are discussed in the social structure of their subgroup, as any other subject of empirical research.

Jean-Claude Lauzon's felons, whether representative of law or disorder, are also peripheral societal characters. *Un Zoo la nuit*'s hero Marcel does not have a home. What is left of his father's apartment is being torn down and integrated into an Italian restaurant. Although befriended by the owners of the restaurant, Marcel and his father are as much outsiders here, because of the language barrier, as they are out of place in general society. Lauzon's film defines a society of drug dealers, prostitutes, homosexual cops on the take, and prison corruption which isolates the hero from his father.

Jésus de Montréal is a modern-day version of Saint Genêt, the actor who becomes his role. Daniel is converted through the effort of understanding the character he is playing and through new eyes seeing, perhaps for the first time, Quebec society as it really is, in all its hedonistic pursuit of money. The actor's trade, like others discussed here, is and has been traditionally, a peripheral one. Actors are not part of the mainstream, because they wear masks and pretend to be what they are not. They cannot be trusted because one cannot know them. Arcand's troop is not even part of the mainstream of the acting profession. Their existence is schizoid, escapist, as they hide from themselves and others in the personalities they assume. Arcand's actors undermine and subvert the intent of the Church hierarchy, as biblical Jesus undermined and subverted the religious intent of the Pharisees.

There are at least two images from Yves Simoneau's *Pouvoir intime* which characterize the subversive as portrayed by Quebec filmmakers. The first is the object of the corruptor's and corrupted's enterprise—the armored car—on which is painted in English, "TRUST." Quebecois, as portrayed in these films, no longer have trust, especially not trust in English, seen as the oppressive language which kept Quebec subservient for two centuries. The second image is a visual indexing of the disintegration of the societal union: an overhead tracking shot of a pool table, early in the film. The breaking of the racked balls parallels the filmic diegesis, as the group's structure splits into smaller components, each one going its separate way.

Weinmann's theory about Arcand's intentions in *Jésus de Montréal* leads the reader to question the film's ending and to ask if the film holds out hope for a different vision of Quebec's future. It is true that Daniel's existence helps the Other; it is not spiritual but, instead, physical help because his organs will be used to allow others to live. As for the family, the "roman familial" to which Weinmann repeatedly refers, it is no less forlorn and scattered at film's end than the gang in *Pouvoir intime*, or Marcel's pointless life in *Un Zoo la nuit*, or the desolate university crowd at the end of *Le Déclin*. Yet there appears to be a hopeful vision. Daniel Coulombe's disciples will form a theater group to continue his work, although even this noble goal seems doomed because it has been incorporated by the same money-oriented lawyer who, earlier in the role of Satan, tried to tempt Daniel with wordly goods. To the extent that *Jésus de Montréal* provides a hopeful epilogue to the desolation with which *Le Déclin* ends, there is truly cause to ask whether subversion will lead to salvation. The answer does not lie in Arcand's next film, *Love and Human Remains*, which was filmed in English. Such a linguisitic decision leads to the final subversive cinematic element discussed here—language—and, in particular, the language of Others.

In a 17 May 1993 article in *Variety* which proclaims, "Québécois Auteurs en Anglais," MaxFilms' producer Jean Frappier notes the growing phenomenon of Quebec directors shooting films in English. Frappier cites the examples of Denys Arcand filming his first English-language film, *Love and Human Remains*, in Montreal and Yves Simoneau, director of *Pouvoir intime*, *Les Fous de Bassan*, and *Dans le ventre du dragon*, who has gone to Hollywood to make such films as *Mother's Boy* with Jamie Lee Curtis and Vanessa Redgrave. Frappier comments: "[Filming in English] is not a question of nationalism, it's a question of realism," adding that while 15 years ago directors would not have worked in English, now many in Quebec believe that the language is safer than before.[5] But a review of certain Quebec films suggests that the seeds of this surprising turnabout, a flirtation with the linguistically forbidden Other in Quebecois filmmaking, were sown in the decade of the 1980s.

Quebec's 1977 Bill 101 and its predecessors Bill 22 (1974) and Bill 63 (1969) have forbidden English—the linguistic Other—in exterior signage and tolerated it in schools reserved for children of Anglophone parents. But the language question has always been alive in Quebec cinema where the language of Others, especially English, is used not only by native speakers of English but by Francophones too. The issue of the secure position of the French language notwithstanding, anyone unfamiliar with filmmaking in Montreal might be struck by the irony that, despite 24 years of government language policy favoring French, Denys Arcand, arguably Quebec's leading director, had made a film in a language other than his own.

Linguistic otherness in Quebec film, moreover, is not limited to English. Cofinancing, primarily with France, has introduced a linguistic element deceptively different, simultaneously a familiar and other music, swathed in extra-Quebecois resonances, which can produce the effect of distancing to the Quebecois ear as easily as the use of English. Furthermore, the language of immigrants, principally Italian, is often heard in scenarios of the 1980s. Critics of Quebec's language policy, resident and nonresident Canadian Anglophones principally, are joined by other Québécois concerned about the effect of language policy on provincial immigration. Critics of Quebec's ethnocentric language policy, such as Réal La Rochelle, speak of a desirable "métissage" in regard to Quebec's cinema. Eshewing assimilation into the international or Hollywood cinematic world vision, La Rochelle vaunts the creativity explicit in the multicultural nature of the Quebecois reality which produces its distinctiveness. La Rochelle deplores the politically correct ethnocentrism which has produced films he dubs unexportable banalities: "[Son] ouverture à divers apports culturels québécois non francophones fait partie d'une résistance à l'ethnocentrisme tous azimuts qui a marqué les projets politico-culturels depuis plus d'une décennie et dont l'échec, justement, est régénérateur."[6]

La Rochelle not only defines *métissage* in Quebec cinema, but also allows us to compare successful films with the failures he sees in *Maria Chapdelaine* and *Les Plouffe*. Of his list of successful films — *On est au coton, Gina, L'Acadie, L'Acadie, Les Ordres, La Bête lumineuse, Sonatine, Caffè Italia, Montréal* — he says:

> Ces films québécois . . . ont en commun d'être des films métis, c'est-à-dire d'abord et avant tout de ne pas être, comme dans la peinture à numéros, des copies qu'on veut aussi conformes que possible aux présumées normes conduisant aux Oscars d'Hollywood ou aux Césars de Paris, celles qu'on croit tirer des seuls manuels de gestion et de rentabilité commerciales... . Les films métis québécois n'ont d'abord rien à voir avec ces productions de type "wasp." Ils se caractérisent par des fusions et des mélanges du cinéma direct documentaire et du cinéma de fiction. Le cinéma québécois parle maintenant italien, créole, anglais, espagnol . . . à travers la culture francophone. A sa façon, souvent indirecte, ce cinéma critique la vague ethnocentriste dont le cinéma québécois a été facilement marqué durant les quinze dernières années. Le cinéma québécois métis est polymorphe et non sectaire . . . tourné vers l'avenir plutôt que vers la nostalgie passéiste, tout en respectant la mémoire culturelle et sociale.[7]

As if the notion of Francophone and other cultural and linguistic fusions were not enough of a palimpsest, the variety of Quebecois French poses an additional consideration to the directors and film producers of Montreal. Each must decide which accent to use as a means of conveying French Canadian culture. The problem is stated most succinctly by Yves Lever in his *Histoire générale du cinéma au Québec*:

S'ajoutant au problème du scénario se pose avec acuité celui de la langue des films. . . . "A Téléfilm, on estime que passé deux millions de dollars, il faut tourner en anglais, ou avec trop de compromis" dit André Lamy, alors directeur général [1985]. Mais avec le français, quel accent adopter? Comme la presque totalité des films se situent en milieux populaires, doit-on, pour le reálisme, adopter un accent familier, nécessairement régional, que même une grande partie des Québécois ne comprendront qu'à moitié? Et même s'ils le comprennent, un accent qui correspond à une image d'eux-mêmes qu'ils n'aiment pas? Durant cette période d'affirmation de soi engendrée par le nationalisme jusqu'au moment du référendum de 1980, et en parallèle avec le théâtre le plus vivant, surtout celui de Michel Tremblay, l'accent populaire des quartiers prolétaires de l'Est de Montréal est devenu, en quelque sorte, la norme difficilement évitable; phénomène sociologiquement intéressant, certes, mais esthétiquement limitatif. Entre le français châtié des comédiens parisiens ou des hommes politiques de France qui nous rendent visite et le "français québécois" du monde ordinaire, le cinéma parvient mal à se situer. En plus de provoquer nombre de frustrations pour les spectateurs locaux, cela pose problème pour la diffusion internationale des films.[8]

A number of important films of the 1980s offer concrete examples of linguistic diversity under discussion here: *Maria Chapdelaine, Jésus de Montréal, Le Déclin de l'empire américain, Les Fous de Bassan, Le Matou,* and *Un Zoo la nuit.* In these films, the otherness of foreign languages and accents appears to have socio-politico-ethical implications and lends a character to these films which beguiles, lures, and threatens. In ironic fashion, the use of linguistic otherness has the effect of subverting the icon of offical language policy and reminding all French-speaking Canada of the fragility of its cultural situation.

Gilles Carle's 1983 *Maria Chapdelaine* underscores the importance of the French language as the transmitter of a unifying culture. Yet the film, like Louis Hémon's novel, also poses the attraction of the foreign language, English, as a threat to that very culture. In novel and film, English is the language of emigration to the United States where Quebecois have gone to work and prosper, like Lorenzo Surpenant, in the textile mills of New England. When, in the final sentences of the novel, Eutrope Gagnon asks Maria whether she still intends to leave, she responds, "no," symbolizing both a rejection of the Other and an affirmation of the status quo, an acceptance of the individual's role as a link in a natural chain binding Maria to a tradition, a culture, a language. The reader is prepared for Maria's rejection of otherness, described so alluringly by Lorenzo, by the well-known passage in which Maria is visited by three ethereal voices of Quebec. The second of these voices, representing the French language as bearer of culture, reminds her that, in the United States, she will live among people speaking a different language, singing different songs. It is instructive to remember that this voice is described by Hémon partly as a priest's sermon. In Carle's film, the priest's voice is supplied by the French actor, Claude Riche. Ironically, Maria's voice of authority speaks in continental French, undercutting the potential *québécitude* of the political-cultural message.

The seduction of the linguistic, in this case cinematic language, is a major theme addressed by Pierre Perrault, cinematic icon and director of the landmark, *Pour la suite du monde*. The cinematic Other, he observes, however enticing, alienates, robbing the soul of its authenticity. The lure of the United States for Maria parallels the lure of American cinematic language: in a word, it is colonizing.[9]

In different forms, two Denys Arcand films address the issue of the language of Others. A film conceived in the 1980s though released in 1990, *Jésus de Montréal* tells the story of a marginal group, actors in the mainstream neither of the theater nor of society. Moreover, their language is punctuated by the use of English. For instance, graffiti scribbled on the door of Constance's loft announce: "101, OK, you bet." With tongue in cheek, Arcand refers to the use of English in exterior signage prohibited by Bill 101, icon of official language policy.

The group of actors, though part of the French linguistic majority, marginalizes itself by its diction. Theirs is not the French of the working class neighborhoods of east Montreal, and their dreams are not those of playing roles in Michel Tremblay's or any other Quebec playwright's plays. They aspire to Shakespearean roles, speaking English. René, who does voice-overs for documentaries, asks to have Hamlet's soliloquy incorporated into the text of the new Passion play. The priest, Constance's lover and former actor, recites speeches in English from *Richard III*. Certainly the most important use of English in *Jésus de Montréal* takes place in Montreal's Jewish Hospital. This locus of English is compared with the locus of French, St. Mark's Hospital, overcrowded and understaffed by overworked and indifferent employees. By contrast, the doctors and staff of Jewish Hospital work in clean, uncrowded surroundings and can respond immediately—albeit too late—to the medical emergency which takes Daniel Coulombe's life. Otherness is Jewish efficiency, and English is its language.

In *Le Déclin de l'empire américain* (1986), Arcand uses a paradigm similar to the marginal society of actors seen in *Jésus*. Here the marginal group is composed of academic intellectuals, all associated with the Université de Montréal. Like the actors in *Jésus*, their speech is corrupted by the use of English and, like the characters in *Maria Chapdelaine*, are beguiled by the United States, emblem of the English-speaking world and of the Other. In *Le Déclin de l'empire américain*, the influence of the Other, the American, the English-speaking, is ubiquitous from the professors' American Ph.D.s to their English-riddled language.

Nonetheless, in the same film, various levels of French spoken in Quebec play a part too. While this American-trained intellectual elite makes puns in English, they encounter another linguistic register, the *joual* of the uncultured Mario. His animal sexual effect on women seems to coincide with his use of substandard French and absence of English, the opposite of the very cultural code which binds the university crowd. Mario does not eat coulibiac, drive BMWs, drink imported beer, or speak English. Mario's *parlure* embarrasses the professors, reminding them that they behave like Others in their own linguistic culture, if *joual* is the language standard from which they are distanced.

Yves Simoneau's 1986 adaptation of *Les Fous de Bassan* reiterates the lure of the Other, the pleasure of the foreign as represented by the English language and the United States, whether its pleasure is seduction by the Florida Keys or travel in a Buick. But the linguistic vehicle for otherness in *Les Fous* is the French language, not English. As with *Maria Chapdelaine*, the exigencies of coproduction pose a certain number of linguistic difficulties because by law, a percentage of roles must be assigned to French and Quebecois actors. It does not pass without notice that the Atkins cousins, icons of desire, are both French actresses, speaking continental French. The lure of the Other, embodied in the reserved Olivia and the sexually aggressive Nora, both objects of Stevans Brown's lust, are manifested by the difference of accent and diction between him and them.

Furthermore, as with the voice of the preacher in *Maria Chapdelaine*, the threat to community solidarity is, once again, the

French of Others. *Les Fous's* preacher (emblem of vice), like the Atkins cousins (emblems of desire), speaks a continental French. Evil is made alluring and authoritative through the idealized diction of the familiar language.

As in *Les Fous de Bassan,* nonfamiliar, continental French is spoken by the figure of evil intent in Jean Beaudin's *Le Matou* (1985). Ratablavasky, the moral and fiscal seducer, speaks the French of France, representing the Other more than linguistically. He is an immigrant. Like other immigrants, he undermines the livelihood of the young Quebecois who open the "binerie." As the ways of foreigners are mysterious, so are Ratablavasky's. Yet he beguiles, and much of the success of his guile derives from his seductive use of language.

In the same film, the role of Ratablavasky's henchman, the Anglophone Slipskin, is to assist his master in ruining the hardworking Francophone couple who represent the heroes of the film. The connivance between foreign elements and native Others, as represented by Slipskin, is indexed inevitably through language. The Anglophone Slipskin (whose name encodes his duplicitous nature) is capable of linguistic deception for, when he speaks French, he seems to be one of the Francophones. Moving between one language and the other, he is the agent of seduction in constant metamorphosis.

Certainly, the problem of language in the 1980s is articulated best on film in Jean-Claude Lauzon's *Un Zoo la nuit.* Two Francophones, father (Albert) and son (Marcel), first find their home surrounded and, subsequently, find themselves evicted by the expanding presence of Others, in this case Italian immigrants. Like the allure of the foreign in other films we have discussed, the Italians, although they have befriended the native Quebeqois, are now in the process of expanding their restaurant, and to complete that process, they must dispossess Albert. This dispossession is as linguistic as it is spatial for, as the redesign of their restaurant proceeds, Albert's space is invaded by Italian-speaking workmen.

The Francophone hero Marcel's nemesis is the cruel, Anglophone cop George whose otherness is also indexed by his homosexuality. In his attempt to impose both his language and sexual preference on Marcel, he becomes, like *Le Matou's* Slipskin, the diabolical agent of subversion. When his attempts at seduction are rejected, first conducted in English and, when unsuccessful, in French, George engages in sadistic revenge.

The otherness of the United States, what film critic Seth Feldman names the "Silent Subject in English Canadian Film," is, as we have seen, a common theme in Quebecois film.[10] In *Un Zoo la nuit*, the lure of the foreign, the Other, the Anglophone, is also represented, not only by the United States as place, but by the person of an American who, in prison with Marcel, conspires with him to murder the Canadian Anglophone, George. The conspirators' conversations are conducted in English, as is George's attempted seduction of Marcel and, eventually, the American's seduction of George. When Marcel and his American friend part, the latter reminds him, in English, that he always has a friend in the States.

Throughout the decade of the 1980s, Quebec cinema (whose production is subventioned, at least in part, by public funds) as a form of public language, appears to overlook the language law by using other languages, particularly English, as working languages. As agent of the Other, the foreign language becomes an icon of subversion of the unilingual and unicultural mission of stated government policy. In regard to cinema, we might conclude, with Marc Levine, that "at the very least, despite Bill 101 and its clear assertion of French as the public language of Quebec, the signs of controversy illustrated graphically that there remained passionate disagreement of the place of English and French in the province through the late 1980s."[11] The use of the language of Others in Quebecois films thus reflects the everyday multicultural quilt, today's Quebec reality, in which context the move to filmmaking in English appears evolutionary, perhaps regrettable, but not revolutionary.

Notes

1. Heinz Weinmann, *Cinéma de l'imaginaire québécois* (Montreal: Hexagone, 1990), 19–20.

2. Ibid., 261.

3. Gilles Deleuze and Felix Guattari, *Anti-Oedipus*, trans. Richard Huxley, Mark Seem and Helen R. Lane (Minneapols: University of Minnesota Press, 1983), 277.

4. Weinmann, 251.

5. Qtd. in Brendan Kelly, "Québéçois Auteurs en Anglais," *Variety*, 17 May 1993.

6. Réal La Rochelle, "Le cinéma québécois en voie d'assimilation ou de metissage?" in *Les Pratiques culturelles* des *Québécois*, ed. Jean-Paul Baillarqeou et al. (Montreal: IQRC, 1986), 217.

7. Ibid., 218–19.

8. Yves Lever, *Histoire générale du cinéma au Québec* (Montreal: Boréal, 1988), 328.

9. Pierre Perrault, "Réflection Impertinentes sur la création cinématographique," in *Essays in Quebec Cinema*, ed. Joseph I. Donohoe (East Lansing: Michigan State University Press, 1991), 69.

10. Seth Feldman, "The Silent Subject in English Canadian Film" in *Take Two*, ed. Seth Feldman (Toronto: Irwin, 1984), 48–57.

11. Marc L. Levine, "Language Policy and Quebec's *Visage* français," *Quebec Studies* 8 (spring 1989): 15.

MATTERS OF DEFENSE

UNCOMFORTABLY IN THE MIDDLE
THE DEPARTMENT OF EXTERNAL AFFAIRS AND CANADA'S INVOLVEMENT IN THE INTERNATIONAL CONTROL COMMISSIONS IN VIETNAM, 1954-73

John Hilliker
Dept. of Foreign Affairs and International Trade
Government of Canada

Donald Barry
University of Calgary

In 1954 Canada, together with India and Poland, accepted membership on the International Commission for Supervision and Control (ICSC) in Vietnam, which was established by the Geneva Conference to oversee the agreement ending an eight-year war in Indochina involving French, Communist, and nationalist forces. The government's decision to participate was consistent with Canada's long-term objective of preventing peripheral conflicts from becoming a source of superpower confrontation. Ottawa's goal was to promote a settlement that would be acceptable to all of the parties in order to enhance the prospects for stability in the region.

At the time there was no expectation that membership on the commission would evolve into a frustrating nineteen-year commitment, although no termination date had been set by the Geneva Conference. As Canadian decision makers considered their options over the years, the reasons for staying seemed more persuasive than the arguments for withdrawing. A new opportunity for Canada to reconsider its position arose between 1968 and 1973, when a final cease-fire agreement was being reached. By this time the government was increasingly determined to avoid becoming involved in another open-ended commitment. At this same time, however, the commitment itself had become a major cause of public controversy, as a result of suspicions that Canada had abetted the deepening and increasingly unpopular U.S. involvement in the Vietnam conflict. This controversy was expressed in some of the literature produced in the decade or so following Canada's withdrawal. Some writers saw the government's actions as fulfilling the "helpful fixer" role that was the lot of the middle power; others attributed its behavior to considerations arising from Canada's relationship with the United States. A review of some of the documents after more time has elapsed suggests that both factors came into play, with the emphasis shifting to the latter near the end of the period, but with concern to achieve a viable settlement never completely abandoned.[1]

Getting In[2]

Canada was caught unawares by the request from the Geneva Conference to serve on the commission. The conference, which took place from 26 April to 19 July 1954, was called to complete the settlement of the Korean conflict and to end the war in Indochina. As a contributor to the UN command, Canada was invited to participate in the discussions on Korea, but it was not asked to attend the sessions on Indochina and did not seek an invitation "lest it lead to further commitments in South East Asia."[3] Accordingly, when the Korean talks ended in mid-June, External Affairs minister Lester Pearson and the other members of the Canadian delegation left Geneva, leaving John Holmes, the department's assistant undersecretary for Far Eastern affairs, to observe the discussions on Indochina. Holmes, however, departed before they ended, concluding that there were no direct implications for Canada. The department, which shared Holmes's view, was therefore surprised when it learned that the Chinese foreign minister, Chou En-lai, had proposed Canada as a member of the commission set up to supervise the application of the cease-fire agreement in Vietnam. India and Poland, with the former as chairman, would also be included.[4] The formal invitation from the conference cochairs, the Soviet Union and the United Kingdom, was issued on 21 July.

The St. Laurent government had reservations about accepting, but it decided to do so in order to sustain the fragile agreement. Its doubts were reflected in a public statement, released on 28 July after the cabinet had agreed to the request, which said that the decision had been taken

only after detailed study of the cease-fire and armistice agreements . . . and with full knowledge and appreciation of the responsibilities and difficulties that will go with membership. There are no illusions about the magnitude and complexity of the task.[5]

As long as the commission focused on such matters as verification of the cease-fire, troop withdrawals, and exchanges of civilian internees, the Canadian, Indian, and Polish delegations worked together reasonably well. When politically sensitive issues began to arise, however, differences emerged. These matters were complicated to deal with because, as James Eayrs has pointed out, the Canadian commissioner occupied a position somewhere between political representative acting on instructions from headquarters and an impartial arbiter. Ottawa's view, according to John Holmes, was that "there was no pretense of being neutral in the broader East-West conflict," but that "the Canadians . . . should . . . act fairly and impartially in deciding on evidence." Holmes believed that the Indians and the Poles were also guided by instructions from home; and for all concerned, the diplomatic aspect of the assignment grew in importance as the issues involved became more political. Ottawa's attitude probably came as no surprise to the Chinese architects of the arrangement.[6] Although Chou En-lai "appreciated our independent attitude," External Affairs had learned during the conference that "he knew on what side Canada stood."[7]

The most serious problems arose in Vietnam, which was divided between the communist Viet Minh in the North and the non-communist regime in the South. During the first "three hundred days," when the main elements of the settlement were to be completed, the issues were largely technical. But complaints related to the transfer of refugees and allegations of Communist subversion in the South soon created political tensions. In approaching these matters the Poles consistently supported the North Vietnamese and the Indians assumed the role of arbiters. Relations among the delegations became strained and negotiations difficult.

The refugee question arose early in the 300 days, which had to be extended by two months to enable the commission to deal with the complaints coming before it. Most of the complaints arose in the North, where the regime put major obstacles in the way of refugees wishing to move to the South. According to Holmes, the Canadians were "shocked" by the actions of the North Vietnamese, exasperated by Polish support for the local authorities, and disappointed by the Indians, whose search for compromise often resulted in the adoption of positions unfavorable to the refugees.[8] In the circumstances, Douglas Ross has pointed out, the Canadians became "mildly partisan," attempting to maintain a balance by "shaping the record" to expose injustice in the North and downplaying criticism of the South.[9]

Getting Caught

Although the Canadians could express their concern about the treatment of refugees by dissenting from the commission's conclusions, the experience was frustrating especially because there was no mechanism for an international response. As a result, by the time the commission completed its initial work in the summer of 1955, when opposing regimes were established in Hanoi and Saigon, withdrawal began to seem attractive to some officials in Ottawa, including the minister. John Holmes did not share this view. "The argument for remaining," he wrote later, "was an argument for maintaining a symbol of the Geneva agreements on the basis of which the parties and their sponsors might some day construct a real peace, after they had recognized the dangers and disadvantages of other courses. It was not so much an argument for staying as an argument against resigning." As he noted at the time, this amounted to "a policy of stalling" rather than "bringing things quickly to a head." The result might be involvement in Indochina "for a very long time" and a commitment to "frustrating labours." But it might also "be the best chance of keeping the peace and holding the line in Asia."[10]

Holmes's advice prevailed, leading to the lengthy commitment that he had foreseen and a full measure of frustration. Contributing to the latter was the issue of subversion in the South by Communist agents from the North. In August 1955 the commission's Indian chairman asked its Legal Committee for a report on whether such acts were covered by the cease-fire agreement and were within the commission's mandate, and if so, how such complaints should be addressed. The committee's majority report, supported by Canada and India, concluded that the commission was both competent and obliged to consider such complaints, and that in doing so it should follow the same procedure that it employed with other issues coming before it.

No action was taken during most of 1956, in part because the commission was occupied with other matters. In October of that year, the Canadian delegation urged that the report be dealt with, in order to preserve the commission's credibility in the South. The Indians, however, insisted on reopening discussions with the Canadians. In early 1957, the Indians produced a much more restrictive definition of subversion than had been agreed to earlier. The result was deadlock which lasted for most of the year.[11]

The subversion question remained in the forefront of Canadian concerns after John Diefenbaker's government replaced that of Louis St. Laurent in the June 1957 general election. A breakthrough was finally achieved in June 1961, when the Indo-Canadian majority adopted a policy statement supporting the commission's right to investigate charges of subversion and stating the intention to refer cases to the Legal Committee. Although the Indians were initially reluctant to act on the allegations, a deteriorating security situation eventually convinced them to do so, making references by majority decision possible by November of that year.

Meanwhile, the United States, which supported the regime in Saigon, was increasing its aid to South Vietnamese forces. Washington justified its action on the grounds that the forces needed effective training in order to deal with the North's subversive activities. This argument was accepted by Ottawa where the main concern was that the Indians not join the Poles in condemning South Vietnam for violations of the cease-fire agreement and possibly demanding the commission's withdrawal. Consequently, it became the delegation's "main task" to see that the buildup of the U.S. military missions "was handled in a manner least likely to jeopardize the future of the Commission and of the Geneva Settlement."[12] The effort succeeded, and the commission approved the increase in April 1960.

The two issues came together in a special report, agreed upon by the Canadians and the Indians and submitted to the Geneva Conference cochairmen in June 1962. In the report the commission accepted the Legal Committee's interim findings on cases referred to it, and acknowledged for the first time that there had been subversion against South Vietnam sponsored by the North. The Legal Committee was to produce a detailed documentary account. The report also acknowledged that the "military arrangements" between the United States and South Vietnam amounted to "a factual—though not a formal—military alliance," but it recorded the South's assurance that these arrangements would stop when the North ended "all acts of aggression and [began] to respect the Geneva agreements."[13] Although the document was a clear acknowledgment that the peaceful conditions envisaged at Geneva had not materialized, it was an important success from Canada's standpoint in that it suggested that Indian policy was becoming more supportive and secured "an effective Commission reference to the long-standing problem of subversion."[14]

Canada's main priority following publication of the special report was adoption of the Legal Committee's detailed investigation, which was to provide a basis for action on the South's complaints against Hanoi. Agreement with the Indians proved elusive, however, and by the time Lester Pearson's government came to power in the spring of 1963, the commission's activities had almost ground to a halt. Likewise, no action was taken on new allegations of subversion brought against Hanoi by the Canadian delegation.

Paul Martin, the new secretary of state for External Affairs, expressed support for the 1962 report.[15] A review of the commission's priorities conducted by the delegation in Saigon in September recommended a renewed effort "to get the Commission's work moving again," the first step being the early completion of the Legal Report.[16] The department agreed but advised against sudden action. It also informed the delegation of the results of a headquarters review of Canada's role on the commission, which concluded that "no fundamental changes are possible at this time and that we must therefore ensure that the Canadian Government is in a position to carry out its functions . . . on the basis of the best and most complete advice possible." Having been caught off guard by recent U.S. pressures on the Diem government of South Vietnam to introduce political reforms after it attacked political opponents, the department also asked the delegation to expand its information gathering to include American "intentions and capabilities."[17]

The Legal Report was finally completed in December and was given to the Canadian, Indian, and Polish governments in February 1964. Although Ottawa was not reassured by its soundings regarding India's plans to proceed with the report, the department, with the support of the high commissioner in Delhi, decided to adopt a "soft line" approach.[18] The department's frustration, however, was clear in a message to the high commissioner, which described the lack of progress as a "dereliction of our responsibilities in light of what is known of increasing support being received from

North Vietnam by Viet Cong [South Vietnamese insurgents]." The commission's inactivity reflected "not only on present Commission and its members but on very principle of international peace-keeping." The high commissioner raised Ottawa's concerns with Indian authorities but received only an undertaking to study the matter.[19]

Canada's membership on the commission led to an expansion of its role in the spring of 1964, when the government agreed to a request from the U.S. administration to open a confidential communications channel between Washington and Hanoi, through the commissioner in Saigon. The assignment arose of talks between the secretary of state, Dean Rusk, and Pearson and Martin in Ottawa on 30 April and between Pres. Lyndon Johnson and the prime minister in New York on 28 May. The Americans were concerned that North Vietnam was planning to take advantage of the instability following the assassination of Diem the previous November by stepping up their aid to North Vietnamese insurgents, and they wanted a means of conveying their determination to support the new government in Saigon. They saw the Canadian commissioner, who had easy and inconspicuous access to Hanoi and was respected by both sides, as a reliable conduit.[20]

The assignment was given to the incoming commissioner, Blair Seaborn, who began his appointment earlier than planned for this purpose. It was agreed in follow-up discussions that the mission (code-named "Bacon") would be under Canadian government control in order to protect Seaborn's independence. All communications would be routed through Ottawa which reserved the right to review and amend them, although it would not take responsibility for their content. The prime minister signed a letter for Seaborn to present to North Vietnam's leaders, authorizing him to relay messages between the two sides.[21]

Seaborn made his first visit to Hanoi in mid-June. Although there were no breakthroughs, North Vietnamese and U.S. authorities affirmed that they wanted the channel maintained. The assignment became more delicate when the United States bombed North Vietnamese patrol boats and storage depots on 4 August in retaliation for allegedly unprovoked attacks on American vessels in the Gulf of Tonkin. Four days later, the embassy in Washington forwarded a message from the State Department for Seaborn to present to North Vietnamese authorities on his next visit to Hanoi. The note bluntly stated the U.S. version of events and warned of further retaliation if the attacks were repeated. Exercising the government's right to control the content, the minister directed Seaborn to delete parts that were not clear or appeared to compromise Canada's role as an intermediary. "Our commitment to pass messages faithfully does not mean we can be expected to play the role of unthinking mouthpieces," the department told the embassy in Washington.[22] Even the modified message drew an angry response from Prem. Pham Van Dong. Nonetheless, he told Seaborn that he found the channel useful and wanted it kept open.

In Saigon, meanwhile, the delegation's frustration over its inability to expedite the commission's work led it to question whether Canada should remain a member. External Affairs decided that Canada should continue in the belief that withdrawal in the absence of well-documented evidence of the commission's ineffectiveness would be queried by the public and that it would jeopardize participation in any future conference on Vietnam. The commission, however, was sharply divided over the position to take on the Gulf of Tonkin issue and the U.S. response. The United States stepped up its reprisals on 7 February 1965 when it launched a campaign of air strikes against the North, called "Operation Rolling Thunder." When the Polish and Indian delegations issued a special message condemning the U.S. action, the Canadian delegation, on instructions from the minister, tabled a minority report drawing attention to North Vietnam's violations of the Geneva agreement.[23]

Despite the view expressed in the minority report, concern grew within the government that the deepening U.S. military involvement could expand the war. Pearson hinted at his misgivings in speeches in Ottawa on 10 February and in New York on 10 March. Encouraged by unnamed "persons highly placed in the United States government who were loyal to Johnson but disagreed with his Vietnam strategy and hoped to moderate it," he began to consider how he might intervene in the debate.[24] The prime minister was scheduled to give an address on international peacekeeping at Temple University in Philadelphia on 2 April. He asked External Affairs to include in the speech a suggestion that Washington consider a temporary suspension of the air attacks to test Hanoi's willingness to begin peace talks. Martin, who shared Pearson's concerns but was well aware of U.S. sensitivity to public criticism regarding Vietnam, informed the prime minister that the requested text had been added. He cautioned, however, that "a proposal of this kind would be more effective if it were put forward, in the first instance, privately to President Johnson."[25] Pearson agreed.

On 30 March Pearson discussed Vietnam with Marquis Childs, chief Washington correspondent for the *St. Louis Post-Despatch,* whom he had known since his diplomatic posting in Washington in 1942-46. At the prime minister's request, Childs also met with Martin, suggesting to him that "Canada could play a vital role by making practical suggestions" for the moderation of U.S. policy and that the prime minister's forthcoming speech would offer an opportunity to do so. The minister was dubious, pointing out that Canada "had brought a lot of pressure to bear on the United States and other countries for the purpose of getting negotiations started," but that "under present circumstances our public position should not be expected to run strongly and obviously counter to the United States position."[26]

Childs saw it differently. He telephoned the minister's departmental assistant from Washington on 1 April, asking him to pass on to the prime minister his view "that the general lines of Mr. Pearson's speech would 'not be resented in Washington.'"[27] The "general lines" of the speech put the prime minister at odds with the minister. The latter recalled that he threatened to resign when Pearson, after arriving in Philadelphia, told him that he intended to add the bombing pause proposal. Charles Ritchie, the ambassador in Washington, advised Pearson to give the White House an advance copy, but he refused. The planned address was consistent with a warning that he had given in a 1951 speech that there might be occasions when Canada would publicly disagree with U.S. foreign policy.[28] Moreover, by withholding the text, Pearson avoided any "arm-twisting" by Johnson. Ritchie believed that Pearson knew that a "blow-up" was likely to follow.[29]

In his speech that evening Pearson praised U.S. aims in Vietnam and expressed the hope that Canada could continue to support them, and then put forward the bombing pause suggestion. Johnson's hostility toward the proposal was evident when he met Pearson for lunch the next day at his Camp David retreat. The prime minister seemed surprised by the force of the president's reaction for, according to John English, his face was "ashen" when the two men held a press conference shortly before Pearson returned to Ottawa. As English saw it, the speech reduced whatever chances Canada may have had of influencing Washington's policy on Vietnam and the flow of information from U.S. sources, which Ottawa already considered unsatisfactory, declined even more.[30]

Meanwhile, the "Bacon" channel remained open, if only barely. Seaborn had returned to Hanoi in February, but was received at a low level. In late May the United States, after briefly suspending the bombing attacks, asked that he take a message to Hanoi indicating willingness to work toward a solution based on reciprocal de-escalation and seeking clarification of peace conditions recently announced by North Vietnam. To Pearson's surprise, Seaborn was met by senior authorities, including the foreign minister, Nguyen Duy Trinh, but their response led him to suggest that Ottawa not encourage the United States to use the channel again. "It is not . . . producing significant results and seems only to be exacerbating DVRN [Democratic Republic of Vietnam] antagonism and annoyance with Canada," he said. Martin concurred.[31]

Disappointment with Operation Bacon was underlined when External Affairs learned from the embassy in Paris that the head of North Vietnam's delegation in France had discussed his government's views on a settlement with French officials prior to Seaborn's visit to Hanoi. Pearson was annoyed that neither the French nor the Americans, who had known of the exchange, had informed the government. By this time public speculation about Seaborn's role had also begun to cause concern. On 7 June Martin told Parliament that Seaborn had met with Trinh, although he did not reveal that the commissioner had brought a message from the Americans. Ten days later Johnson paraphrased parts of Seaborn's report during a press conference, saying that the document had come from a foreign diplomat who was acting as his representative. The revelation increased media speculation about Seaborn's activities, but Ottawa did not publicly acknowledge his role.

The department's undersecretary, Marcel Cadieux, summarized the situation for the minister in September, before Seaborn's last visit to Hanoi. The mission had "proved disappointing in terms of results achieved," Cadieux said, and "public interest and speculation about" his activity had "tended to reduce the possible usefulness of this channel." Martin accepted the undersecretary's suggestion that Ottawa inform U.S. authorities about Seaborn's visit while expressing doubt about the advisability of giving him special instructions. No such instructions were offered and this effort to promote communication between Washington and Hanoi effectively ended.[32]

In the meantime, the commission's operations continued to concern the Department of External Affairs. Since the fall of 1964 the commission had acted on only three South Vietnamese complaints against Hanoi, largely in response to the Canadian delegation's effort, as opposed to twelve citations against Saigon. Despite frequent appeals from Ottawa, including two personal messages from Martin to India's foreign minister, Delhi had given no indication that it was prepared to take a more balanced approach. As a result, the department launched another review of Canada's participation in the commission in the summer of 1965. Once again it judged that withdrawal was not advisable. By remaining, Canada would bring its long experience to bear in the interest of achieving a workable settlement. It would also have a persuasive reason to resist possible U.S. pressure to support the military effort against the North, which would have been opposed by Canadian public opinion. Membership, however, was becoming increasingly awkward since the government, while declaring support for American objectives, was participating in a body that accepted evidence of South Vietnamese and U.S. violations of the Geneva agreement, but refused to apply the same scrutiny to the North.[33]

Accompanying the concern about the intensification of U.S. military involvement was a growing belief that Ottawa needed a "forward diplomatic posture." Drawing upon the experience of the Seaborn missions, discussion centered on the possibility of a new initiative to explore the possibilities for negotiations. Impetus was provided when, on Christmas Eve, Washington began a thirty-seven-day bombing pause followed by a major peace initiative. The department favored action through the commission, but Martin, convinced that China was the key to peace in Vietnam, wanted a mission that would include Peking as well as Hanoi. In his view, the most appropriate person was Chester Ronning, who had recently retired from the department. Ronning had been born in China, spoke Mandarin, and was personally acquainted with some of China's leaders. He also had a longstanding invitation to visit Peking. With Pearson's reluctant agreement, the plan was put into action under the code-name "Smallbridge," chosen at random from the Ottawa telephone book.[34]

Ronning would have to overcome major challenges. U.S. officials were concerned that Hanoi would interpret the dispatch of another intermediary as a sign of weakness, and they also had misgivings about Ronning, who was a known admirer of North Vietnam's president, Ho Chi Minh, and a harsh critic of South Vietnamese leaders. The Chinese refused to see him, on the grounds that Ottawa supported U.S. policy in Vietnam, so his meetings in March 1966 were limited to Saigon and Hanoi. Ronning was encouraged by his discussions with Pham Van Dong, who indicated that his government could begin talks with Washington if the

United States unconditionally ended all military action against the North. The State Department was briefed by Ronning on his return, and decided to draft a response; Martin directed that plans be made for another visit.

The U.S. message to Hanoi, however, merely asked North Vietnam to clarify its position, and Canadian efforts to make it more substantive proved fruitless. V.C. Moore, the new Canadian commissioner in Saigon, was in favor of maintaining the channel, but he warned that Canadians would lose credibility in Hanoi if they came "only as a mouthpiece to American propaganda."[35] On reading Moore's telegram, Pearson observed, "We should take this message seriously. It would be a sad ending to our initiative in this matter if we became merely an instrument of U.S. propaganda or for putting the DVRN on the spot."[36] Departmental officials shared Moore's doubts, but the minister decided that Ronning should proceed with the visit in order to maintain the link with Hanoi. Suspicious that Washington was about to step up its air war against the North, he instructed Ronning to report to Ottawa first and to give U.S. officials in the field only the general tenor of his talks.

Ronning reached Saigon on 13 June, following a short stay in Hong Kong, where he again failed to obtain an invitation to visit Peking. Although his meetings in Hanoi from 14–18 June were unproductive, North Vietnamese officials indicated that they did not want the channel closed. Ronning and Martin briefed William Bundy, the State Department's assistant secretary of state for Far Eastern affairs, in Ottawa shortly thereafter, but there were no signs of flexibility in the U.S. position. As Martin put it, "It was evident that we were looking at matters through opposite ends of the telescope."[37] On 29 June the United States began bombing oil installations in North Vietnam.

Martin later accepted the view of External Affairs that the commission should be employed as an instrument for exploring the possibilities for a negotiated settlement. The minister visited Warsaw and Moscow in November 1966. He was not successful, however, in persuading Polish and Soviet authorities to support a commission initiative. They argued that there could be no progress until the United States unconditionally ended the bombing. Later that month Dean Rusk suggested to the minister that Canadian, Indian, and Polish officials meet in Geneva to consider a potential role for the commission in arranging a peace conference. Given Poland's position, Martin and his advisors were skeptical. More promising, the department told the minister, was a proposal by

Roger Fisher of Harvard University that had attracted India's interest. The plan called for a commission-sponsored conference of all interested parties to provide advice on possible action to promote a settlement. The Indian government had invited Canadian and Polish representatives to Delhi for discussions. The department's ideas on the proposal were reviewed with the State Department which gave an encouraging response. The minister agreed to send officials to Delhi for a preliminary exchange of views, but Poland's negative response scuttled the initiative.[38]

External Affairs officials continued to explore the prospects for commission action in 1967 amid signs of growing public uneasiness regarding Ottawa's policy toward the war. Reports that exports of military equipment to the United States under the Canada-U.S. Defense Production Sharing Agreement had increased as a result of American military requirements in Vietnam and published allegations that a Canadian commission staff member in Hanoi had been supplying intelligence information to the Americans added impetus to the criticism. In mid-February, Martin responded in Parliament, drawing attention to Ronning's missions and to attempts to promote a settlement through the commission. And in April, he introduced a four-point plan for ending the war which called for a measure of reciprocal disengagement, an agreed ceiling on military activity, an end to hostilities, and a return to the cease-fire provisions of the Geneva agreement.[39] He also asked O.W. Dier, Moore's successor as commissioner, to give North Vietnamese leaders the text of the plan. Pham Van Dong rejected it, emphasizing that there could be no peace talks until the United States unconditionally halted the bombing.

By this time there were indications that the Pearson government might repeat its call for an end to the air strikes. On 10 May the prime minister spoke in Parliament of his "increasing anxiety" over Vietnam and referred to the need "to bring our worries and anxieties to the notice of those who are more immediately and directly involved in the hope that our advice and counsel will be of some help."[40] Three days later Walter Gordon, the president of the privy council, went further in a speech in Toronto, urging Pearson and Martin "to continue to do everything in their power to press the Americans to stop the bombing."[41]

Although Gordon claimed that the prime minister privately agreed with "ninety-eight per cent" of what he had said, Pearson and Martin took issue with him for breaching cabinet solidarity and for trespassing on the External Affairs minister's territory. With the opposition pressing the government, Pearson called a special cabinet meeting on 17 May, after which he reported that he had stated "in very considerable detail what the policy of the government was. . . . We all agreed that was the right policy to follow and we all agreed that as members of the cabinet we would follow that policy and say or do nothing that would make its implementation more difficult."[42]

Despite the difficulty it caused the government, Gordon claimed that his speech had considerable public support—as might have been expected from opinion polls which had shown disagreement with U.S. policy since early 1966. The department was against responding to this pressure by publicly urging Washington to change its approach. In a memorandum to the undersecretary, the Far Eastern division opposed a suggestion, made by the embassy in Paris, that a group of leaders from countries friendly to the United States urge President Johnson to stop the air attacks. "Any appeal or concerted action, especially if publicly mounted by political leaders of countries allied to the U.S.," the memorandum said, "would be seen as 'ganging up' and would be deeply resented by the President."[43] This assessment was borne out when Pearson and Martin met Johnson at the prime minister's summer residence at Harrington Lake, after the president's visit to Expo '67 in Montreal, and pressed him to end the bombing. Johnson refused to do so without a corresponding concession from Hanoi. Further efforts by Martin to make the case for a bombing halt during the spring meeting of NATO foreign ministers in June also came to naught.

Later that month, three former senior members of External Affairs—Escott Reid, Douglas LePan, and A.F.W. Plumptre—released a statement urging the United States to stop the air strikes without conditions as a first step toward negotiations and calling on countries with troops in South Vietnam not to increase their forces after Washington and Hanoi had begun peace talks. It also asked the Canadian government to call on other governments to support the plan.[43] Pearson told Parliament that, "these proposals do not in any way conflict with government thinking."[44] Marcel Cadieux did not share this view, warning in a memorandum that no "useful purpose would be served by putting public pressure on the Americans to stop the bombing without reciprocity."[45] Martin instructed the Canadian commissioner to visit Hanoi to determine whether there had been any change in North Vietnam's views, but his soundings were negative. By then the minister had concluded that "the time had come to speak out publicly against the bombing."[46] In a speech to the U.N. General Assembly on 27 September, he called for an end to the attacks as a first step to getting peace talks under way.

Encouraged by a speech made by President Johnson in San Antonio, Texas, two days later, which suggested that the United States was prepared to soften its conditions for beginning discussions with Hanoi,[47] Martin continued to explore ways of bringing the two sides to the negotiating table. He expressed interest in a Japanese proposal for mutual guarantees for the United States and North Vietnam by a group of third countries, instructing Canadian officials to cooperate in developing the plan. The idea was discarded, however, after reports that Foreign Minister Trinh had said in late December that Hanoi would begin peace talks once the bombing had stopped. In early January Martin instructed Dier to deliver a letter to North Vietnamese authorities seeking confirmation of Hanoi's position, but they refused to amplify Trinh's statement. Canadian officials concluded that the North was not interested in meaningful discussions.

Unbeknownst to them, Trinh's comment was the most recent development in a secret dialogue begun by Washington and Hanoi in the summer of 1967, which had led to Johnson's San Antonio speech.[49] A further step was taken on 31 March when the president announced that the United States would limit air strikes to an area just north of the demilitarized zone between North and South Vietnam, and declared that he would not seek reelection. Johnson's statement did not resolve the issue, but it did lessen the pressure on the Canadian government to try to modify U.S. policy. Pearson, who was also about to retire from politics, responded by observing that it was now "strictly up to the communist side to reciprocate and show their desire to end the war by negotiation rather than force."[50]

Getting Out

As a result of the changes in Washington and Ottawa, the Canadian government once again had the opportunity to consider its options in Vietnam. In External Affairs, the Far Eastern division thought that the best course for the new prime minister, Pierre Trudeau, was to maintain a "wait and see" attitude after he assumed office on 20 April 1968. He was able to do so throughout the national election campaign that began three days later, for foreign policy in general, and Vietnam in particular, were not prominent among the issues raised.[51] Once confirmed in power by the voters on 15 June,

Trudeau was committed to reviewing all aspects of Canadian foreign policy. He could be expected to be open to change on Vietnam, for he had been a critic of U.S. actions before entering politics, and he was skeptical of the "helpful fixer" role implicit in Canada's peacekeeping activities. He was likely, however, to resist any action that might antagonize the U.S. government without a persuasive compensating advantage for Canada.[52]

In Paris, meanwhile, peace talks had begun between the United States and North Vietnam, and on 22 May 1968 the State Department approached the embassy in Washington for Canada's views on improved supervisory machinery. In responding, the embassy acted on Ottawa's instructions and emphasized that there could be no commitment to Canadian involvement unless the objectives and terms of reference of any new arrangement were satisfactory. Even so, it was recognized at the official level and also by the new minister, Mitchell Sharp, and apparently by the prime minister that an invitation if it came would be difficult to refuse. It was, therefore, in Canada's interest to provide the Americans with further information, based on its experience on the ICSC, that might secure improvements in any agreement reached in Paris. Canada provided the information on 13 March 1969, by which time the talks had been broadened to include South Vietnam and the Viet Cong (first as the National Liberation Front and later as the Provisional Revolutionary Government). It was discouraging, however, that frequent warnings against presenting Canada with a fait accompli, as had happened in 1954, seemed to have little impact in Washington.[53]

Without satisfactory conditions for a new supervisory agency, officials acknowledged, Canada risked becoming involved in "a messy, imprecise and essentially unworkable solution" in Vietnam. At the same time, there were numerous considerations that would make refusal difficult, notably the maintenance of good relations with the United States and other interested countries; the consequences for the government's commitment to pursue a more active policy in Asia; and the opportunity to develop closer ties with the only Francophone states in the region. Against this background, the Department of External Affairs concluded and the minister agreed that the cabinet ought to be briefed on the "full range of implications" for Canada in either accepting or refusing continuing involvement in Vietnam.[54]

In response to this initiative, the cabinet decided, on 15 January 1970, that "Canadian participation [in supervision of a cease-fire] should make a real contribution to peace and orderly political and economic development in the area, that no commitment should be of indefinite duration, that the supervisory organization should have adequate resources for its work and immediate access to any part of the territory to be supervised, and that its reports should go to a continuing political authority which would make them public, as might any of the participating supervisory powers."[55] Marcel Cadieux, who had recently been named ambassador in Washington, was instructed to use this document to reinforce Canada's earlier messages when making his introductory calls. He did so, but in the absence of prospects for an early resolution of the conflict there was little opportunity for effective follow-up.[56]

The Canadian position nonetheless remained clear. The booklet on the Pacific in the government's foreign policy review, for example, indicated a willingness to be helpful in a new peacekeeping arrangement in Vietnam, but only if conditions along the lines of those set out by the cabinet seemed likely to be met.[57] Disappointingly, this message did not seem to have been fully absorbed by the Americans when they let it be known, on 25 October 1972, that the Paris talks at last seemed ready to produce a cease-fire, and indicated a day later that the parties were agreed that it should be supervised by an international commission that Canada, along with Poland, Hungary, and Indonesia, would be asked to join. The decision came at an awkward moment for Canadian negotiators, for Trudeau's government was facing a test at the polls on 30 October which would reduce it to a precarious minority in the House of Commons. In the United States, Richard Nixon's administration was to be returned a few days later. Although the results there were much more favorable to the incumbent, the bilateral relationship was in a delicate phase as a result of measures taken in Washington the previous summer to deal with U.S. balance of payments problems. The Canadians, therefore, had to be concerned about linkages between decisions on Vietnam and efforts to settle cross-border economic issues.[58]

The way Canada should respond to the invitation to join the supervisory commission became a subject of lively debate with External Affairs, with the poles represented by Cadieux in Washington and the commissioner in Saigon, David Jackson. Although troubled by lack of consultation by the Americans (which he explained in terms of the diffuseness of U.S. decision making), Cadieux had a number of reasons for urging cooperation: the adverse effect that the "pessimistic judgment" implicit in a Canadian refusal would have on international confidence in the peace process; the possibility of using "a certain modest leverage" in Moscow and Peking to get the commission off to a good start; and the opportunity to generate some goodwill useful in economic negotiations with the United States. He, therefore, recommended concentrating on an effort (which the Americans had indicated willingness to support) to influence the commission's terms of reference, with a view to serving for a limited period of six months to a year. By this time, he thought, Canada's persuasiveness, at least in the Communist capitals, would probably be exhausted.[59] These did not seem like very good ideas in Saigon, where Jackson expected the conflict to continue, for reasons internal to the peninsula, long after U.S. withdrawal. He discounted Canada's potential effect on international opinion and questioned the value of its influence in major capitals, since he did not expect the Vietnamese parties to be amenable to outside pressure. He doubted that the North would agree to acceptable terms of reference for the commission and suggested that, as a result, service might turn out to be open-ended and might do Canada more harm than good in its bilateral relations with the United States. The best course for Canada, therefore, was to take a decision against serving, and to make its intentions clear in Washington.[60]

The undersecretary, A. E. Ritchie, received Jackson's representations with sympathy but also with reserve, citing Canada's reputation for peacekeeping, which implied "that we must show cause for refusing," and concern for the effect of withdrawal on the bilateral relationship with the United States. The ideal, he explained in a telegram to Saigon on 27 November, was "to determine what are minimum conditions with which we would be prepared to live if they were accepted," and, if suitable terms could not be worked out, to have established grounds for refusal that would be credible in Canada, the United States, and elsewhere.[61] In pursuit of the latter objective, Canada insisted on knowing the terms of reference before agreeing to take part in truce supervision. It maintained this position without effect until 24 January 1973, three days before the Paris agreement was signed, when it finally received the documents creating the new supervisory body, the International Commission of Control and Supervision (ICCS).

The government was now faced with making a rapid choice between the options identified by Cadieux and Jackson. Circumstances favored the former, for Canada had had to make contingency plans for joining the ICCS at the same time as it avowed that it was keeping its options open. As well, there were the various

assurances, public and private, of Canada's willingness to be helpful in the right circumstances, and a commitment announced on 2
November to make the ICSC delegation staff available in the initial
stages of the peace process. Whether or not expectations thus created in Washington were justified, Cadieux warned of the danger
to bilateral relations of disappointing them. The position taken by
the government indicated that it had heeded Cadieux's warning
and absorbed some of the suggestions he had made for dealing
with it. Declaring that "a first look" suggested that "the conditions
and considerations which we communicated to the parties have to
some degree contributed to the terms which have been agreed on,"
External Affairs minister Sharp announced that Canada would
make an initial commitment limited to sixty days, during which
time it would decide on its future course after studying the documents and assessing its experience on the new commission.[62]

In charge of the Canadian delegation on the new commission
was the ambassador to Greece, Michel Gauvin. He was considered,
Sharp recalled later, to have the "right qualifications" to carry out
an "open-mouth" policy that the government had decided on in
order to avoid being reduced to ineffectual silence by the rules of
the new body, as had happened under the ICSC. Canada, in other
words, would consider itself free to publicize not only its own
views but the proceedings of the commission as a whole.[63] Gauvin,
who arrived in Saigon on 29 January, was also determined to keep
Canada's options open. It was his intention, he reported in his first
assessment, to do "everything . . . through leadership and initiatives" to make the commission effective, so that "when we . . . have
had enough, we will be free to withdraw with honour and with no
. . . need for excuse."[64]

Gauvin's advice would remain crucial to Canadian decision
making on future involvement in the commission as a result of the
unsatisfactory outcome of an international conference, which was
attended by the parties to the agreement. The UN secretary general,
the permanent members of the Security Council, and the participants on the commission, attended the conference in Paris on 27
February, in order to guarantee the settlement. Sharp, who led the
Canadian delegation, had as his main object the acknowledgment
of an effective "continuing political authority," preferably the secretary general, to receive reports from the commission and decide
on the action to be taken. The other participants were unenthusias-
tic, and the best that Sharp could achieve was that reports would
be circulated to the secretary general and to the other signatories of

the act produced by the conference. Further international action would be possible only if the conference were reconvened at the joint request of the United States and North Vietnam or at least six unspecified signatories to the act. Wishing to support the "spirit of the act," Canada once again had to "suspend judgment until it had had an opportunity to review carefully the new arrangements in light of Canadian experience in the ICCS."[65]

To "evaluate Canadian experience in the ICCS," Sharp visited Indochina, stopping in Tokyo en route, between 13 and 18 March 1973. Another objective of the journey, according to Arthur Andrew, director general of the department's Asia and Pacific bureau at the time, was to test optimistic U.S. accounts of the peace process against a much less encouraging picture merging from Canadian reports from Saigon.[66] The trip confirmed the latter view, but also added to international pressure coming from other quarters (Sharp later mentioned the United Kingdom and China in addition to the United States and the Asian countries that he had visited[67]) to remain on the commission. There was still room for debate before making a final decision.

In Washington Cadieux remained concerned about the effect on bilateral relations of what might seem to be precipitate withdrawal, because of the importance Nixon attached to a settlement and the difficulty that the United States might encounter in finding a suitable replacement for Canada. "I know," he acknowledged, "that it is easier to make such a recommendation from here than from Vietnam or from Ottawa," but in his view Canada should remain for another nine months, that is until the end of the calendar year.[68] Gauvin, on the other hand, contended that the open-mouth policy had "demonstrated publicly time and again that ICCS does not . . . work," that Canada should remain for no longer than another ninety days, and that this should not be regarded as a further trial period after which it might change its mind.[69] In Ottawa, the undersecretary also the shorter time period, but was inclined to retain some flexibility when a commitment was made.[70]

The government's decision, announced on 27 March, was closer to Gauvin's preference than to Cadieux's, but contained an element of compromise that would not have been welcome in Saigon. Canada would remain on the commission for another sixty days, at the end of which there would be a grace period of a further thirty days during which the parties could search for a successor. If, however, there were "a substantial improvement in the situation in Viet-Nam or some signs of an imminent political settlement,"

Canada might revisit this decision.[71] "I hope you will find that it presents a fair assessment of situation and that it does not . . . attempt to justify a new trial period on grounds that ICCS might even yet be viable in role assigned to it under agreements," the undersecretary cabled to Saigon. Other considerations had influenced the decision: the need for flexibility to respond to developments in Vietnam, avoidance of a long "lame duck" period on the commission, concern for relations with the United States, and anticipated difficulty in selling an immediate decision to withdraw to the Canadian public, "which identifies this country with peacekeeping in all its aspects."[72]

The government had to decide on its further plans by the end of May. There were only "two readily identifiable parties" to whom Canada was concerned to justify a decision to leave, Gauvin was told by telegram on 8 May — the domestic public, "especially as represented in H[ouse] of C[ommons]," and the United States. Attention focused on the latter, partly because Canadians' response to the announcement of 27 March had been favorable, and also perhaps because of pressure being exerted at this time by cabinet ministers concerned about linkage with bilateral economic issues in which they had an interest.[73]

A complicating factor in dealing with the United States, Gauvin suggested, might be the success of the open-mouth policy, which had operated to the benefit of that country and South Vietnam. Cadieux, on the other hand, was becoming more optimistic about the prospects of getting out, especially since Nixon was being weakened by the Watergate scandal. The United States, External Affairs acknowledged, would be "inconvenienced" if Canada left the commission, but its reaction should be "manageable."[74] Of the three choices open to Canada at the end of May — full membership on the commission, another extension, or withdrawal, the department favored the last as the only one consistent with positions the government had taken so far and consistent with realities in Vietnam. This was the course chosen, although the government did agree to a request from Nixon's assistant for national security affairs, Henry Kissinger, to remain an extra month, to give more time to find a successor and to avoid complicating discussions he was having in Paris with the North Vietnamese.[75]

In formulating a justification for the government's decision, the department wanted to avoid casting doubt on the Paris agreement. Gauvin agreed with this objective, and thought that the blame should be laid on North Vietnam and the Provisional Revolutionary

Government for subverting the settlement and on the Communist members of the commission for helping them do so. W.T. Delworth, the ambassador to Indonesia (who had had much experience with Vietnam through service on the ICSC and in the Far Eastern division in Ottawa), contended that withdrawal would be the "most dramatic possible expression of our judgment that task [of supervision] is impossible." The Canadian announcement, he argued, should make it clear that the reasons were to be found in the "totality of [the] situation," that is in a combination of problems arising from the agreement and from the circumstances prevailing in Vietnam.[76]

On 29 May Sharp announced the government's decision to withdraw from the commission, the only qualification being willingness to consider a temporary extension to supervise elections held under the terms of the Paris agreement, in the unlikely event (which did not come to pass) that they took place. Sharp stressed that he was not criticizing the Paris agreement, but otherwise his statement made some allusion to the "totality of the situation." Canada, he declared, was adhering to what he had said on 27 March: since "the Canadian concept of the functioning of the International Commission [had] not been accepted," it was time for a change. It was not upon the ICCS, however, that a final settlement in Vietnam would depend, but upon the parties to the peace agreement. "It is only if the parties are co-operating in a strict observance of the agreement and are willing to use the ICCS as a means of reinforcing the agreement that the commission can perform its function with any hope of success."[77] This approach seems to have had the desired effect in Washington. "We regret it, but we understand it," was Kissinger's verdict in a press conference the same day.[78] Nixon, Trudeau noted in his memoirs, "was very angry . . . and . . . called me some nasty names."[79] That outburst, however, was private, and did not become known until later. At long last, Canada had set a date for getting out of its burdensome and frustrating commission responsibilities in Vietnam, without its action becoming either a destabilizing factor in the peninsula or a major irritant in bilateral relations with the United States.

The views expressed are those of the authors and not necessarily those of the Department of Foreign Affairs and International Trade.

Notes

1. The mediatory function is considered most closely in the works cited below by John Holmes and Douglas Ross, while considerations involving the United States are emphasized in those by James Eayrs, Victor Levant, and Charles Taylor.

2. This section and the following one are adapted from John Hilliker and Donald Barry, *Canada's Department of External Affairs: Coming of Age, 1946–1968* (Montreal and Kingston: McGill-Queen's University Press), 1995.

3. R.A. MacKay, ed., *Canadian Foreign Policy, 1945–1954: Selected Speeches and Documents* (Toronto: McClelland and Stewart, 1971), 323.

4. John W. Holmes, "Geneva, 1954," *International Journal* 22, no. 3 (1967): 470–71. Commissions were also established with the same membership for Cambodia and Laos.

5. Canada, Department of External Affairs, "Statement on Canadian Membership on the International Commission for Vietnam, Laos and Cambodia," 28 July 1954, Statements and Speeches (SS) 54/30.

6. John W. Holmes, *The Shaping of Peace: Canada and the Search for World Order, 1954–1957* (Toronto: University of Toronto Press, 1982), 2:208; James Eayrs, *In Defence of Canada, Indochina: Roots of Complicity* (Toronto: University of Toronto Press, 1983), 63–69.

7. New York (UN) to Ottawa, 30 June 1954, telegram 525, Department of External Affairs (DEA) file 50052-40.

8. Holmes, "Geneva, 1954," 474, and *Shaping of Peace*, 2:211.

9. Douglas A, Ross, *In the Interests of Peace: Canada and Vietnam, 1954–1973* (Toronto: University of Toronto Press, 1984), 121.

10. Holmes, *Shaping of Peace*, 2:215–16.

11. Christopher Dagg, "Canada, the International Commission on Vietnam, and the Question of Subversion: Chronological Survey 1954-February 1965 [Draft]," n.d., Dagg Papers, Vancouver, private collection of Christopher Dagg.

12. Undersecretary to Secretary of State for External Affairs (SSEA), 1 March 1960, DEA file 50052-A-13-40.

13. International Commission for Supervision and Control in Vietnam, *Special Report to the Co-Chairmen of the Geneva Conference on Indo-China*, Saigon, 2 June 1962, Cmnd 1775 (London: Her Majesty's Stationery Office, 1962).

14 Dagg, "Canada, the International Commission in Vietnam and the Question of Subversion."

15 Paul Martin, *A Very Public Life, vol. 2, So Many Worlds* (Toronto: Deneau, 1985), 423.

16. Saigon to SSEA, 17 September 1963, dispatch 373, with enclosure "Memorandum to the Commissioner," 10 September 1963, DEA file 21-13-VIET-ICSC-1.

17. Ottawa to Saigon, 18 October 1963, dispatch Y-155, ibid.

18. Ottawa to Saigon, 3 April 1964, telegram Y-269, also 20 March 1964, telegram Y-240, DEA file 21-13-VIET-ICSC.

19. Ottawa to Delhi, 6 April 1964, telegram Y-270, ibid., Dagg, "Canada, the International Control Commission in Vietnam and the Question of Subversion."

20. W.T. Delworth, "A Study of Canadian Policy with respect to the Vietnam Problem, 1962–1966," 17 September 1973, Department of Foreign Affairs and International Trade, Corporate Communications Division, Historical Section, p. 6; also "Draft Meeting with Mr. Rusk in the office of the Prime Minister," 30 April 1964, DEA file 20-1-2-USA; *Foreign Relations of the United States, vol. 1, Vietnam, 1964* (Washington, D.C.: Government Printing Office, 1972), 1:394–96.

21. Delworth, "A Study of Canadian Policy," 10.

22. Ottawa to Washington, 12 August 1964, telegram Y-606 in ibid, appendix, also Martin, *A Very Public Life*, 2:429–30.

23. International Commission for Supervision and Control in Vietnam, *Special Report to the Co-Chairmen of the Geneva Conference on Indo-China*, Saigon, 13 February 1965, Cmnd 2609 (London: Her Majesty's Stationery Office, 1965); also Dagg, "Canada, the International Control Commission in Vietnam and the Question of Subversion."

24. Bruce Hutchison, *The Far Side of the Street* (Toronto: Macmillan, 1976), 354.

25. SSEA to prime minister, 29 March 1965, DEA file 20-CDA-9, Pearson, L.B.

26. John Hadwen (office of the SSEA) to file, 31 March 1965, L.B. Pearson Papers, National Archives, Series N3, vol. 281.

27. Hadwen to file, 1 April 1965, ibid.

28. "Canadian Foreign Policy in a Two-Power World," 10 April 1951, SS 51/14.

29. Lawrence Martin, *The Presidents and the Prime Ministers* (Toronto: Doubleday, 1984), 224–25.

30. John English, *The Worldly Years, The Life of Lester Pearson, vol. 2, 1949–1972* (Toronto: Alfred A. Knopf, 1992), 2:362–68, McGeorge Bundy, "Canada, the Exceptionally Favored: An American Perspective," in *Friends So Different, Essays on Canada and the United States in the 1980s*, ed. Lansing Lamont and J. Duncan Edmonds (Ottawa: University of Ottawa Press, 1989), 238–39.

31. Saigon to Ottawa, 10 June 1965, telegram 480 and undersecretary to USSEA, 11 June 1965, DEA file 20-22-VIETS-2-1; also Delworth, "A Study of Canadian Policy," 36.

32. Undersecretary to SSEA, 20 September 1965, DEA file 20-22-VIETS-2-1; also Delworth, "A Study of Canadian Policy," 42, and Canada, House of Commons, Debates (CHCD), 7 June 1965, p. 2038.

33. Undersecretary to SSEA, 25 August 1965, DEA file 21-13-VIET-ICSC-4., Delworth, "A Study of Canadian Policy," 42.

34. Delworth, "A Study of Canadian Policy," 56–61, 65–67; undersecretary to SSEA, 6 December 1965, DEA file 21-13-VIET-ICSC; Martin, *A Very Public Life*, 2:436–37; English, *The Worldly Years*, 371–72.

35. Saigon to Ottawa, 6 June 1966, telegram 450, in Delworth, "A Study of Canadian Policy," appendix.

36. Quoted in Delworth, "A Study of Canadian Policy," 84.

37. Martin, *A Very Public Life*, 2:442.

38. Documents on DEA files 21-13-VIET-ICSC-11 and 20-22-VIETS-2-1.

39. CHCD, 13 February 1967, pp. 12962–66, Canada, House of Commons,

Standing Committee on External Affairs, *Minutes of Proceedings and Evidence*, 11 April 1967, pp. 312–15.

40. CHCD, 10 May 1967, 57.

41. Notes for Remarks by the Honourable Walter L. Gordon to the Sixth Arts of Management Conference, Toronto, Ontario, 13 May 1967, DEA file 20-22-VIETS-2-1.

42. Policy statement, Vietnam, 17 May 1967, ibid; also Walter Gordon, *A Political Memoir* (Toronto: McClelland and Stewart, 1977), 284.

43. Far Eastern Division to undersecretary, 18 May 1967, DEA file 20-22-VIETS-2-1.

44. Escott Reid, *Radical Mandarin: The Memoirs of Escott Reid* (Toronto: University of Toronto Press, 1989), 373.

45. CHCD, 27 June 1967, 1984.

46. Undersecretary to SSEA, 7 July 1967, DEA file 20-22-VIETS-2-1.

47. Martin, *A Very Public Life*, 2:454.

48. President Lyndon B. Johnson, "Answering Aggression in Viet-Nam," *U.S. Department of State Bulletin*, 57, 1478 (23 October 1967): 519–22.

49. Briefing Material for Mr. Trudeau, "Vietnam," 10 April 1968, DEA file 20-22-VIETS-2-1.

50. Prime Minister's Office, Press Release, 1 April 1968, Pearson Papers, N9, vol. 46.

51. Far Eastern Division to Ralph Collins (assistant undersecretary), 17 April 1968, and enclosure, DEA file 21-13-VIET-ICSC-11; Charles Taylor, *Snow Job: Canada, the United States and Vietnam* (Toronto: Anansi, n.d. [1974?]), 139.

52. J.L. Granatstein and Robert Bothwell, *Pirouette: Pierre Trudeau and Canadian Foreign Policy* (Toronto: University of Toronto Press, 1990), 7; Taylor, *Snow Job*, 141; and, on the foreign policy review, Bruce Thordarson, *Trudeau and Foreign Policy: A Study in Decision-Making* (Toronto: Oxford University Press, 1972).

53. A.S. McGill (office of SSEA) to H.B. Robinson (deputy undersecretary), 23 October 1968, Far Eastern Division memorandum, 14 November 1969, DEA file 21-13-VIET-ICSC-12.

54. Far Eastern Division to undersecretary, 28 May 1969, also undersecretary to SSEA, 27 November 1968 and 21 July 1969, and minute by SSEA, n.d., ibid.

55. SSEA, *Viet-Nam: Canada's Approach to Participation in the International Commission of Control and Supervision October 25, 1972 - March 27, 1973* (Ottawa: Information Canada, 1973), 2.

56. Ottawa to Washington, 29 January 1970, letter GFE-111, Washington to Ottawa, 23 April 1970, telegram 1248, DEA file 21-13-VIET-ICSC-12.

57. SSEA, *Foreign Policy for Canadians: Pacific* (Ottawa: Information Canada, 1970), 24; Ross, *In the Interests of Peace*, 326.

58. Victor Levant, *Quiet Complicity: Canadian Involvement in the Vietnam War* (Toronto: Between the Lines, 1968), 214. See also Robert Bothwell, *Canada and the United States: The Politics of Partnership* (Toronto: University of Toronto Press, 1992), 106–8.

59. Washington to Ottawa, 28 October 1972, telegram 3934, also 25 November 1972, telegram 4249, DEA file 21-13-VIET-ICSC-12. For an extended discussion of opinion in the department at this time, see Ross, *In the Interests of Peace*, 324ff.

60. Saigon to Ottawa, 31 October, 17 November, and 9 December 1972, telegrams 1578, 1579, 1672, and 1802, ibid.

61. Ottawa to Saigon, 27 November 1972, telegram GPP-132, ibid.

62. CHCD, 24 January 1973, 595; Washington to Ottawa, 23 January 1973, telegram 257, DEA file 21-13-VIET-ICCS-1973. Levant (*Quiet Complicity*, 231) and Taylor (*Snow Job*, 153–59) point out that the agreement fell far short of meeting Canadian conditions. Taylor contends that it was Canada's strategy to use this shortfall to justify early withdrawal from the commission.

63. Mitchell Sharp, *Which Reminds Me . . . A Memoir* (Toronto: University of Toronto Press, 1994), 213.

64. Saigon to Ottawa, 1 February 1973, telegram ICCS14, DEA file 21-13-VIET-ICCS-73.

65. SSEA, *Viet-Nam*, 20, 22.

66. Arthur Andrew, *The Rise and Fall of a Middle Power: Canadian Diplomacy from King to Mulroney* (Toronto: Lorimer, 1993), 118.

67. SSEA, *Viet-Nam*, 24.

68. Washington to Ottawa, 22 March 1973, telegram 1007, DEA file 21-13-VIET-ICCS-73.

69. Saigon to Ottawa, 27 March 1973, telegram ICCS550, ibid.

70. Undersecretary to SSEA, 8 March 1973, and minute by undersecretary, n.d., ibid.

71. SSEA, *Viet-Nam*, 26.

72. Ottawa to Saigon, 27 March 1973, telegram GPP-64, DEA file 21-13-VIET-ICCS-73.

73. Ottawa to Saigon, 8 May 1973, telegram GPE-495, ibid.; Taylor, *Snow Job*, 174–75.

74. Undersecretary to SSEA, 22 May 1973, also Saigon to Ottawa, 12 May 1973, telegram ICCS1140, DEA file 21-13-VIET-73; Levant, *Quiet Complicity*, 246. On the open-mouth policy and domestic opinion in the United States, see Gareth Porter, *A Peace Denied: The United States, Vietnam, and the Paris Agreement* (Bloomington: Indiana University Press, 1975), 225–26.

75. Washington to Ottawa, 23 May 1973, telegram 1795, DEA file 21-13-VIET-ICCS-73.

76. Jakarta to Ottawa, 21 and 25 May 1973, telegrams 1002 and 1054, also Saigon to Ottawa, 22 May 1973, telegram ICCS1216.

77. CHCD, 29 May 1973, 4195.

78. Washington to Ottawa, 29 May 1973, telegram 1836, ibid.; Levant, *Quiet Complicity*, 246.

79. Pierre Elliott Trudeau, *Memoirs* (Toronto: McClelland and Stewart, 1993), 218. On the involvement of Trudeau and his foreign policy adviser, Ivan Head, in

the Vietnam issue, see Ivan Head and Pierre Trudeau, *The Canadian Way: Shaping Canada's Foreign Policy, 1968–1984* (Toronto: McClelland and Stewart, 1995), 108–84.

THE END OF THE CANADA-UNITED STATES DEFENSE RELATIONSHIP

Joseph T. Jockel
St. Lawrence University

Joel J. Sokolsky
Royal Military College

Introduction

The Canada-United States defense relationship, just like the Cold War that necessitated and sustained it, is over. As the two countries become economically closer, especially with the establishment of the Canada-United States Free Trade Agreement (FTA) and more recently the North American Free Trade Agreement (NAFTA), defense entanglements have been moving in the opposite direction.

The bilateral defense relationship consisted of two central elements. The first was the joint protection of North America against nuclear attack. In the earlier days of the Cold War, Canadian airspace and territory were nothing short of essential to detect and potentially destroy any attacking Soviet bombers. Many Canadians remember that John Foster Dulles once called their country, because of its location between the United States and the Soviet Union, "a very important piece of real estate." Americans and Canadians built several vast radar networks spanning the continent, coordinated fighter/interceptor aircraft operations of the U.S. and Royal Canadian air forces, and in 1957 placed what became a single system under the operational control of the North American Air Defense Command (NORAD) whose commander in chief was always an American general with a Canadian deputy. Had the call to Washington warning of impending attack ever come, it might well have been a Canadian general on the line.

As the threat to North America shifted from manned bomber to the intercontinental ballistic missile (ICBM) and submarine launched ballistic missile (SLBM), (and as the United States shifted from active defense to reliance on deterrence), NORAD adapted, becoming in 1981 the North American Aerospace Defense Command whose prime function was warning and attack assessment. The importance of this function to the credibility and functioning of the American offensive nuclear posture meant that NORAD placed Canada in a unique position relative to other U.S. allies. No other foreign military personnel were as close to the central strategic nuclear forces upon which collective western defense rested as were those of Canada.

The second element of the defense relationship was a focus on the defense of Western Europe, especially through the North Atlantic Treaty Organization (NATO), of which both countries were founding members and to which both contributed military forces, including the deployments of standing air and ground formations in Western Europe itself. This NATO focus was, of course, a continued reflection of the basic North American interest in preventing any potentially hostile power from establishing hegemony over Europe, a shared interest that had taken both Canada and the United States in the First and Second World Wars.

For Canada, NATO membership was always far more than just a way to pursue a fundamental security interest. It was a ticket into the "big leagues" of international diplomacy. Moreover, it seemed to offset the ties with the behemoth to the south. As the distinguished Canadian diplomat and scholar John Holmes put it, "Canadians also saw NATO as a counterweight . . . it would give Canada a multilateral forum in which, by combining with other lesser powers, it could make its weight be felt and so be relieved, at least psychologically, of the inhibitions of life with one gigantic neighbour."[1] The United States, for its part, not only welcomed Canada's NATO participation but throughout much of the Cold War fretted whenever Ottawa began to talk about reducing Canadian air and ground forces in Europe or even pulling them out, lest the solidarity of the alliance be threatened.

North American and NATO roles became the raison d'être of the Canadian Forces (CF) and the essence of their military professionalism. Functional ties with the U.S. armed forces became very close. This was particularly true of the air forces because of

NORAD. But it was also the case for the navies which shared anti-submarine warfare (ASW) responsibilities related to the protection of both North America and Europe.

Today, it is evident that the geographic focus of whatever security cooperation may crystallize between the two countries is shifting "out of area," that is outside North America and Western Europe. But it is far from clear how extensive and enduring these new forms of bilateral military cooperation will be.

North America

To argue that the Canada-United States defense relationship has ended is not to say that strictly bilateral military cooperation in North America has terminated or will soon terminate. Rather, collaboration in the direct defense of the continent will continue its already marked decline into strategic marginality.

The Clinton administration's July 1994 statement *A National Security Strategy of Engagement and Enlargement,* scarcely mentions North American defense.[2] This is also the direction in which Canadian policy is moving. A January 1995 government statement by Ottawa emphasized that "direct threats to Canada's territory are diminished" and that future challenges to Canadian security are increasingly likely to be of a nonmilitary nature, that is, economic, environmental and demographic.[3]

Even before the Cold War's formal end, the level and tempo of Canada-United States defense relations, particularly in NORAD, had been decreasing. By the late 1980s, the frequency of Soviet *Bear* bomber flights near North America was dramatically reduced, as were Soviet submarine patrols.[4] Washington cut back on plans contained in the 1985 Canada-United States Air Defense Modernization Agreement, which had provided for a modest revitalization of continental air defenses, especially against air- and sea-launched cruise missiles. A new line of radars across northern Canada and Alaska was built, but now will operate on much reduced capacity. Of the four modern air defense radar installations envisaged in 1985 for the United States, two were canceled, one was deactivated, and the last put on part-time alert status. U.S. funding for air defense forward operating locations in northern Canada was completely cut off by Congress.

Accordingly, the classic air defense mission against massive bomber attack has been put on the backburner. Forces for this mission have been put in what NORAD calls a "regeneration" category with expectation that there would be as much as a two-year strategic warning of any resurgent air threat. There are no longer NORAD "war plans" but "concept plans" for North American air defense.[5]

With the North American air defense mission waning and with the threat of large scale ballistic missile attack all but gone, focus has shifted to the possible role of Colorado Springs as part of a multinational "global warning initiative" designed to meet the threat of the proliferation of weapons of mass destruction and missile technology.[6] The possibility also remains that the United States might deploy a limited ballistic missile defense (BMD) system in North America or limited theater missile defenses (TMD) for protection abroad, especially for U.S. forces deployed overseas.

It is far from clear, however, how much emphasis the United States intends to put into North American BMD. The Clinton administration is continuing the emphasis on TMD. Although the new Republican-controlled Congress tried to speed up the fielding of a BMD system to defend the United States,[7] the current legislation requires only that a BMD system be "developed by 2003, with Congress having to vote again before it can be deployed."[8]

Ottawa has indicated that it is open to including some reference to further BMD roles in a renewed NORAD agreement. Yet even if the United States does move to deployment after the turn of the century, Canada will not be needed for the central role geography required it to play in North American air defense. No systems critical for BMD need to be located in Canada or operated by Canadians. This is a continuation of a trend that was under way well before the Cold War ended. No system to detect ballistic missiles has ever been placed in Canada or operated by the Canadian Forces. If Canada does become involved in missile defense, it is far more likely that it will be as part of a NATO-wide program for TMD outside North America.

Canada's sixteen surface warships (including twelve new patrol frigates), its plans to augment the country's naval presence in the Pacific, and more recent changes to the underwater surveillance system will make the Canadian maritime contribution to continental defense actually better than it is at present.[9] The Canadian and U.S. navies can be expected to maintain close contact and cooperation. But with the dramatic decline in post-Soviet naval power, purely national sovereignty protection duties, as opposed to bilateral roles, are much more likely to be the main focus of the Canadian Navy in the waters surrounding North America, as evidenced by its actions against Spanish fishing vessels in the spring of 1985. The only naval building now under way in Canada is for a fleet of short-range Maritime Coastal Defence Vessels. In the 1980s there was significant Canadian concern about the operation of foreign, including American submarines in the Arctic, which led to the proposal in a 1987 Canadian White Paper to acquire a fleet of nuclear-power attack submarines (SSNs) capable of under-ice operations. Tensions rose with the U.S. Navy, which found the prospect of operating in conjunction with the Canadians under the ice decidedly unwelcome and doubted Canada's ability to pay for SSNs and operate them effectively. The plan was abandoned in 1989 and the current Canadian government appears only marginally interested in what might be going on beneath Arctic waters.

In the past, Canada's security relations with the United States have been problematic in domestic politics. This is because Canadian governments have been caught between their support for collective defense, which has made military cooperation with the United States essential, and popular fears that national sovereignty and independence would be compromised by too close an association with the nuclear-armed giant to the south. The close working relationship between the Canadian and American air forces and bureaucracies has, in particular, always lent a faint air of illegitimacy to NORAD. The suggestion was that the Canadian military, eager to play in the big leagues, has promoted an integration of defense efforts of which the political leadership has not always been fully cognizant. Should not Canada's real role in international affairs be that of a "peacemaker" and not a "powder monkey"?[10]

In the present international circumstances, with no real threat to North America, the military relationship with the United States — especially NORAD — might be expected to encounter criticism in Canada as anachronistic business as usual at the expense of a new, more independent, Canadian defense policy. Moreover, with NAFTA binding Canada ever more closely to the United States economically, Ottawa might have anticipated a new reaction against continued military ties with the Americans.

The passing of the Cold War , however, has weakened the "peace movement" in Canada, depriving it of its ability to combine fear of nuclear war with Canadian nationalism. NORAD renewed in 1996, ceased to be an issue in Canada. But if the peace movement has been deprived of its strongest arguments against bilateral cooperation, so too have pro-defense groups. In the past, they also appealed to nationalist sentiment by contending that cooperation with the United States was an exercise in "defence against help." In other words, if Canada did not monitor its own air and sea approaches, the United States by strategic necessity, would do it, thereby challenging Canadian sovereignty and independence.[11] With the ending of the Cold War, this argument has lost much of its persuasiveness, a fact not lost on Ottawa as it cuts the country's defense budget. The end of the Cold War has also meant that bilateral defense relations are no longer an issue of controversy on the Canadian public policy agenda.

This made it easier for Ottawa and Washington to renew NORAD in 1996 even though there was no compelling defense need to do so. Changes were made in the wording of the agreement reflecting the altered global security environment. Reference was also made to future cooperation in BMD. Regardless of the wording NORAD will still be a pale reflection of its Cold War self.

Nonetheless, there is some merit in preserving an inexpensive hedge against international uncertainties. More concretely and immediately, not renewing would have required making alternative arrangements for the restructuring of vestigial defense collaboration. Such substantive changes would not have been costless in terms of money and attention that would have been required on the part of both governments. And at this point North American defense is not sufficiently high on either Washington's or Ottawa's list of foreign policy priorities to warrant the time, effort, and money required to get rid of it.

NATO and European Security

NATO is even likelier, far likelier in fact, than NORAD to be maintained over the next few decades with both Canada and the United States remaining members. But, the changing nature of the alliance will alter the roles of Ottawa and Washington in a manner that will further diminish the importance of the bilateral defense relationship.

Despite many early, and now decidedly premature obituaries, NATO has remained the dominant security organization in Europe and is poised to expand both geographically and functionally. Building upon the Partnership For Peace (PfP) initiative, the alliance has formulated a set of principles and procedures for the admission of new members from Eastern Europe. Revising military strategy, it is seeking more mobility and flexibility through the idea of Combined and Joint Task Forces (CJTF). The alliance, as evident in Yugoslavia, is taking a more active role in peace support operations.

What is clear is that neither will succeed. American leadership is essential but the nature of the United States' role in Europe will change from that of a guarantor of West European security against a common threat to that of the key organizer of multilateral efforts to cope with instances of instability throughout the continent. In this new role, however, Washington will have a measure of discretion as to the extent of its involvement. As many, if not most, European problems will not directly threaten U.S. vital interests, the president and Congress will be able to select where and when the United States will exercise a leadership role.

For Canada, the disappearance of the Soviet threat has broken the link between its security and that of Europe. Also gone is the old argument that NATO provides a counterweight to close defense ties with the United States. Moreover, as Washington and the alliance turn their attention eastward, with the possible admission of more strategically important members, Canada's place and influence within allied councils will diminish from its already reduced stature. The political significance which Washington used to attach to Canadian participation in NATO will fade into marginality. All of this will hasten what is already a clear Canadian policy of disengagement from NATO.

Well before the Cold War ended, Canadians reluctantly came to accept their inability to build trade flows with Europe into a "counterweight" to economic ties with the United States. The Canada-U.S. FTA and NAFTA can be taken as formal confirmation of Canada's economic future as a North American country. In addition, just like the United States, Canada today trades more across the Pacific than across the Atlantic.

To be sure, in recent defense and foreign policy white papers, Ottawa continues to proclaim its allegiance to the transatlantic ideal and to support NATO expansion.[12] But in the 1990s, as Kim Richard Nossal of McMaster University recently has pointed out, "the notion of Canada as a European nation will remain a conceit, for few Canadians seem willing to embrace the costs that would give the fine sounding rhetoric of transatlantic projection concrete meaning."[13]

Those real costs that could still tie Canada to Europe would include defense dollars. The Cold War was scarcely over when the Canadian government announced in 1991 that the country's two military bases in Europe, both located in Germany, would be closed and that the Canadian military presence in Europe would be reduced to a token force of 1,100, to be stationed at a British or U.S. base. A year later, Ottawa abandoned even this political symbolism. Canada's two fighter squadrons and armored brigade group would be brought home. Over the next two years, drastic cuts were made to the Canadian forces. By the end of the decade the regular force will drop to 60,000.

Nevertheless, the *1994 Defence White Paper* states that Canada will maintain "multi-purpose, combat capable armed forces able to meet the challenges to Canada's security both at home and abroad."[14] It will continue to supply naval forces to the alliance, crews for the NATO Airborne Warning and Control aircraft and individual personnel for various allied staff positions. And in Canada it will retain air and ground forces which could be sent to Europe. Despite overall force reductions, some 3,000 personnel will be added to the land forces. In the event of a major overseas contingency, Ottawa would be prepared to send land, sea and air forces simultaneously and "this could conceivably involve in the order of 10,000 military personnel."[15]

But this reconfiguration entails an even greater Canadian retreat from European defense than many realized. The white paper does not earmark these potential expeditionary forces for NATO alone. Rather it states that they will be available for contributions to international security in general "within a UN framework, through NATO, or in coalitions of like-minded countries." As the white paper acknowledges, a major crisis in Europe might find the very hard-pressed and undermanned Canadian forces deployed elsewhere requiring difficult and protracted redeployments.[16] Combined with continued budgetary pressures, it is not at all certain that Canada will be able to maintain a militarily meaningful contribution to European security.

Many Canadians would protest immediately that their country has more than demonstrated its continuing commitment to European security by its long-standing participation in the international efforts under way in the former Yugoslavia. In June 1995 there were more than 2,000 Canadian troops in Croatia and Bosnia, making it one of the leading contributors—and this when U.S. ground involvement was limited to a small presence in Macedonia and a field hospital in Croatia.

It would be a mistake, though, to see Canada's recent peacekeeping efforts as proof of a permanent commitment to

European security. In effect, Ottawa backed into Yugoslavia, thinking that it would be like other "classic" U.N. operations in which Canadian forces have been involved and which entailed the deployment of lightly armed multinational forces between combatants who had already stopped fighting. In Croatia and Bosnia, of course, there was precious little peace to keep. At first, Canadians took pride in the prominent role their blue berets were playing. But as the fighting continued and when Canadian troops were taken hostage, Canadians back home grew increasingly frustrated. It was also frustrating for them to see their country excluded from the high-level contact group of countries attempting to broker a peace. On several occasions, Ottawa resisted the strong temptation to pull out lest it be seen as reneging on a commitment and undermining efforts.

Those commitments, however, were begun under the previous government. For its part the Chrétien government has been less enthusiastic about the Yugoslavian role. It continually sought to block and then only grudgingly accepted American-sponsored demands that air strikes be used to punish the Serbs for not respecting safe areas. The pattern was "one of . . . seizing every opportunity to reduce the size and exposure of Canadian troops."[17] After the 1995 summer offensive, Canada joined other U.N. forces in leaving Croatia. Then, following NATO's massive air assault on the Bosnian Serbs and the U.S. brokered cease-fire, the prime minister announced "with pleasure" that the Canadians would be withdrawn from Bosnia by November 1995 because "the mission was over."[18]

The problem for Ottawa was that the mission was not over. President Clinton made a major commitment of American power and prestige in order to lead NATO in securing the 21 November 1995 settlement in Bosnia. The alliance likewise put its credibility to European security on the line. Thus as much as the Chrétien government would have liked to have put Bosnia behind it, the Clinton initiative put Ottawa in a difficult position.

On the one hand, as NATO's 60,000 person force for Bosnia was to have a war fighting capability, this was the opportunity for Ottawa to redeem itself in the eyes of its allies as well as to live up to the promises of the white paper, and deploy a sizable combat-capable force in support of the alliance. This would also have been consistent with the white paper's call for NATO to take a more active role in peacekeeping.

On the other hand, given defense department budget and man-power cuts, the heavy peacekeeping commitments of recent years and public opinion, Canada was in no position to send a major force back into Bosnia, particularly one that have to wage war against violators of the peace agreement. Moreover, the Chrétien government could have claimed that Canada had done more than its share in the Balkans and done so when the Europeans proved themselves incapable of solving the problem on their own and the United States was reluctant to become more heavily involved. Finally, after the experience of the last few years and the dominant American role in the NATO initiative, there should be no more illusions in Ottawa about having any influence over the Bosnian peace process, whatever the Canadian contribution.

Not surprisingly therefore, the reaction in Ottawa to the American call for support was ambivalence. After the Canadian foreign minister, speaking in Washington, at first said Canada would participate in the NATO force, but then both he and the prime minister backed away from a pledge to send combat forces, saying that Canada would participate "only if absolutely neces-sary."[19] Canada was the last NATO country to decide on the size of its commitment. While attending the December 1995 NATO meet-ing, the foreign minister noted that although Canada was a staunch supporter of peacekeeping, "this is not a decision like those in the past on the subject of real traditional peacekeeping of the United Nations; it is something else. . . . We could spend much more money in the reconstruction element of the package than on the military package. But obviously we will have to consider the need of NATO, the demands in regards to troops, how much has been already contributed by others."[20] In its deliberations, the cabinet considered a range of options from sending a token support force of about 200 to the dispatch of more than 2,000 combat troops.[21]

Ottawa's eventual decision to send a force of 1,000 troops re-flected its ambivalence toward the operation and the domestic con-straints. Given the nature of the mission and the dangers, the force was more heavily armed than previous Canadian units in the for-mer Yugoslavia and had the authority to defend themselves under the more "robust rules of engagement" that NATO operated under. But more than half the force, 500–600, were assigned to support British soldiers by providing a headquarters unit, including com-munications staff, west of Sarajevo and only 300 to 400 were com-bat troops. Ottawa also made clear that the deployment would be for only one year. In justifying the small size of the force, Minister of National Defence David Collenette cited Canada's then three-year-long participation in U.N. peacekeeping in Yugoslavia: "This is what Canadians would expect us to do."[22]

There is little doubt that in making this commitment, Ottawa was trying to mend fences with NATO. As Mr. Collenette noted, Canada had a "moral obligation" to support the alliance[23] at this "historic time for NATO."[24] In the final analysis, though, the decision can be explained simply by the continuing Canadian desire not to be entirely left out of a major American-led western undertaking.

While it was unlikely that Canada would have chosen not to participate in the Bosnian effort at all, it is equally unlikely, given the obvious reluctance on Canada's part and the size of the force, that this will be seen in Europe and Washington as a reaffirmation of Canada's commitment to NATO. Rather, it will be viewed as further evidence of a desire to distance Ottawa from the alliance's new role in coping with Europe's ethnic instability.

No doubt the Clinton administration would have preferred a larger, more combat capable, Canadian contribution as it rounded up the NATO posse for Bosnia. However the United States was not going to put any pressure on Canada to do more. Militarily and operationally it made little difference. Given Canada's continuing budgetary crises and recent policy decisions, there was little the United States could do. More significantly, such entreaties would not have been worth the effort. It was far more important for the Clinton administration to garner West European contributions and the participation of some of the PfP countries, especially Russia. Had the U.S.-brokered settlement on Bosnia floundered on the killing fields of Yugoslavia or in Congress, then little importance will have been attached to Ottawa's reluctance to become involved or the size of Canada's commitment.

Whatever now happens in Yugoslavia, Canada will retain its seat at the perhaps soon-to-be enlarged NATO table. Its diplomats and senior military officials will participate in allied affairs and its small forces will continue to exercise with those of older allies and PfP nations. But in Europe as in North America, the Canada-U.S. defense relationship will continue to slide from marginality to obscurity.

Out of Area and the Future of U.N. Peacekeeping

As the two central elements of the bilateral defense relationship-North American and NATO-diminish, attention is increasingly focused on Canada-U.S. security links "out of area." There are two broad dimensions to collaboration: regional security arrangements, including ad-hoc coalitions formed under U.S. leadership and peacekeeping operations. During the Cold War, Canada had very little involvement in American-led regional security efforts. Ottawa did not even join the Organization of American States (OAS) until 1989. Nor did Canada participate in any limited wars or interventions between the Korean War and the Gulf War.

There was, however, an implicit and sometimes explicit collaboration between Canada and the United States in the realm of U.N. peacekeeping. This was based upon a compatibility between Canada's desire to use peacekeeping partly as a way to project a more independent identity externally and U.S. national security interests. For the United States, U.N. peacekeeping operations were used to fill a political vacuum and prevent Soviet intervention, cool conflict between allies, monitor agreements negotiated by U.S. officials, or serve "U.S. foreign policy goals of the moment."[25] While Canadians often viewed peacekeeping as a neutral activity in the context of the dominant East-West struggle, Washington welcomed and appreciated Canada's participation precisely because Ottawa was a loyal Western ally.[26] Nevertheless, peacekeeping remained marginal to global security relations and between 1979 and 1988, the United Nations in general fell into great disfavor with the Reagan administration.

Since the end of the Cold War, the United States and Canada have collaborated in a range of multilateral operations from the peace enforcement of the Gulf War to efforts at peacekeeping in Somalia and Haiti. But it is premature to conclude that the two countries are about to engage in a new joint approach to international security threats despite the continuing commitment of both to multilateralism. For here too, the relationship is changing as each country adopts different approaches to regional conflicts and instability.

When Washington does feel itself "bound to lead," it will seek out followers. But for the United States, multilateralism is a tool to be used when it can support the achievement of American interests. As then Ambassador Madeleine Albright told a Senate Committee in 1994, "When threats arise, we may respond through the U.N., through NATO, through a coalition, through a combination of these

tools or we may act alone. We will do whatever is necessary to defend the vital interests of the United States."[27]

For Canada, acting alone is rarely an option, thus multilateralism has always been viewed as a necessary means to achieve broad
foreign policy objectives. Under the current government, the prime
Canadian interest abroad is economic—to promote trade and multilateral regimes favorable to its vulnerable, open economy. As one
moves away from concrete matters of dollars and cents, Canadian
internationalism often tends to be an amorphous amalgam of vague
concepts which simply equate Canada's well-being with broad
global stability and unabashed claims that Canadians have certain
virtues that make them especially well qualified to promote that
stability. As a recent parliamentary review of foreign policy concluded:

> foreign policy matters to Canadians. They have deep-rooted values that
> they carry over into the role they want Canada to play—nurturing dialogue
> and compromise; promoting democracy, human rights, economic and so-
> cial justice; caring for the environment; safeguarding peace; and easing
> poverty. And they can offer corresponding skills-mediating disputes; coun-
> selling, good governance in a diverse society; helping the less fortunate;
> and peacekeeping.[28]

What this approach often obscures is the reality that most cases
of regional conflict or instability will not even indirectly affect
Canadian economic or security interests. Ottawa is often simply
looking to participate actively in global affairs. Lacking any solid
basis in vital national security interests, Canada does not see its
commitment to multilateralism as requiring it to assume a greater
share of the military burden for regional security especially where
this could entail high- intensity conflict as part of a coalition. The
limited Canadian involvement in the Gulf War, though fully supportive of the U.S.-led coalition, reflected Ottawa's modest assessment of what Canada could be expected to contribute.[29] Ottawa
may still believe that Washington is "bound to lead," but it does
not always hold that it is necessarily bound to follow.

Canada is showing a new interest in the countries of the Far
East and Latin America. Prime Minister Jean Chrétien's most publi-
cized trade missions have been to these two areas.[30] Ottawa believes that as Canada seeks out new trading opportunities, there
should be some commensurate augmentation in military links with
regions and countries outside the traditional North Atlantic

triangle. The *1994 White Paper* reflects this state of affairs. It documents how Canadian interest in the security of the Asia Pacific region has become much more active—through the encouragement of regional security dialogues such as the Asia Regional Forum, the Council for Security Cooperation in Asia Pacific, and the Canadian Consortium on Asia Pacific Security. Canada will expand the current program of bilateral military contacts with a variety of Asian nations, including Japan, South Korea, and members of the Association of South East Asian Nations.[31]

Increased Canadian military ties in Latin America, the Pacific and elsewhere might involve some cooperation with the United States. But this new interest cannot be equated with a Canadian commitment to the security of these regions, a commitment necessitating greatly expanded military operations. Thus it is unlikely that beyond staff talks, exchanges of information and the occasional port visit and participation in joint exercises, Canada is prepared to bind itself to concrete regional security arrangements. The emphasis upon naval ties is noteworthy since they are a relatively inexpensive way to maintain a nominal "global" presence. Forces that exercise together will not necessarily fight together. Indeed, the attractiveness of these new links seems to rest for the most part in their relatively low political, and above all financial, costs. Canada, it may be said, is more interested in "conference" than military-backed confidence-building measures.

In short, the key motivating factor behind expanding military ties is economic not traditional military security. Recently a high-level Canadian military delegation went to China to establish contacts with the Peoples Liberation Army and to explore opportunities for military exports.[32] A cruise by Canada's newest warship into the Persian Gulf was likewise intended to promote Canadian defense products. To this extent, Ottawa and Washington might well find themselves in a competitive rather than cooperative situation overseas.

For the United States, Canada's shallow commitment to regional security and any future war-fighting coalitions is of little import-even less than in the Cold War when some political symbolism was attached to Canadian diplomatic support. The U.S. military knows full well that Canadian forces lack the capability to make a significant military contribution out of area. Moreover, for the United States, promoting regional security will depend upon cooperation with regional powers and, at times, powerful external actors such as France and Britain, and even Russia. If Washington cannot persuade these other nations to follow its lead, then it will either act alone, if its vital interests are deemed to be at stake, or it will not act at all.

With NORAD, NATO, and ad-hoc coalitions waning in importance for Canada, U.N. peacekeeping has emerged, for the first time, as the de facto top priority in Canadian defense policy. And, as Dennis Stairs of Dalhousie University has observed, the 1994 parliamentary reviews of defense and foreign policy "established beyond any doubt that there was massive support in the country at large" for peacekeeping.[33] Thus, even as Ottawa was pulling its troops out of Yugoslavia, and hedging on whether to participate in NATO's peace enforcement efforts there, the government was launching new foreign and defense policy initiatives designed to strengthen the U.N.'s peacekeeping capabilities and to augment Canada's contribution to them. In early September 1995, Mr. Collenette announced that as many as 3,000 additional members of the Canadian Forces would be available for peacekeeping operations, putting the total number at more than 20,000 out of combined armed forces of soon-to-be 60,000. He also stressed that the UN, not NATO, "should take the lead in setting the broad context for all security initiatives and in giving direction for multilateral operations."[34]

Later that month, Canada tabled a report at the U.N. entitled *Towards A Rapid Reaction Capability For the United Nations*.[35] Based on the idea of the "Vanguard Concept," the report called for nations to maintain an enhanced multinational standby force of up to 5,000 troops to be assembled and deployed on short notice under the operational control of a small permanent operational headquarters. This force would "buy time for diplomatic efforts and prepare the ground work for a longer-term traditional peacekeeping operation." The report also contained proposals for other improvements to the United Nations' approach to crisis management in the area of early warning and logistics.[36] "This report," Mr. Collenette stated, "illustrates the Government's commitment to ensuring a vigorous and effective United Nations at a time of increased demand for peacekeeping."[37]

In the early post-Cold War years, Canada-U.S. compatibility in peacekeeping seemed to grow and hold greater potential as the Bush administration embraced U.N. peacekeeping as a useful tool. Between 1988 and 1993, some twenty new operations were begun with Canada participating in nearly all of them and with considerable American diplomatic, logistic, and financial support.[38] The

U.S. military began incorporating peacekeeping into its doctrine and training.[39] The "Canadianization" of American defense policy seemed to be at hand.

But rather than heralding the beginning of a new phase in bilateral relations, the proliferation of peacekeeping in the early 1990s now appears as a false start in efforts to order the new world disorder. After some early successes, it began to turn sour in Somalia and finally collapsed in the Yugoslavian nightmare. By July 1995, the United States owed nearly $650 million on its peacekeeping budget assessments and nearly $530 million to the U.N.'s regular budget.[40] Peacekeeping had become "unAmerican."

Under attack at home by the Republican congressional majority, which included criticism of peacekeeping in the *Contract With America*, in May 1994 the Clinton administration issued Presidential Decision Directive 25 (PDD-25), *U.S. Policy on Reforming Multilateral Peace Operations* which tempered the earlier enthusiasm and placed limits and conditions on future U.S. involvement in U.N. peacekeeping operations.[41]

It is not that Washington wants the United Nations to get out of the peacekeeping business, but rather that as many of these operations cross the line between classic peacekeeping and peace enforcement, the United States will insist upon its own methods of making the U.N. more "vigorous and effective." This might mean removing operations from the UN altogether which, according to then Ambassador Albright, "has not shown a capacity to respond decisively when the risk of combat is high" and when "military credibility is what is required" to keep the peace.[42]

Thus, as it assumed the leadership role in Yugoslavia in the summer of 1995, Washington was determined not to repeat the mistakes of the United Nations Protection Force. In making his case for the dispatch of U.S. troops to Bosnia as part of the NATO mission, President Clinton assured the American people that "unlike the UN forces" they would have the "authority to respond immediately" to attacks. "America," he warned, "protects its own. Anyone, anyone, who takes on our troops will suffer the consequences. We will fight fire with fire, and then some."[43]

Testifying before a U.S. Senate Committee, Joint Chiefs of Staff Chairman General John Shalikashvilli stressed that any force sent into Bosnia had to be sized "sufficiently large so when they have to go in they are robust enough to take care of themselves." He added that he wanted to ensure the force would not be "pushed around" the way the UN troops had been."[44] In the minds of many

Americans, peacekeeping, as it was practiced by the UN in Bosnia and elsewhere has been "discredited."[45] Put more bluntly by *Washington Post* columnist Charles Krauthammer, "peacekeeping is for chumps."[46]

For Canadians, whose troops bravely, honorably and usefully served the United Nations in the former Yugoslavia, these may appear as an inaccurate and indeed unfair assessments. Nevertheless, the more the U.N.'s velvet glove takes advantage of NATO's iron fist, there is little doubt whose hand holds the leash on what former Defense Secretary Perry assured Congress would be "the biggest, toughest, the meanest dog in town"[47] operations which are contracted out to American-led coalitions because they hold the potential for high intensity combat may increasingly be beyond Canada's capacity, militarily and politically.

Recent trends and changes in peacekeeping also appear to be having an impact on Canadian conduct and not only in the case of Bosnia. Despite its decision to augment available forces for peacekeeping and the proposal for a new U.N. "vanguard force," the Chrétien government has moved away from the activism of the Mulroney years. At the end of 1993, Canada had nearly 5,000 peacekeepers in U.N. operations. With the end of the U.N. operation in Yugoslavia, Canada had only 900 peacekeepers, nearly all in two UN operations—on the Golan Heights, which dates back to 1974, and in Haiti.[48]

Still, there remains a role for classic peacekeeping, and this is where Canada with declining, yet highly skilled forces, can continue to make a contribution to regional stability. The Canadians can be part of more lightly armed U.N. troops which go into areas where all parties consent to the deployment or where prior American intervention has eliminated opposition by force and insured that there is a peace to keep, as in Haiti. For these operations, a new U.N. operational headquarters and rapid reaction force, along the lines Canada has proposed, might be useful for the United States, although the Clinton administration has stated that it will not commit its U.S. forces in advance to the United Nations.

Any reform of peacekeeping, whether American ground forces participate in specific operations or not, will require U.S. backing as Washington makes major change in New York a condition of its continued support for peacekeeping. And while Washington will no doubt encourage Canada to sustain its interest, many other countries can now be called upon to contribute, including former Warsaw Pact nations and former Soviet republics whose participation will carry more political significance for the United States than Canada's participation. Indeed, the Clinton administration has encouraged PfP nations to train for peacekeeping operations, and in October 1995 U.S. and Russian troops held a joint peacekeeping exercise in the United States.

In an ironic twist, what has happened is not the Canadianization of American defense policy but the Americanization of peacekeeping in a manner that may well deprive Ottawa of the opportunity to use this activity to cut a distinct (unAmerican) international figure. In the long run, trends in both American and Canadian policy suggest that Canada-U.S. collaboration in multilateral peacekeeping may well have reached its high-water mark.

Conclusion

There is no need to regret the end of the Canadian-U.S. defense relationship. After all, it is the result of victory in the Cold War-a victory that amply justified the close collaboration of those decades. Moreover, the decline of this relationship will have benefits for both countries and a positive impact on any future military collaboration.

The dream of the anti-American English Canadian nationalist has come true: Canada is no longer "partner to behemoth" or "powder monkey" on the American national security ship of state. For Canadians and the Ottawa government, it means that they need fear no more "annihilation without representation" or agonize over the threat to their independence and sovereignty as a result of very close military collaboration with the United States. Canada will still live in the shadow of the United States, now the world's sole superpower, but Canada and the United States will be free to conduct bilateral military relations in a way that more clearly reflects the enormous disparity in military power, international status, and global responsibilities between the two.

The benefit of all this is that frictions which have arisen in the bilateral relationship because of Canadian sovereignty concerns over defense issues will wane. They will arise again only if Ottawa itself chooses to become more heavily involved in American-led activities whether in North America through an accelerated NORAD BMD role, in Europe through NATO actions in the East, or "out of area" through participation in coalitions and U.S.-backed U.N. peace enforcement efforts.

What is coming to an end is the cooperation between Canada and the United States in the defense of the West-not all military links between the two countries. This will continue in a scaled-back NORAD, in Europe through minimal alliance ties, and at the United Nations through participation in classic peacekeeping. Ottawa will no doubt wish to sustain these links for the sake of Canada's international standing as a G-7 nation, as part of the Canadian identity and self-perception, and for the sake of maintaining a high degree of professionalism within the Canadian forces. At the same time, given Canada's declining interest in NATO and the tenuous nature of new forms of "out of area" cooperation, strictly North America security may, by virtue of simple geography and costs, come to represent Canada's most important military link with the United States, even as NORAD and other forms of continental military ties fade.[49]

What could bring even this reduced level of bilateral collaboration to a complete end would be Canada's domestic woes-namely the unresolved national unity question. The razor thin "non" vote in the 30 October 1995 Quebec referendum afforded only a reprieve, not a pardon for a federal government which badly misjudged the strength of separatism. English Canadians may "love" Quebec, but it is clear they and their provincial governments are unwilling to recognize and entrench Quebec's distinctiveness in the Canadian constitution. The final chapter in the Canada-U.S. defense relationship could come about simply because Canada itself may come to an end.

This article is based on a paper released in 1996 simultaneously by the Queen's University Centre for International Relations and the Center for Strategic and International Studies in Washington, D.C.

Notes

1. John W. Holmes, *Canada: A Middle-Aged Power* (Toronto: McClelland and Stewart, 1976), 128.

2. United States, White House, *A National Strategy of Engagement and Enlargement* (Washington, D.C., July 1994)

3. Canada, Department of Foreign Affairs and International Trade, *Canada and the World* (Ottawa, 1995), 24. See also, Canada, Department of National Defence, *1994 Defence White Paper* (Ottawa: Minister of Supply and Services, 1994), hereafter cited as *1994 White Paper*.

4. Briefing by Maj. Gen. J. D. O'Blenis, Commander, Fighter Group Canadian NORAD Region, Ottawa, 31 May 1990.

5. Remarks by Deputy CINCNORAD Major General J.D. O'Blenis to a conference on "Rethinking the Canada-United States Military Relationship," Ottawa, 19–20 March 1994.

6. Lt. Col. David Bashow, "NORAD, Past, Present and Future," *Forum* 8 (fall 1993): 80.

7. Eric Schmitt, "Foreign Policy Plan of G.O.P. Is Set Back Over Missiles," *New York Times*, 16 February 1995, A9.

8. Helen Dewar, "Senate Backs Missile Plan, Adds Funding for Weapons," *Washington Post*, 7 September 1995, A2.

9. Canada, Department of National Defence, Maritime Command, *The Naval Vision: Charting The Course for Canada's Maritime Forces into the 21st Century* (Halifax, 1994), 17–25.

10. See for example, James Minifie, *Peacemaker or Powder Monkey: Canada's Role in a Revolutionary World* (Toronto: McClelland and Stewart, 1960) and John W. Warnock, *Partner to Behemoth: The Military Policy of a Satellite Canada* (Toronto: New Press, 1970).

11. Nils Orvik, "The Basic Issue in Canadian National Security: Defence Against Help, Defence To Help Others," *Canadian Defence Quarterly* 11 (May-June 1983): 3–7.

12. *1994 White Paper*, 35.

13. Kim Richard Nossal, "A European Nation? The Life and Times of Atlanticism In Canada," in *Making a Difference: Canada's Foreign Policy in a Changing World Order*, ed. John English and Norman Hillmer (Toronto: Lester Publishing, 1992), 96.

14. *1994 White Paper*, 2.

15. Ibid., 34.

16. Ibid.

17. Paul Koring, "Canadian Troops to Go Back to Bosnia," *Globe and Mail*, 19 October 1995, A16.

18. Qtd. in Ibid.

19. Paul Koring, "Chrétien Hedges on Bosnia Mission," *Globe and Mail*, 20 October 1995, A5.

20. Helen Branswell, "Canada Tries to Cool Expectations about Role in Peace Enforcement," *Ottawa Citizen*, 6 December 1995, A6.

21. Jeff Sallot, "Canada Commits Force of 1,000 to Bosnian Mission," *Globe and Mail*, 7 December 1995, A1.

22. Ibid, A1, A6.

23. Jeff Sallot, "'Moral Obligation' Seen in Bosnia," *Globe and Mail*, 6 December 1995, A1, A6.

24. Sallot, "Canada Commits," A6.

25. Marjorie Ann Browne, "United Nations Peacekeeping: Historical Overview and Current Issues," *CRS Report for Congress* (Washington, D.C.: Congressional Research Service, The Library of Congress, 31 January, 1990), i.

26. J.L. Granatstein, "Peacekeeping: Did Canada Make a Difference? And What difference Did Peacekeeping Make to Canada?" in *Making a Difference*, ed. English and Hillmer, 231.

27. United States, Congress, Senate, Committee on Armed Services, Subcommittee on Coalition Defense and Reinforcing Forces, Hearing, 12 May 1994,

United Nations Peace Operations (Washington, D.C.: Government Printing Office, 1994), 5–6.

28. As quoted in Heather Smith, "Seeking Certainty and Finding None: Reflections on the 1994 Canadian Foreign Policy Review," *Canadian Foreign Policy* 3 (spring 1995): 122.

29. See, Andrew Cooper, Richard Higgot, and Kim Nossal, "Bound to Follow? Leadership and Follwership in the Gulf Conflict," *Political Science Quarterly* 106 (fall 1993): 391–410.

30. Prime Minister Chrétien, along with a group of provincial Premiers, embarked to China in the fall of 1994 in an attempt to increase trade relations between Canada and the Far East. In early 1995 a similar delegation traveled throughout Latin America in a similar attempt to increase Canadian business in that region as well. This is line with the general trend in Canadian foreign policy under the Liberals. See, Andrew Cohen, "Canada in the World: The Return of the National Interest," *Behind The Headlines* 52 (summer 1995).

31. *1994 White Paper*, 37.

32. Rod Mickleburgh, "Canada Holds Talks with Chinese Military," *Globe and Mail*, 18 March 1995, A1, A13.

33. Denis Stairs, "The Public Politics of the Canadian Defence and Foreign Policy Review," *Canadian Foreign Policy* 3 (spring 1995): 105.

34. Jeff Sallot, "Collenette Orders Increase in Peacekeeping Force Abroad," *Globe and Mail*, 11 September 1995, A5.

35. Canada, *Towards A Rapid Reaction Capability For the United Nations* (Ottawa, September 1995).

36. *Defence Newsletter* (Dalhousie University, Halifax, N.S.), 14 (September 1995): 4.

37. Canada, Department of Foreign Affairs and International Trade, *News Release*, No. 176, "Canada Tables Its Report on A Rapid Reaction Capability for the UN," 26 September 1995.

38. Victoria Holt, *The U.S. Role in United Nations Peace Operations* (Washington D.C.: Council for a Livable World Education Fund, 1994), 4.

39. See for example, U.S. Department of the Army, *FM 100-23: Peace Operations* (Washington D.C., December 1994).

40. Marjorie Ann Browne, "United Nations Peacekeeping: Issues for Congress," *CRS Issue Brief* (Washington, D.C.: Congressional Research Service, The Library of Congress, 22 September 1995), 15.

41. The White House Presidential Decision Directive 25, *The US Policy on Reforming Multilateral Peace Operations*, unclassified version, (Washington, D.C., 6 May 1994).

42. U.S., Congress, *United Nations Peace Operations*, 5.

43. Text of President's remarks of 27 November 1995, *New York Times*, 28 November 1995, A6.

44. Eric Schmitt, "As Prospects in Bosnia Brighten G.O.P. Doubts a Need for G.I.," *New York Times*, 22 September 1995, A12.

45. Robert Burns, "U.S. Troops in Line to Keep Peace in Bosnia," *Herald Sun* (Durham, N.C.), 16 September 1995, A1, A3.

46. Charles Krauthammer, "Peacekeeping is for Chumps," *Saturday Night*, November 1995, 73.

47. John Diamond, "Officials Try to Sell Senate on Sending Troops to Bosnia," *Herald-Sun*, (Durham, N.C.), 18 October 1995, A4.

48. Paul Koring, "Dropping the Peacekeeping Torch," *Globe and Mail*, 7 October 1995, A10.

49. Joel J. Sokolsky and David Detomasi, "Canadian Defense Policy and the Future of Canada-United States Security Relations," *American Review of Canadian Studies* 24 (winter 1994): 538.

OF NEWSPAPERS AND NARRATIVES

COVERAGE OF CANADIAN POLITICAL AND ECONOMIC AFFAIRS IN THREE MAJOR U.S. NEWSPAPERS

William W. Joyce
Michigan State University

To a considerable extent what we know about a nation, its people and institutions is controlled by the media: newspapers, news magazines, and television constitute the major sources of information from which images about a nation are created.[1] Senior government officials learn about other nations through a variety of sources, some of which are first hand, but they too, are greatly influenced by the media. When a president, premier, or prime minister of one nation expresses interest in another nation, Canada, for example, for whatever reason, we can expect the media to discover that same interest. [2] The media can play a powerful role in framing and setting an agenda for public opinion and public action.[3] There is a growing body of knowledge attesting to the critical influence of perceived image in the crafting of foreign policy.[4] Kenneth Boulding's insightful comment on images is particularly relevant here: "A nation is a complex of images of the persons who contemplate it. [Policy makers] do not respond to the objective facts of the situation . . . but to their 'image' of the situation."[5]

This article centers on "images" of Canada presented in the U.S. press. Issues of the *New York Times, Wall Street Journal,* and *Washington Post* published before and after the general elections of 1993 were analyzed to determine the extent and nature of coverage

accorded Canada's political and economic affairs during this tu-
multuous period. The analysis encompassed these elements:

1. How Canada's coverage compared with that of other
   nations of the world.
2. The nature of the content of stories published.
3. Major themes of stories on Canada's general elections and
   its participation in the North American Free Trade
   Agreement (NAFTA).

A few previous studies have assessed Canada's images in the
foreign press. David Hutchison's 1994 study examined Canadian
coverage in six British newspapers in 1991 and again a year later
during the national referendum of 1992. The second phase of his
study yielded three times the coverage that Canada received a year
earlier and claimed that some of the more recent coverage was inaccurate, highly biased, opinionated, and some in cases blatantly
offensive: Fred Langan, a journalist at the *Telegraph* (London) described the citizens of Manitoba as a "million stubborn, bitter people living in a cold, isolated place," New Brunswick as "a feudal
place of fish, trees, and potatoes, ruled by several rich families"
and the Northwest Territories as "Home to Indians, Eskimos who
like to be called Innuit, and eccentric whites who live in
Yellowknife." He called British Columbia "lotus land," Ontario
"probably the most Canadian place in Canada," and Quebec, "What
all the fuss is about."[6]
  Characteristic of articles about the referendum, according to
Hutchison, was their tendency to editorialize about important implications of Quebec's departure from Canadian confederation.
Though such reporting can provoke interest in Canada, it can produce unintended biases, one of which was the lack of attention
given to attitudes in the western provinces toward secession.
  T. A. Keenleyside and Peter Gatti investigated the treatment of
Canada by major U.S., British, and French newspapers (the
Washington Post, the *Times of London*, and *Le Monde*, respectively).
They found that, in terms of frequency of coverage, Canada ranked
35th among the nations of the world in *Le Monde*, 29th in the *Times*,
and 17th in the *Post*. Stereotypical images of Canada surfaced in all
three papers.[7]
  Despite the dissimilarity of these studies, they are in accord on
one important point: the United States press gives Canada limited
coverage in proportion to its importance to the United States. The

coverage Canada receives in the U.S. press belies its stature as our leading trading partner.[8]

The Study

Issues of the *New York Times, Wall Street Journal*, and *Washington Post* published from 1 September 1993 to 31 December 1993 were analyzed for their coverage of political and economic events in Canada and elsewhere in the world. This period was selected because it encompassed one of the most volatile times in recent Canadian history — a period likely to elicit extensive coverage from the U.S. press. The most significant event was the Liberal Party's landslide victory in the October general elections and the election of Jean Chrétien as prime minister. The importance of the Liberals' stunning return to power after a nine-year hiatus can be discerned from these statistics: their 25 October victory reduced the Torys' House of Commons strength from 155 seats to only 2 — by far the worst defeat in the history of any Canadian political party — and gave Chrétien's Liberals a comfortable 177-seat majority. Concurrent with the destruction of the Tory Party, two regional parties, the Eastern Bloc Quebecois and the Western-based conservative, populist Reform Party, gained fifty-four and fifty-two seats respectively. Their victories signaled a widening of the anti-and pro-Federalism rift and added to the ominous challenges confronting Prime Minister Chrétien and his Liberal Party.

These dramatic changes in Canada's landscape were accentuated by other problems, both economic and political: Canada's $26 billion federal deficit; a foreign debt load of $225 billion — the largest among the industrialized nations of the world — and an 11.2 percent unemployment rate, also among the world's highest; lukewarm domestic support for Canadian participation in the North American Free Trade Agreement; growing hostility toward government; and Chrétien's refusal to endorse special status for Quebec (one Bloc Quebecois poster read, "Christ had his Judas; Quebec has its Chrétien").

The *New York Times, Wall Street Journal*, and *Washington Post* were selected for their outstanding reputations as news sources and also because of the likelihood that they would be good sources of coverage of Canadian affairs. The *Journal* and *Times* can be regarded as national newspapers, as evidenced by their widespread distribution throughout the United States.

During the four-month study, 122 issues of the *Times* and *Post* and 88 of the *Journal* were analyzed for a total of 332 issues. The discrepancy can be attributed to the *Journal's* five-day-a-week publishing schedule, which contrasts with the seven-day-a-week schedule of the *Times* and *Post*.

A four-member team coded and analyzed the newspapers. Their analysis procedures, based on the work of Ole Holsti,[9] yielded a coder reliability established at 88 percent. The analysts examined the front page, the first section, and the international/foreign news, editorial, business, and "op-ed" sections for content on Canada and other nations. For a nation or a Canadian story to be counted in this study, it must have received at least ten lines of coverage of political and/or economic news. Stories centering on other topics (sports, travel, the fine arts, etc.) were excluded from the study. Canadian stories were analyzed in a variety of dimensions; the results are reported in the next section.

Findings

Coverage of Canadian political and economic affairs in the *New York Times, Wall Street Journal*, and *Washington Post* varied considerably. In terms of frequency of coverage determined by the number of times a nation was the subject of a news story on its political or economic affairs, Canada's ranking of thirtieth in the *Times* was equal to that of the new nation, Georgia, and slightly lower than that of North Korea. Canada fared better in the *Wall Street Journal*, attaining a ranking of 10th, which is slightly below France and slightly above Somalia. Canadian coverage in the *Times* received the lowest ranking, thirtieth, alongside Sri Lanka.

These findings demonstrate that despite the turmoil associated with the fall 1993 elections and its entry into the NAFTA, Canada received limited attention in two of the three major U.S. newspapers used in the study. Since these papers consistently cover more international stories than other U.S. papers while maintaining huge nationwide circulations, it becomes apparent that with the exception of the *Journal* the U.S. press is providing its citizenry with exceedingly sparse coverage of Canada.

Tables 1-3 show the approximate length of the Canadian stories as well as their titles. It was difficult to determine the precise length of each story, owing to the inclusion of photos, charts, and other visuals in some stories; moreover, there were some variations in the number of characters per line of type between the three newspapers. Titles of stories cited in these tables were expanded to include subtitles in an effort to convey maximum information about each story.

During the four-month period observed, the *Journal* published more stories on Canada (27) and devoted more lines of print (2,739) than did the *Times* or *Post*. The *Journal's* extensive Canadian coverage over the duration of this study is remarkable, as this paper published only 88 issues, compared to the 122 issues published by both the *Times* and the *Post*.

The length of Canadian stories varied considerably within and between the three newspapers. Though the *Post* ran fewer Canadian articles (17) than the *Journal* (27) and the *Times* (20), the *Times* (20), the *Post's* stories tended to provide greater depth and more intensive coverage of Canadian issues than those of the other two papers. Thirteen of the *Post's* 17 Canadian stories were between 100 and 200 lines in length, while 11 of the *Time's* 20 stories and 7 of the *Journal's* 27 stories were this length. Even more revealing perhaps, is the high number of Canadian stories of 100 lines or fewer in two of these newspapers. Twenty of the *Journal's* 27 stories (78%) and 9 of the *Times'* 20 stories (52%) were 100 lines or fewer.

From this analysis of the number and length of stories in the three newspapers we can conclude that although the *Wall Street Journal* ran the most stories on Canada, this paper's stories tended to be shorter and more condensed than those in the other two newspapers; indeed, more than a few bore a resemblance to stories commonly appearing in *USA Today*. Judged in terms of depth of coverage of Canada stories, the *Washington Post* was the winner.

Table 4 reports data on the frequency and content of the Canadian stories in the three newspapers. This table attests to the paucity of press coverage Canada received in the fall of 1993. With the largest number of Canadian stories and the least detailed coverage, the *Wall Street Journal* carried an article on Canada about once in every three issues. In contrast, a story on Canada appeared in the *Washington Post* about once every five issues. Finally, the reader will note that stories on the general elections and Canada's participation in NAFTA tended to dominate Canadian coverage in the *Times* and *Post*, but not in the *Journal*.

Table 1. Canadian Stories in the *New York Times*,
1 September - 31 December 1993.

Date/Approx. Length	Title
1 Sept./80 Lines	"A Mythical Medical Monster" (Douglas Copeland)
8 Sept. /65 Lines	"Canadian to Call General Election; Campbell Expected to Make Announcement Today and Set Vote for October 25" (Clyde H. Farnsworth)
15 Sept./98 Lines	"Premier of Quebec to Quit in January; Ottawa to Lose Strong Voice for Keeping the Province within the Federation" (Clyde H. Farnsworth)
15 Sept./212 Lines	"UAW and Ford Bargain Past Deadline for a Strike" (James Bennet)
22 Oct./108 Lines	"A New Party in Western Canada Growing on Protest and Populism" (Clyde H. Farnsworth)
24 Oct./137 Lines	"Voting in Canada Can Affect Relation with the U.S."
25 Oct./68 Lines	"Canada Votes Today with Polls Suggesting a Victory by Liberals" (Clyde H. Farnsworth)

(table 1 cont.)

26 Oct./264 Lines	"Governing Tories in Canada Routed by Liberal Party; Quebec Bloc Gains; Voters Wait Jobs, Which May Mean New Talks on Free-Trade Pact"* (Clyde H. Farnsworth)
27 Oct./269 Lines	"Canadian with Mandate; Joseph Jacques Jean Chrétien"* (Clyde H. Farnsworth)
27 Oct./64 Lines	"Redrawing the Map in Canada"**
27 Oct./167 Lines	"U.S. Says Chrétien Will Not Undo NAFTA"
28 Oct./116 Lines	"Chrétien Says He Wants Changes in Trade Accord" (Clyde H. Farnsworth)
28 Oct./47 Lines	"New Canada Party Surges in Election; Disgruntled Voters in West Give Reformists a Voice" (Timothy Egan)
30 Oct./56 Lines	"Canada's Quarrel with NAFTA" **
31 Oct./134 Lines	"Quebec Bloc Set for Ottawa Role: Leader of the New Separatist Opposition Asserts Focus will be on Economics" (Clyde H. Farnsworth)

---

* Front page story
** Editorial

(table 1 cont.)

9 Nov. /253 Lines	"Canada Links Trade Pact to an Accord on Subsidies" (Clyde H. Farnsworth)
13 Nov./151 Lines	"Two Towns Do Battle Over Canada's Rain Forest"
22 Nov./38 Lines	"Canada Renews Call to Modify Trade Pact"
13 Dec. /235 Lines	"Canada's Morals Police: Serious Books at Risk?" (Sarah Lycell)
13 Dec. /66 Lines	"Campbell Resigns as Tory Leader in Canada" (Clyde H. Farnsworth)

**Editorial

Total Lines: 2,702

Table 2. Canadian Stories in the *Wall Street Journal*,
1 September - 31 December 1993.

Date/Approx. Length	Title
23 Sept./199 Lines	"Family Rift Threatens McCain Food; Canadian Village Watches Its Livelihood at Stake" (Christopher J. Chipello)
27 Sept./33 Lines	"McCain Brothers Pursue an Out-of-Court Settlement"
11 Oct./80 Lines	"Canadian Mining Companies Prepare for Big Exploration Program in Cuba" (Rosanna Tamburri)
11 Oct./79 Lines	"Quebec's Independence Advocates Set for Gains in National Elections" (Christopher Chipello)
14 Oct./33 Lines	"Canada's Liberal Party Looks Likely to Win Vote"
26 Oct./225 Lines	"Canada Election Won by Liberals Led by Chrétien; Party Seeks to Rework NAFTA among other Disputes with U.S. on Trade!" (John Urquhart)
27 Oct./110 Lines	"Canadians Take Account"*

---

*Front page story

(table 2 cont.)

27 Oct./80 Lines	"Canada's Newly Elected Liberal Party Is Backed by Nation's Business Groups" (John Urquhart)
28 Oct./170 Lines	"Canadian Banks Set Their Sights on Insurance Business; Big Changes are Predicted for Sector in Wake of Deregulation" (Larry Grenberg)
28 Oct./61 Lines	"Integrated Health Services to Acquire Unit of Canada's THZEC for 86 Million"
28 Oct./61 Lines	"Canada Awaits Liberals' Move on Central Bank" (John Urquhart)
9 Nov./61 Lines	"MacDonald's Staff wants a Break Today at Canada Franchise; Teenage Employee Triggers First Campaign to Unionize a Fast Food Operation" (Mark Heinzl)
10 Nov./125 Lines	"Study Raises a Warning Flag about Canadian Health Care" (Ron Winslow)
23 Nov./74 Lines	"Ontario Anti-Smoking Law Aims to Cut Cigarette Sales in Half by Decade's End" (Mark Heinzl)
26 Nov./61 Lines	"Ratings are Cut on Ontario's Debt by Two Services" (Andrew Willis)

(table 2 cont.)

26 Nov./80 Lines	"Canadian Airlines Clears Big Hurdle in Deal with AMR" (Rosanna Tamburri)
30 Nov./73 Lines	"Canada's Liberal Government Predicts a Record High Deficit in Fiscal 1994" (John Urquhart and Christopher J. Chipello)
3 Dec./96 Lines	"Canada Clears NAFTA, Claims Improvements; Liberal Party Says it Won Changes to Trade Pact on Unfair Pricing Codes" (John Urquhart and Rosanna Tamburri)
3 Dec./116 Lines	"Jones Intercable Enters Accord with BCE Inc." (Mark Robichaux)
8 Dec./135 Lines	"A Canadian Judge Tries—Unsuccessfully— to Silence the Media" (Murray B. Light)
14 Dec./9 Lines	"Air Canada Plans Airbus Deal"
14 Dec./27 Lines	"Canada Ex-Prime Minister Resigns as Party Leader"
15 Dec./16 Lines	"Quebec Premier-Designate Named"
16 Dec./70 Lines	"Ford Plans Sharp Boost in Shipments between Mexico, the U.S. and Canada" (Robert L. Simison)

(table 2 cont.)

Dec. 16/59 Lines   "Socal Gas Offers Settlement to Producers in
                                    Canada to Renegotiate Supply Pact"

20 Dec./40 Lines   "U.S.-Canada Panel Seeks an End to Lumber
                                    Duties"

27 Dec./26 Lines   "Ontario, Quebec End Rules on
                                    Discriminatory Trade"

Total Lines: 2,739

Table 3. Canadian Stories in the *Washington Post,*
1 September - 31 December 1993.

Date/Approx. Length	Title
1 Sept./116 Lines	"Canada Closes Section of Atlantic to Fishing; 12,000 Expected to Lose Jobs; Dwindling Supply of Cod Leaves Scientists Mystified" (Anne Swardson)
9 Sept./169 Lines	"Elections in Canada Due October 25; New Tory Premier Faces Restive Voters" (Charles Trueheart)
15 Sept./154 Lines	"Quebec Premier Announces Resignation: Anti-Separatist Bourassa Leaving as Nationalists Showing Strength" (Charles Trueheart)
28 Sept./205 Lines	"Canadians Adapting to New Era of Trade; Workers Learn Lessons of Competition" (Anne Swardson)
10 Oct./171 Lines	"Quebec Separatists Seek Voice in Ottawa; Party Aims to Dominate Province's Delegation to Parliament after October 25 Vote" (Charles Trueheart)
18 Oct./188 Lines	"Coalition Possible for Canada as Tories Sink in Polls"* (Charles Trueheart)

*Front page story

(table 3 cont.)

18 Oct. /139 Lines	"Reform Party's Populist Appeal Winning Support Across Canada" (Charles Trueheart)
24 Oct./164 Lines	"Quebecer Chrétien Looks West to Win Canadian Premiership" (Charles Trueheart)
25 Oct./126 Lines	"Exasperated Canadians Jump for Jays: The Thrill of Victory, The Agony of Politics" (Anne Swardson)
26 Oct./115 Lines	"Canadian Liberals Win Vote: New Cabinet to Lead a House Divided Over Quebec's Future"* (Charles Trueheart)
26 Oct./72 Lines	"New Government Faces Threat of U.S. Wheat Quota" (Anne Swardson)
27 Oct./201 Lines	"Canada's Voters Awake to New Political Order; 2 out of 3 Replaced in Lower House"* (Charles Trueheart)
27 Oct./87 Lines	"Clinton Rejects Renegotiating Trade Pact" (Anne Devroy)

———————

*Front page story

(table 3 cont.)

28 Oct./156 Lines   "Canadian Still Seeks Changes in NAFTA; Premier-Elect wants to Renegotiate Points" (Anne Swardson)

30 Oct./65 Lines   "U.S. Tells Canada, Mexico Side Agreements are Vital" (Peter Behr)

5 Nov./143 Lines   "Chrétien Takes Charge in Canada; Prime Minister Starts Out Tough on Federal Spending, Quebec"

18 Nov./64 Lines   "New Barriers Traded for Votes" (Anne Swardson)

Total Lines: 2,335

Table 4. Canadian Stories in the *New York Times, Wall Street Journal,* and *Washington Post,* 1 September - 31 December 1993.

No. Lines of Print	*NYT*	*WSJ*	*WP*
Canadian Stories	2,702	2,739	2,335
No. Issues Published	122	88	122
No. Canadian Stories	21	27	17
Avg. No. Canadian Stories per Issue	0.17	0.30	0.14
No. Canadian Stories on Elections/NAFTA	17	12	15
Canadian Stories on Elections/NAFTA as a % of Total	80%	44%	88%

Table 5. Type of Canadian Stories in the *New York Times*, *Wall Street Journal*, and *Washington Post*, 1 September - 31 December 1993.

	NYT	*WSJ*	*WP*
No. Issues	122	88	22
No. Canadian Stories	21	27	7
Avg. No. Issues per Story			
Banking		1	
Communications		1	
Constitutional Rights	1	1	
Ecology	1		
Energy		1	
Fishing		2	
Food		2	
General Elections	10	7	10
Health	1	3	
Inter-Provincial		1	
Labor Management	1	2	
Mining		1	
NAFTA	7	1	5
Ontario		1	
Quebec	1	2	
U.S.-Canada Issues		1	1

Table 5 provides a more intensive analysis of the Canadian stories in the three newspapers. Some stories had to be multi-coded because they centered on more than one topic. This was especially true with stories on the general elections and Canada's participation in the North American Free Trade Agreement. Moreover, some stories pertaining to both the general elections and NAFTA were classified in accordance with the category receiving the greater emphasis. Some examples: "Voting in Canada Can Affect NAFTA, Expected Victory by Liberals Tomorrow May Bring Call to Reopen Trade Talks" (*New York Times*, 24 October 1993); "Canada Clears NAFTA, Claims Improvements; Liberal Party Says it Won Changes to Trade Pact on Unfair Pricing Codes" (*Wall Street Journal*, 3 December 1993); "Canadian Still Seeks Changes in NAFTA: Premier-Elect Wants to Renegotiate Points" (*Washington Post*, 28 October 28 1993).

Typically, stories on other topics were carried by only one of the three newspapers; rarely did comparable stories surface in the other papers. For example, a *Times* article on constitutional rights of Canadians, "Canada's Morals Police: Serious Books at Risk?" (13 December 1993) centers on rigorous application of Canada's anti-obscenity laws, while a second article entitled "A Canadian Judge Tries – unsuccessfully – to Silence the Media," (*Wall Street Journal*, 8 December 1993), probes issues of freedom of speech. Both articles were grouped under the heading, "Constitutional Rights." Similarly, the vast majority of the business-related stories were carried by one newspaper, the *Wall Street Journal*, and rarely appeared in the other papers.

Themes of stories on the general elections and NAFTA are presented in tables 6 and 7 respectively.

Table 6. Coverage of Canadian General Elections by the *New York Times*, *Wall Street Journal*, and *Washington Post*, 1 September - 31 December 1993.

Theme of Stories	*NYT*	*WSJ*	*WP*
1. Quebec Premier Boarassa Resigns	x	x	x
2. Kim Campbell accused of running unfocused, erratic campaign			x
3. Voters in cantankerous, punitive frame of mind; political choices unappealing			x
4. New party in west growing on protest and populism	x		x
5. Voting in Canada can affect NAFTA	x		
6. Polls suggest Liberal Party victory	x		
7. Liberal Party steamrolls opposition	x	x	x
8. Rise of Bouchard's Bloc Quebecois and Manning's Reform Party raise spectre of Canadian disunity	x	x	x
9. Newly elected members of Parliament lack experience			x
10. Chrétien's mandate: jobs, trade, budget deficit, and national unity	x	x	x
11. Chrétien seeks to keep Canada independent of the U.S.	x	x	x
12. Liberal Party backed by business groups; Chrétien picks pro trade Cabinet	x	x	
13. Liberal Party predicts high deficit in 1994		x	
14. Bloc Quebecois will form official opposition in House of Commons			x
15. Campbell resigns as Tory leader	x	x	x

Table 7. Coverage of NAFTA by the *New York Times, Wall Street Journal,*
and *Washington Post,* 1 September - 31 December 1993.

Theme of Stories	*NYT*	*WSJ*	*WP*
1. Chrétien seeks to renegotiate NAFTA	x	x	x
2. Clinton rejects renegotiation of NAFTA	x	x	x
3. U.S. restriction on Canadian durum wheat exported to U.S. could disrupt Canadian ratification of NAFTA			x
4. Canada's private sector unprepared for FTA in 1989, may not be prepared for NAFTA either			x
5. Ford plans sharp boost in shipment of cars between Mexico, U.S., Canada		x	

Only five of the fourteen—Bourassa's resignation, the Liberal Party's stunning victory, the rise of the Bloc Quebec and the Reform Party, Chrétien's desire to keep Canada independent of the U.S., and Kim Campbell's resignation—were dominant, pervasive themes in all three newspapers.

Six weeks prior to the general elections, there was growing evidence that Kim Campbell was running an unfocused, erratic campaign, voters were in a cantankerous, punitive frame of mind and the Bloc Quebecois and Reform Party were flourishing. One politician claimed that voters were so disenchanted with the general elections that "Bugs Bunny could win 20 per cent of the vote if his name were on the ballot," wrote Charles Trueheart of the *Washington Post*.[10] Only the *New York Times* would later predict that the Liberals would win the election.

Other significant themes that appeared in the three newspapers included Voting in Canada can affect NAFTA (*New York Times*) and Newly elected members of Parliament lack experience (*Washington Post*). The former was one of the few themes in the three newspapers that explored relationships between the general elections and NAFTA via a series of provocative scenarios. The latter theme appeared solely in the *Post*, and commanded front-page status: "two of every three candidates elected will be newcomers to Parliament, most of them to political office of any kind" wrote Charles Trueheart (*Washington Post*, 27 October 1993). The situation ". . . could turn the House of Commons into an explosive laboratory of reform."[11]

Table 7 discloses themes of stories on Canadian participation in the North American Free Trade Agreement. Five themes emerged from the stories on NAFTA that appeared in the three newspapers. Only the first two themes—Prime Minister Chrétien's desire to renegotiate NAFTA and President Clinton's rejection of this request—appeared in all three newspapers. The publicity given these issues is probably warranted, especially because renegotiation of NAFTA was a campaign promise that Chrétien had made to the Canadian people prior to the Liberal Party's stunning victory in the 1993 general elections. More important, there is additional evidence attesting to the legitimacy of Chrétien's request: many Canadian concerns were not addressed in NAFTA, including a subsidies code, an anti dumping code, dispute resolution mechanisms, and the same energy protection as Mexico. Clinton, of course, saw renegotiation of NAFTA as a dangerous risk, one that could undermine passage of NAFTA in Congress. Ann Swardson, one of the *Post*'s Canada experts, wrote "with an economy one tenth the size of the U. S.'s Canada depends far more on trade to earn its livelihood. Moreover, Canada's economy was believed to be more hidebound, less efficient and more vulnerable to lower priced imports and relocation of factories to nations with cheaper labor."[12]

Each of the three remaining themes in table 7 surfaced in only one of the three newspapers. Themes (3) and (4), which were drawn from stories in the *Washington Post*, appear to have considerable long-range significance. The battle over U.S. restrictions on importation of Canadian durum wheat continues to rage today, and the private sector of the Canadian economy seems unable to deal effectively with the U.S.-Canada Free Trade Agreement or with NAFTA four years later.

Conclusion

This study documents the lack of sustained attention given to Canada by the U.S. press. Conducted during one of the most volatile periods in recent Canadian history—a period likely to elicit extensive U.S. press coverage—the data showed that the press coverage accorded the general elections and NAFTA was at the expense of other newsworthy events likely to interest U.S. readers. Indeed, during the four-month span of the study, the vast majority of the Canadian coverage of the *New York Times* and *Washington Post* was focused on the general elections and NAFTA. Other important topics of interest with political and economic relevance including health care, the state of the Canadian economy, and a variety of related social, environmental, and constitutional issues received almost no attention in the three papers.

The type of coverage accorded Canadian issues is another concern. Though most of the stories on Canada published in the *Times* and *Post* were written by established, respected Canada experts, such as Clyde Farnsworth (*Times*) and Anne Swardson and Charles Trueheart (*Post*), stories in the *Journal* were written by a variety of reporters, few of whom provided the detailed, insightful, well-researched reporting characteristic of better stories in the other two papers. Clearly, the *Post* and *Times* provided far more in-depth coverage of Canadian events than the *Journal*, but once the elections were over in late October and the post-election analyses had been published, news on Canada virtually vanished from the three papers. The worst offender, the *Post*, published only two stories on Canada in November and December of 1993.

The United States ignores Canada perhaps because the U.S. media ignore Canada. The political climate and the political character in Canada are changing rapidly. Fueled by high unemployment, the dramatic growth of contentious regional parties, and one of the highest national debts in the world, the new politics emerging in Canada are likely to produce sudden, perhaps often unanticipated changes in the not-too-distant future. The facts are that the ruling Progressive Conservative party's strength in the House of Commons plummeted from 155 seats to 2 seats in the 1993 elections; that the secession vote failed in Quebec in 1995 by less than ½ of 1 percent; that the incumbent Liberal government carried one province in the 1997 general election. We are looking at a lengthy and unendurable destabilization in a country that has borrowed the happy metaphor of "peaceable kingdom." It is to the advantage of the United States and other world powers to keep abreast of developments in Canada. The media must be a vital witness.

Acknowledgments

The author is grateful to Mary Joyce, Joshua Oberts, Theodore Rancour, Colin Francis, Debra Carpenter and Marian Stoll for their valuable contributions to this chapter.

Notes

1.   T. A. Keenleyside and Peter Gatti, "Still the Great White Blank? Canada in the American, British and French Press," *American Review of Canadian Studies* 22 (spring 1992): 39-64.

2.   Donald Flournoy et al., *Media images of Canada: U.S. Media Coverage of Canadian Issues and U.S. Awareness of Those Issues*, Ohio Journalism Monograph Series, No. 3, (Athens: E.W. Scripps School of Journalism, Ohio University, 1992).

3.   Janice Hanson and Constantina Skanavis, "A Comparative study of Canadian-U.S. Media Perspectives of the Environment at Risk." Paper presented to the conference of the Association for Canadian Studies in the United States, New Orleans, Louisiana, 1993, 17-21.

4.   Keenleyside and Gatti, 39.

5.   Kenneth Boulding, "National Images and International Systems," in *International Politics and Foreign Policy*, ed. James N. Rosenau (New York: Free Press, 1969), 422-31.

6.   David Hutchison, "The Reporting of Canada in the British Press," *British Journal of Canadian Studies* 9, no. 1 (1994): 1-14.

7.   Keenleyside and Gatti.

8.   Guido Stempel, "Preface," in Flournoy.

9.   Ole Holsti, *Content for the Social Sciences and Humanities* (Reading, Mass.: Addison-Wesley, 1964).

10.   Charles Trueheart, "Elections in Canada Due October 25," *Washington Post*, 9 September 1993, A-29.

11.   Charles Trueheart, *Washington Post*, 27 October 1993, 1.

12.   Ann Swardson, "Canadian Workers Learn Lessons of Free Trade," *Washington Post*, 28 September 1993, A-32.

KALEIDOSCOPIC CULTURE
THE NATION WITHOUT A NARRATIVE

Elspeth Cameron
University of Toronto

The Meech Lake debates, the Charlottetown Accord, the 1992 Referendum, the 1993 General Election and the 1995 Referendum in Quebec all illustrate clearly that Canadians are far from having a common concept of nationhood. Many have expressed the opinion—indeed many have expressed the hope—that Canada will fragment into some loose association of political and economic entities. Public discussion has focused almost exclusively on political, economic and constitutional issues. But we must also take heed of those deeper truths of national sensibility which, in their expression, we call culture.

I want to explore the changing ideological context in Canada. This ongoing process of acculturation is partly the result of the imaginative representations of identity by Canadian artists and the shape of Canadian cultural institutions, and is at the same time the context within which those same artists and institutions must function. I also want to comment on the ways in which culture is funded in Canada, since the ideological context and the mechanisms for funding the arts are interrelated.

At the end of World War II, Canada clearly identified itself as a place of two nations. Hugh MacLennan's classic, *Two Solitudes*, dramatized the inconsistent, even incompatible, values held by those two entities. English Canadians, he argued, are rooted in a Protestant, Puritan, rational tradition, somewhat biased in favor of science and industry and somewhat biased against art. French Canadians, in contrast, are rooted in a Catholic, Jansenist, mystic tradition, uncomfortable with the advance of science and comfortable with the emotional expressiveness of art.[1]

The Royal Commission on Bilingualism and Biculturalism, the "B and B," as it was called, established in the early 1960s, reflected this dichotomy, thereby influencing the development of a number of cultural measures and regulations. Such measures — especially language regulations that enshrine French as the language of commerce and education — have ensured that the French Canadian culture will not be assimilated by the English Canadian culture. Assimilation has always been a threat mainly because of the North American and increasingly, a global market preference for English. The advent of computers and the Internet have probably confirmed this preference for the foreseeable future.

MacLennan's *Two Solitudes* was misunderstood. Or rather, the realities of history and of contemporary political and economic needs, proved more powerful than art in shaping the two-nation myth. The sentimental conclusion to that novel (wherein the all-Canadian boy, half French/half English and with a fondness for hockey, marries an American girl and resolves the national schizophrenia) extols an unabashed assimilation of the French. The very term "Two Solitudes," which MacLennan intended as a model for harmonious cohabitation, now stands for prickly and irreconcilable differences between two partners who are close to divorce. It is worth noting that this preoccupation with "two nations" does not take into account any other national groups in Canada. The first peoples, for example, are completely overlooked. What endures is a perception of Canada, both from within and from beyond its borders, as a country with two languages, two religions and two cultures.

In 1947, with a post-war population of little more than twelve million, Prime Minister William Lyon Mackenzie King called for increased immigration "to enlarge the population of Canada" which was too small "to hold so great a heritage as ours."[2]

King, of course, meant the *British* heritage. It never occurred to him that encouraging immigration might transform that heritage.

Nor did it occur to the B and B Commission that it would discover that already, in the mid-1960s, one-quarter (soon, one-third) of the nation was neither French nor English! Moreover, what was yet to be appreciated was that these national groups: Italian, Greek, Pakistani, Japanese, German, Polish, Ukrainian — would express anxiety about being marginalized and consigned to a perpetual lower status in this bilingual/bicultural state. As was surely fitting for those who had been enjoined to maintain "our great heritage," these communities wanted to help formulate a Canadian culture. The views of this third "solitude" were recorded in the fourth volume of the B and B report, almost as an afterthought. The title of that volume, *The Contribution of Other Ethnic Groups*, suggests actions completed rather than actions contemplated, or not yet begun.

In her Afterword to *The Journals of Susanna Moodie*, Margaret Atwood observed that *all* Canadians are immigrants. This is surely evident in our culture which many observers have noted is constructed of layer upon layer of veneer. But as the twentieth century draws to a close, we have come to accommodate an international, multiethnic identity which includes such figures as Japanese-Canadian painter Takao Tanabe, Australian novelist Janette Turner Hospital and Trinidad writer Neil Bissoondath. Michael Ondaatje, co-winner of the Booker Prize, is of Sri Lankan and Dutch descent. *The English Patient* is not only not set in Canada but has only one Canadian character.

Since the B and B report made visible the hitherto invisible facts about the other "solitude," Canada has been recognized and has recognized itself as a a multi-cultural nation. In his 1971 reply to the B and B, Pierre Eliott Trudeau confirmed that "We believe that cultural pluralism is the very essence of Canadian identity. Every ethnic group has the right to preserve and develop its own culture and values within the Canadian context." Trudeau saw no inconsistency or problem in the coexistence of multiculturalism and bilingualism: "To say that we have two official languages is not to say we have two official cultures."[3]

Despite the credence given multiculturalism since the mid-1960s, and despite the creation of a multicultural directorate within the Department of the Secretary of State in 1973, no legislation was passed to enforce the rights of ethnic groups. In fact, the multiculturalism directorate set three goals which clearly demonstrated that multiculturalism was supposed to exist within the bi-partite English/French culture:

* to help maintain ethnic culture
* to foster cross-cultural understanding
* to integrate immigrants through teaching the two official languages.

Furthermore, there was not nearly as much money made available through this office as there was for mainstream cultural activities through the Canada Council and similar veteran agencies. The Francophone attitude to the emergence of multiculturalism has been unrelentingly hostile. A Quebec cleric stated in Le Droit in 1976: "We cannot help but see this as an insidious and steady shift away from biculturalism toward a crushing of Francophonie's special needs under the political weight of multiculture."[4]

Rene Levesque put it this way: "Multiculturalism is really folklore. It is a red herring . . . to obscure the Quebec business, to give an impression that we are all ethnics and do not have to worry about special status for Quebec."[5]

The 1982 Charter of Rights and Freedoms—a document with profound implications for Canadian identity—upheld the ideal of multiculturalism without articulating ethnic rights or detailing clear obligations. Article 27 describes multiculturalism simply as a "quality of Canadian life" and promises that all other articles of the Charter will be interpreted in a manner consistent with multiculturalism. The double standard implicit here has been addressed by Robert Harney in a 1988 article in Daedelus:

> It is not at all unusual or destructive of consensus in the political discourse for French Canadian spokesmen and those of aboriginal peoples to describe policies that encourage acculturation and assimilation into anglophone Canada as cultural genocide. Very few Canadians would, however, tolerate expressions of a similar kind about the rights of ethnic groups.[6]

When Mackenzie King spoke in 1947 of "our great heritage" 50 percent of Canadians were of British descent, 30 percent of French descent. Forty years later, less than 40 percent were from either British or French background. The Multicultural Act of 1987 affirmed this reality but did not provide mechanisms that would enforce its goals.

The multicultural myth "decentralized" Canadians' perception of their land. Whereas the "two-nation" view focused on the central Canadian conflict between the English and the French, the multicultural sanction has strengthened regional affiliations and allegiances to the Prairies, the Maritimes, the Pacific coast or to the North. This sanction was fostered by artists who might once have been distressed to be known as a "regionalist" but who began to take pride in expressing the special sensibilities of their immediate environments.

One of the most important consequences of multiculturalism and the coincident new pride in regionalism has been the way in which Canada's aboriginal peoples—one thinks of playwright Thomson Highway and poet/dramatist David Daniel Moses—have asserted their rights and cultures through mainstream artistic productions. No longer are Canada's first peoples content to be stereotyped as quaint carvers of the North or as ceremonial curiosities dressed up in folk costume for royal visits. To regard Canada as the "two nation" land of French and English is to overlook the crucial fact that both these nations had colonized and exploited the original owners. Severely marginalized, virtually ignored, the first peoples now argue that they ought to be reinstated to a special place of privilege vis-à-vis both the two "founding nations" and their multicultural successors. As the provisions of the Charlottetown Accord made clear, there is a third view of Canada in which the first peoples are seen to have parallel powers aside from, but contingent upon, those of both the "founders" and the multicultural groups.

These three "ideological conceptualizations" are clearly incompatible. We cannot regard French Canada as a "distinct society" *and* simultaneously accept Canada as a collection of ethnic communities among which French Canada would have a diminished status as simply one among many ethnic or religious or linguistic groups. And if the special place of the first peoples is to be recognized, neither of the other two definitions of Canada can remain quite as they were.

Is Canada, then, a nation without a coherent narrative which characterizes its essence? Is such a narrative conceivable in a country where the appropriation of *artistic voice* is a continuing issue? Does a White writer have the capability, even the right, to produce a novel from the point of view of a Black, Asian, or Aboriginal character? Can an English critic make reliable judgments on the work of a French Canadian artist? Does the unfamiliarity of Cree narrative structures prevent a non-Cree editor from appreciating—and therefore recommending—a collection of stories for publication? Is there to be one artistic canon that defines Canada? If so, who is to be assigned the authority to shape this canon? One thing seems clear: whenever a center takes shape, those marginalized by such features as race, color, or language are suspicious and press for greater visibility. The result of this cultural dynamic is an

ever-shifting definition of center and margin. This multiplicity of
voices emerging, extending, enhancing, and complicating the national narrative and, consequently, the canon(s) is like a kaleidoscope wherein the same fragments are always present but in an
ever-shifting relationship to one another.

The government of Canada, with its assumed and major responsibility for funding the arts, is faced with the virtually impossible task of shaping the narrative, by shaking the kaleidoscope.
The roots of present arts funding policies can be traced to the post-
World War II years when the Massey-Levesque Commission, established in 1947, explored the role government might play in
encouraging culture. The assumption was that the encouragement
of culture was in the best interest of Canadians. This best interest
was already being served by the National Gallery, the Canadian
Broadcasting Corporation and the National Film Board. The Massey
Report went on to make a number of recommendations, most
important of which for this discussion was the creation of the
Canada Council in 1957. That Council, then as now, is at the center
of an arts-funding network that is both federalist and decentralized. Very shortly, the provinces established their own arts councils; more recently, metropolitan organizations have emerged. This
trend in arts-funding has both inspired and echoed that of the perception of the national identity — moving from broad outline to
smaller units of greater diversity and complexity.

The system of funding is a hybrid of British and American
practices. The result, like our national identity, could be called a
"plurality of pluralities." The Canada Council was a copy of the
Arts Council of Britain established during World War II. In that the
private sector is expected to share in the subsidies to cultural proj-
ects, we resemble the American effort wherein the federal government does not play as vital a role in arts funding as it does in
Britain or Canada.

How much money is involved? Not as much as in Germany
where 8 or 9 percent of annual government expenditure goes to
culture, France, where 4 to 5 percent is expected. Since the early
1960s, Canada has allocated about 1.6 percent annually to cultural
programs, half of which goes to the CBC. This currently translates
to about 2.5 billion dollars in support of the National Gallery, the
National Archives, the National Film Board and the Canada Council (which receives about 120 million dollars a year).With recent
cuts to this cultural affairs budget exceeding cuts in other areas of
federal funding, the inference is to be made that the government

policy is shifting away from public appropriations to incentives for private sponsorship.

The provinces collectively spend a little less than 1 percent of their budgets, three hundred million a year, on cultural. Ontario, for example, pays for TV Ontario, The Royal Ontario Museum, the Art Gallery of Ontario, the Heritage Foundation, and the Ontario Arts Council (which alone receives 35 million dollars). Provincial budget cuts, too, will undermine this support.

Many see in Canada's diversity of arts funding a great advantage for artists, programs, and institutions because the sharing of the burden and the authority ensures maximum artistic freedom of expression. This is confirmed by arts critic Robert Fulford who has long argued that individual artists and companies whose art is not easily acceptable to everyone stand a better chance with two or three arts councils than with one. Uniformity, whether the uniformity of politicians or of arts bureaucrats then becomes harder to impose.

The most vital cultural issue for Canada now is who decides the various levels of funding for the arts. And that, in turn, depends on what perception of Canada decision makers hold. A "two-nation" view means large allocations to protect and encourage the French-Canadian heritage, not only in Quebec, but in New Brunswick, Manitoba, Ontario, and elsewhere. But if Canada is viewed as what historian J.M.C. Careless calls "a loose league of survivor states" — each confronting the others, especially French Canadians and the first peoples, as contenders for the same pieces of the federal funding pie — who says what about where cultural funding is designated diminishes the potential for French Canada's special status, or that of Aboriginal peoples. No decision can avoid the inference of a political position. But question of quality remains. Though there is certainly a danger of representational funding replacing funding by merit, it has become clear that there are no absolute criteria for quality and merit, since these are relative to ethnicity, gender, and education.

A number of cultural pundits think Canada is on a fulcrum between past and future, wondering where to go next. The overwhelming anxiety produced by federal and provincial attempts to balance their budgets has upstaged cultural concerns. Yet those same cuts will focus these issues more keenly. Dramatic cuts in spending on the arts necessitate even more precise definitions of which among the plethora of arts and artists deserve funding.

Notes

1. Hugh MacLennan, *Two Solitudes* (New York: Duell, Sloan and Pearce, 1945). .

2. Hansard, *House of Commons Debates*, 1 May 1947, 2644–47.

3. As cited by Robert F. Harney in "'So Great a Heritage as Ours': Immigration and the Survival of the Canadian Polity" *Daedelus* (fall 1988): 72.

4. Rev. Leger Comeau, "Multiculturalism—A Francophone Viewpoint," *Second Canadian Conference on Multiculturalism Report* (Ottawa: Minister of State, Multiculturalism, 1976), 27.

5. Rene Levesque, "Education in a Changing Society: A View from Quebec," in *Canadian Schools and Canadian Identity*, ed. A. Chaiton and N. McDonald (Toronto: Gage Educational Publishing, 1977).

6. Harney, *op. cit.*

CONTRIBUTORS

Louis Balthazar teaches political science at Université Laval and is co-author of *Contemporary Quebec and the United States: 1960–1985.*

Donald Barry is co-author of *Canada's Department of External Affairs: Coming of Age: 1946-1968.* He teaches at the University of Calgary.

D. M. R. Bentley is on the faculty of the Department of English at the University of Western Ontario. He is the editor of *The Essays and Reviews of Archibald Lampman,* published in 1996.

Elspeth Cameron is the biographer of Earle Birney and Irving Layton. She is a member of the English Department faculty at the University of Toronto.

Paul A. Demers is writing a doctoral dissertation on Fort Drummond at Michigan State University.

Henry Garrity teaches Quebec Literature and Film at Bowling Green University State University.

John Hilliker is head of the historical section of the Department of Foreign Affairs and International Trade. He is the author of *Canada's Department of External Affairs: The Early Years, 1909-1946.*

Victor Howard taught Canadian Studies at Michigan State University for twenty-five years.

Daniel Jacobson was professor of Geography and Teacher Education at Michigan State University prior to his recent death.

Joseph T. Jockel is professor of Canadian Studies at St. Lawrence University. His books include Canada and International Peacekeeping.

William W. Joyce is Director of the Canadian Studies Center at Michigan State University and a professor of teacher education.

Philip Kokotailo is a specialist in Canadian Literature and Culture on the faculty of University School, Huntington Valley, Ohio.

Henry A. Regier is professor of Zoology and member of the Institute for Environmental Studies at the University of Toronto.

Joel J. Sokolsky is a professor of political science at the Royal Military College of Canada and a senior fellow at the Queen's University Center for International Relations.

Gordon Stewart is the author of *The American Response to Canada Since 1776*. He teaches Canadian History at Michigan State University.